Law and Inhumanity

In *Law and Inhumanity*, Luigi Corrias explores fundamental philosophical issues underlying the law and politics of atrocity crimes within international criminal justice. Focusing on understanding the experiences of victims and perpetrators, Corrias draws on numerous disciplines to construct his conceptual framework while also using several case studies to examine important issues including references to 'humanity' in the discourse on atrocity crimes; the need for a first-person plural perspective of a 'We' within international criminal justice; the experiences of dehumanisation of both victims and perpetrators; the temporalities of suffering and justice; and the tension between individual criminal responsibility and structural violence.

Luigi Corrias is Associate Professor in the Department of Legal Theory and Legal History at Vrije Universiteit Amsterdam. He is the author of *The Passivity of Law: Competence and Constitution in the European Court of Justice* (2011), for which the Netherlands Association for Philosophy of Law awarded him the Prize for the Best Dissertation in Legal Philosophy in the Netherlands and Belgium in 2009–2010. For his research on *Law and Inhumanity*, he received a fellowship from the Netherlands Institute for Advanced Study in the Humanities and Social Sciences (NIAS-KNAW) in 2019–2020.

Law in Context

Since 1970, the Law in Context series has been at the forefront of a movement to broaden the study of law. The series is a vehicle for the publication of innovative monographs and texts that treat law and legal phenomena critically in their cultural, social, political, technological, environmental and economic contexts. A contextual approach involves treating legal subjects broadly, using materials from other humanities and social sciences, and from any other discipline that helps to explain the operation in practice of the particular legal field or legal phenomena under investigation. It is intended that this orientation is at once more stimulating and more revealing than the bare exposition of legal rules. The series includes original research monographs, coursebooks and textbooks that foreground contextual approaches and methods. The series includes and welcomes books on the study of law in all its contexts, including domestic legal systems, European and international law, transnational and global legal processes, and comparative law.

Books in the Series

Acosta: *The National versus the Foreigner in South America: 200 Years of Migration and Citizenship Law*

Alaattinoğlu: *Grievance Formation, Rights and Remedies*

Ali: *Modern Challenges to Islamic Law*

Alyagon Darr: *Plausible Crime Stories: The Legal History of Sexual Offences in Mandate Palestine*

Anderson, Schum & Twining: *Analysis of Evidence, 2nd Edition*

Ashworth: *Sentencing and Criminal Justice, 6th Edition*

Barton & Douglas: *Law and Parenthood*

Baxi, McCrudden & Paliwala: *Law's Ethical, Global and Theoretical Contexts: Essays in Honour of William Twining*

Beecher-Monas: *Evaluating Scientific Evidence: An Interdisciplinary Framework for Intellectual Due Process*

Bell: *French Legal Cultures*
Bercusson: *European Labour Law, 2nd Edition*
Birkinshaw: *European Public Law*
Birkinshaw: *Freedom of Information: The Law, the Practice and the Ideal, 4th Edition*
Blick: *Electrified Democracy: The Internet and the United Kingdom Parliament in History*
Broderick & Ferri: *International and European Disability Law and Policy: Text, Cases and Materials*
Brownsword & Goodwin: *Law and the Technologies of the Twenty-First Century: Text and Materials*
Cane & Goudkamp: *Atiyah's Accidents, Compensation and the Law, 9th Edition*
Clarke: *Principles of Property Law*
Clarke & Kohler: *Property Law: Commentary and Materials*
Collins: *The Law of Contract, 4th Edition*
Collins, Ewing & McColgan: *Labour Law, 3rd Edition*
Cowan: *Housing Law and Policy*
Cranston: *Making Commercial Law Through Practice 1830–1970*
Cranston: *Legal Foundations of the Welfare State*
Darian-Smith: *Laws and Societies in Global Contexts: Contemporary Approaches*
Dauvergne: *Making People Illegal: What Globalisation Means for Immigration and Law*
David: *Kinship, Law and Politics: An Anatomy of Belonging*
Davies: *Perspectives on Labour Law, 2nd Edition*
Dembour: *Who Believes in Human Rights?: Reflections on the European Convention*
de Sousa Santos: *Toward a New Legal Common Sense: Law, Globalization, and Emancipation*
Diduck: *Law's Families*
Douglas-Scott: *Brexit, Union, and Disunion: The Evolution of British Constitutional Unsettlement*
Dowdle: *Transnational Law: A Framework for Analysis*
Dupret: *Positive Law from the Muslim World: Jurisprudence, History, Practices*
Emon: *Jurisdictional Exceptionalisms: Islamic Law, International Law, and Parental Child Abduction*
Estella: *Legal Foundations of EU Economic Governance*
Fortin: *Children's Rights and the Developing Law, 3rd Edition*
Garnsey: *The Justice of Visual Art: Creative State-Building in Times of Political Transition*
Garton, Probert & Bean: *Moffat's Trusts Law: Text and Materials, 7th Edition*
Ghai & Woodman: *Practising Self-Government: A Comparative Study of Autonomous Regions*
Glover-Thomas: *Reconstructing Mental Health Law and Policy*
Gobert & Punch: *Rethinking Corporate Crime*
Goldman: *Globalisation and the Western Legal Tradition: Recurring Patterns of Law and Authority*
Haack: *Evidence Matters: Science, Proof, and Truth in the Law*
Harlow & Rawlings: *Law and Administration, 4th Edition*

Harris: *An Introduction to Law, 8th Edition*
Harris, Campbell & Halson: *Remedies in Contract and Tort, 2nd Edition*
Harvey: *Seeking Asylum in the UK: Problems and Prospects*
Herring: *Law and the Relational Self*
Hervey & McHale: *European Union Health Law: Themes and Implications*
Hervey & McHale: *Health Law and the European Union*
Holder & Lee: *Environmental Protection, Law and Policy: Text and Materials, 2nd Edition*
Jackson & Summers: *The Internationalisation of Criminal Evidence: Beyond the Common Law and Civil Law Traditions*
Jeutner: *The Reasonable Person: A Legal Biography*
Kennedy: *Inducing Intimacy: Deception, Consent and the Law*
Kostakopoulou: *The Future Governance of Citizenship*
Kreiczer-Levy: *Destabilized Property: Property Law in the Sharing Economy*
Kubal: *Immigration and Refugee Law in Russia: Socio-Legal Perspectives*
Lewis: *Choice and the Legal Order: Rising above Politics*
Likosky: *Law, Infrastructure and Human Rights*
Likosky: *Transnational Legal Processes: Globalisation and Power Disparities*
Lixinski: *Legalized Identities: Cultural Heritage Law and the Shaping of Transitional Justice*
Loughnan: *Self, Others and the State: Relations of Criminal Responsibility*
Lunney: *A History of Australian Tort Law 1901–1945: England's Obedient Servant?*
Maughan & Webb: *Lawyering Skills and the Legal Process, 2nd Edition*
McGaughey: *Principles of Enterprise Law*
McGlynn: *Families and the European Union: Law, Politics and Pluralism*
Mertens: *A Philosophical Introduction to Human Rights*
Miller: *An Introduction to German Law and Legal Culture: Text and Materials*
Moffat: *Trusts Law: Text and Materials*
Monti: *EC Competition Law*
Morgan: *Contract Law Minimalism: A Formalist Restatement of Commercial Contract Law*
Morgan & Yeung: *An Introduction to Law and Regulation: Text and Materials*
Nash: *British Islam and English Law: A Classical Pluralist Perspective*
Ng: *Political Censorship in British Hong Kong: Freedom of Expression and the Law (1842–1997)*
Nicola & Davies: *EU Law Stories: Contextual and Critical Histories of European Jurisprudence*
Norrie: *Crime, Reason and History: A Critical Introduction to Criminal Law, 3rd Edition*
Norrie: *Rethinking Criminal Justice: Punishment, Abolition And Moral Psychology*
O'Dair: *Legal Ethics: Text and Materials*
Oliver: *Common Values and the Public–Private Divide*
Oliver & Drewry: *The Law and Parliament*
Palmer & Roberts: *Dispute Processes: ADR and the Primary Forms of Decision-Making, 1st Edition*

Palmer & Roberts: *Dispute Processes: ADR and the Primary Forms of Decision-Making, 3rd Edition*

Picciotto: *International Business Taxation*

Pieraccini: *Regulating the Sea: A Socio-Legal Analysis of English Marine Protected Areas*

Probert: *The Changing Legal Regulation of Cohabitation, 1600–2010: From Fornicators to Family, 1600–2010*

Qiao: *The Authoritarian Commons: Neighborhood Democratization in Urban China*

Radi: *Rules and Practices of International Investment Law and Arbitration*

Reed: *Internet Law: Text and Materials*

Richardson: *Law, Process and Custody*

Roberts & Palmer: *Dispute Processes: ADR and the Primary Forms of Decision-Making, 2nd Edition*

Rowbottom: *Democracy Distorted: Wealth, Influence and Democratic Politics*

Sauter: *Public Services in EU Law*

Scott & Black: *Cranston's Consumers and the Law*

Seneviratne: *Ombudsmen: Public Services and Administrative Justice*

Seppänen: *Ideological Conflict and the Rule of Law in Contemporary China: Useful Paradoxes*

Siems: *Comparative Law, 3rd Edition*

Stapleton: *Product Liability*

Stewart: *Gender, Law and Justice in a Global Market*

Tamanaha: *Law as a Means to an End: Threat to the Rule of Law*

Taylor: *Fortin's Children's Rights and the Developing Law, 4th Edition*

Tuori: *Properties of Law: Modern Law and After*

Turpin & Tomkins: *British Government and the Constitution: Text and Materials, 7th Edition*

Twining: *General Jurisprudence: Understanding Law from a Global Perspective*

Twining: *Globalisation and Legal Theory*

Twining: *Human Rights, Southern Voices: Francis Deng, Abdullahi An-Na'im, Yash Ghai and Upendra Baxi*

Twining: *Jurist in Context: A Memoir*

Twining: *Karl Llewellyn and the Realist Movement, 2nd Edition*

Twining: *Rethinking Evidence: Exploratory Essays, 2nd Edition*

Twining & Miers: *How to Do Things with Rules, 5th Edition*

Wan: *Film and Constitutional Controversy: Visualizing Hong Kong Identity in the Age of 'One Country, Two Systems'*

Ward: *A Critical Introduction to European Law, 3rd Edition*

Ward: *Law, Text, Terror*

Ward: *Shakespeare and Legal Imagination*

Watt: *The Making Sense of Politics, Media, and Law: Rhetorical Performance as Invention, Creation, Production*

Wells & Quick: *Lacey, Wells and Quick: Reconstructing Criminal Law: Text and Materials, 4th Edition*

Woodhead: *Caring for Cultural Heritage: An Integrated Approach to Legal and Ethical Initiatives in the United Kingdom*

Yeung and Ranchordás: *An Introduction to Law and Regulation: Text and Materials, 2nd edition*

Young: *Turpin and Tomkins' British Government and the Constitution: Text and Materials, 8th Edition*

Zander: *Cases and Materials on the English Legal System, 10th Edition*

Zander: *The Law-Making Process, 6th Edition*

International Journal of Law in Context: A Global Forum for Interdisciplinary Legal Studies

The *International Journal of Law in Context* is the companion journal to the Law in Context book series and provides a forum for interdisciplinary legal studies and offers intellectual space for ground-breaking critical research. It publishes contextual work about law and its relationship with other disciplines including but not limited to science, literature, humanities, philosophy, sociology, psychology, ethics, history and geography. More information about the journal and how to submit an article can be found at http://journals.cambridge.org/ijc

Law and Inhumanity

Dehumanisation, Silent Claims and Atrocity Crimes

LUIGI CORRIAS

Vrije Universiteit Amsterdam

CAMBRIDGE
UNIVERSITY PRESS

CAMBRIDGE
UNIVERSITY PRESS

Shaftesbury Road, Cambridge CB2 8EA, United Kingdom

One Liberty Plaza, 20th Floor, New York, NY 10006, USA

477 Williamstown Road, Port Melbourne, VIC 3207, Australia

314–321, 3rd Floor, Plot 3, Splendor Forum, Jasola District Centre, New Delhi – 110025, India

103 Penang Road, #05–06/07, Visioncrest Commercial, Singapore 238467

Cambridge University Press is part of Cambridge University Press & Assessment, a department of the University of Cambridge.

We share the University's mission to contribute to society through the pursuit of education, learning and research at the highest international levels of excellence.

www.cambridge.org
Information on this title: www.cambridge.org/9781009418980

DOI: 10.1017/9781009418973

First published 2025

A catalogue record for this publication is available from the British Library

Library of Congress Cataloging-in-Publication Data
Names: Corrias, Luigi, author.
Title: Law and inhumanity : dehumanisation, silent claims and atrocity crimes / Luigi Corrias, Vrije Universiteit Amsterdam.
Description: Cambridge, United Kingdom ; New York, NY : Cambridge University Press, 2025. | Series: Law in context | Includes bibliographical references and index.
Identifiers: LCCN 2025000105 | ISBN 9781009418980 (hardback) | ISBN 9781009418973 (ebook)
Subjects: LCSH: Crimes against humanity (International law) | Crimes against humanity – Law and legislation. | Atrocities – Law and legislation. | Criminal justice, Administration of – Philosophy. | Criminal liability (International law) | International criminal law.
Classification: LCC KZ7145 .C69 2025 | DDC 345/.0235–dc23/eng/20250114
LC record available at https://lccn.loc.gov/2025000105

ISBN 978-1-009-41898-0 Hardback

A Luca

Wir mögen nicht wissen, was das absolut Gute, was die absolute Norm, ja auch nur, was der Mensch oder das Menschliche und die Humanität sei, aber was das Unmenschliche ist, das wissen wir sehr genau.

Theodor W. Adorno

It is sad but true that humankind understands itself partly by the crimes it knows itself to be capable of.

Raimond Gaita

Contents

Acknowledgements

This book could not have been written without the kind help and support of many people. It gives me pleasure to thank them here. I would like to start expressing my gratitude to my colleagues of Vrije Universiteit Amsterdam. Bart van Klink and Wouter Veraart have encouraged me from the very start to pursue this project. In addition, many people have read and commented on earlier drafts of chapters. I would like to thank Tom van den Berg, Bent Bos, Cheyenne Dunk, Gerben Geessink, Ngyen Nath Minh, Sofia Stolk, Wouter Werner and Bertjan Wolthuis for the time they have dedicated to my work and their helpful comments. I especially would like to mention my former colleague Lyana Francot who has been among the most enthusiastic supporters of this book, even when it was only a vague idea. My thanks also go to Tara Rezvani Daryan for helping me with the preparation of the final manuscript with great patience and care.

Others, outside of my institution, also read parts of the manuscript, or provided me with opportunities to present my work. I especially would like to mention Michiel Besters (Erasmus University Rotterdam), Ligeia Quackelbeen (Tilburg University), Shahin Nasiri, Bas Schotel and Marc de Wilde (all at the University of Amsterdam), Roland Pierik (Maastricht University), Ronald Tinnevelt and Bart van Leeuwen (both at Radboud University), Patrick Hayden (University of St Andrews), Sinja Graf (London School of Economics and Political Science), Kertulli Lingenfelter (Max Planck Institute for Comparative Public Law and International Law), Alessio Lo Giudice (Università degli Studi di Messina), Alessandro Ferrara, Paola Chiarella and Alberto Scerbo (all at Università Magna Graecia di Catanzaro) and Ana Lucía Batalla (University of Valencia).

I also acknowledge the permission of Cambridge University Press (CUP) and Routledge to use material previously published with them:

Luigi Corrias, 'Crimes against Humanity, Dehumanization and Rehumanization: Reading the Case of Duch with Hannah Arendt', *Canadian Journal of Law & Jurisprudence: An International Journal of Legal Thought*, 29, no. 2 (2016): 351–70;

Luigi Corrias, 'Law, Time and Inhumanity: Reflections on the Imprescriptible', in *Temporal Boundaries of Law and Politics: Time Out of*

Joint, eds. Luigi Corrias and Lyana Francot (London: Routledge, 2018), 53–70.

These appear in this book in a rewritten form as Chapters 3 and 5.

The Netherlands Institute for Advanced Study in the Humanities and Social Sciences (NIAS-KNAW) has kindly supported the research for this book with an individual fellowship in the spring of 2020. Albeit interrupted by the COVID-19 pandemic and a lockdown, I keep fond memories of the time that I could spend reading, writing and engaging with others in the beautiful NIAS institute. At CUP, I am grateful to Tom Randall, Toby Ginsberg and Gemma Smith for their help. I also want to thank the editors of the Law in Context series, Kenneth Armstrong, Maksymilian Del Mar and Sally Sheldon, for their willingness to accept this book in their prestigious series.

Finally, I would like to thank those closest to me who provide me with the daily hustle and bustle that makes up the beauty of life, even if I do not always realise it. I am immensely grateful to Irina Leichenko for her enduring help and support in matters bookish and unbookish. Her loving confidence in my abilities has been crucial to the writing process. This book is dedicated to my son, Luca, who is the kindest, bravest and funniest person I know. In his unique and unstoppable way, he keeps reminding me of everything that really matters.

Introduction

The concept of humanity seems to have become ubiquitous in international law. From human rights to crimes against humanity and from humanitarian intervention to the common heritage of humanity, international law seems to pivot around notions that, one way or another, invoke humanity. What to make of this? This book sets out to investigate what is at stake in these invocations, especially as they occur within the discourse on the international core or atrocity crimes.[1] Whenever mass atrocities occur, people often turn to the language of humanity and inhumanity to express their grief, claim an injustice or rally others to follow them and resist. This book is born from a fascination with this language and the work it does in the discourse on international criminal law (ICL). What exactly is invoked? How do the law and the politics of humanity work? What is in- and excluded by invoking humanity? How to make sense of the experiences of victims and perpetrators? Is it possible to give voice to those who have been silenced? Such are the questions central to this work.

Theme and Scope

From the beginning, it is important to determine the scope of the project. First, 'humanity' comes in a number of related but separate guises. It would take far more than one book to map all the references within international law.[2] Instead of that gargantuan task, my aim is more modest. The book's field of inquiry is limited to the contemporary uses of 'humanity' in the discourse on international atrocity crimes. To grasp how and why humanity is invoked

[1] This notion is, itself, contested among scholars of ICL; see Christine Schwöbel-Patel, 'The Core Crimes of International Criminal Law', in *The Oxford Handbook of International Criminal Law*, eds. Kevin Jon Heller et al. (Oxford: Oxford University Press, 2018), 768–90, at 771–76. In this book, I will use the notion of core or atrocity crimes to refer to international crimes for which the ICC has jurisdiction, that is, genocide, crimes against humanity, war crimes and the crime of aggression.

[2] For an overview of references to humanity in international law and biolaw, see the contributions to B. van Beers, L. Corrias and W. G. Werner, eds., *Humanity across International Law and Biolaw* (Cambridge: Cambridge University Press, 2013).

requires not only a conceptual analysis, but it also necessitates a look into the normative consequences of the invocation of humanity.

There are specific problems associated with invoking humanity in ICL. Notions such as 'humanity' or 'mankind' are frequently called upon within international law to secure the legal status of a specific territory or area, for example, outer space. In ICL, however, 'humanity' seems to appear without a specific area but refers rather to the entire globe.[3] Hence, ICL's portrayal as global justice by (former) prosecutor at the International Criminal Court (ICC), Luis Moreno Ocampo.[4] At the same time, ICL remains treaty based – the ICC is a good example – and in this way keeps referring to states.

Second, humanity has many meanings in international law. Humanity can be understood both as an entity and as an attitude. As an entity, humanity refers to a class or collective. As an attitude, it signifies benevolence or compassion. The two meanings are related, for compassion is only extended to those who, one way or another, form part of humanity as a collective. This applies to those who we recognise as fellow human beings and to those who, while excluded from humanity, are included in our consideration because it is exactly this attitude that confirms our self-understanding.[5] Furthermore, compassion is mobilised – sometimes in violent ways – by a reliance on the collective, as can be seen in humanitarian interventions with military means.[6] Given this conceptual order, there is, I submit, a primacy of an analysis of the collective level 'We, Humanity' over an analysis on the intersubjective level of individuals. So, there is a conceptual primacy of humanity as a class or collective over humanity as an attitude. Nevertheless, the levels cannot be collapsed into one another.

What interests me primarily is how in the experience of the atrocity crimes humanity is formed but also contested, thus laying bare that the agents are socially situated in a world and related to others. As I will focus on the legal-political context of the atrocities, I will not only analyse the agent from the

[3] Antoine Garapon, 'Judging the Past: Three Ways of Understanding Time', in *Temporal Boundaries of Law and Politics: Time Out of Joint*, eds. L. Corrias and L. Francot (London: Routledge, 2018), 15–32.

[4] L. Moreno Ocampo, 'The International Criminal Court: Seeking Global Justice', *Case Western Reserve Journal of International Law* 40 (2008): 215–26. For a critical view, see Sarah MH Nouwen and Wouter G. Werner, 'Monopolizing Global Justice: International Criminal Law as Challenge to Human Diversity', *Journal of International Criminal Justice* 13, no. 1 (2015): 157–76.

[5] For a thorough investigation of this argument, see Didier Fassin, *Humanitarian Reason: A Moral History of the Present*, trans. R. Gomme (Berkeley, CA: University of California Press, 2012).

[6] There exists a huge amount of literature on humanitarian intervention, when it is allowed, and by which means. For a concise overview of arguments and literature from a philosophical perspective, see Thomas M. Franck, 'Humanitarian Intervention', in *The Philosophy of International Law*, eds. Samantha Besson and John Tasioulas (Oxford: Oxford University Press, 2010), 531–48 and Danilo Zolo, 'Humanitarian Militarism?', in *The Philosophy of International Law*, eds. Samantha Besson and John Tasioulas (Oxford: Oxford University Press, 2010), 549–65.

singular perspective but also from the plural point of view. In other words, I will zoom in on how a reference to the first-person plural of a 'we' plays a pivotal role in the discourse on the atrocity crimes.

Third, taking the atrocity crimes as my starting point entails that humanity appears negatively, that is, as inhumanity. When we turn our attention to the notion of humanity within the founding documents of ICL, we can see that it only occurs a few times. Taking them in chronological order, there is, first, a mention in 1945 in the so-called Nuremberg Charter, part of the Agreement establishing the International Military Tribunal (IMT). In article 6 sub c crimes against humanity were defined. The notion of a crime against humanity is also defined in article 5 of the Statute of the Yugoslavia Tribunal (1993), article 3 of the Statute of the Rwanda Tribunal (1994) and article 7 of the Rome Statute of the ICC (1998). Furthermore, it is defined in article 2 of the Statute of the Special Court for Sierra Leone (2000) and article 5 of the Cambodia Tribunal (2004). Between 1945 and the 1990s, crimes against humanity were also mentioned in the Convention on the Non-Applicability of Statutory Limitations, in article 1 (b) (1968), together with genocide and the crime of Apartheid. Finally, in the 1998 Rome Statute of the ICC, we find the phrase 'the conscience of humanity'.

Moreover, 'humanity' is intimately connected to notions that themselves play a significant role in legal, political, and moral thought. Examples include the notions of (human) dignity and dehumanisation. What transpires when one looks at the 'family resemblances' between these concepts and the way in which they are used in international legal discourse is that lawyers mostly refer to 'humanity' whenever 'it' is violated. In other words, international legal discourse features humanity in a negative guise, or at least the specific sub-field I am focusing on regards 'humanity' from the perspective of the negative.[7] Hence, this book is centred on law and *inhumanity*.

While humanity keeps being invoked in legal and political contexts, critics have pointed out the violence often inherent in these invocations. It is a violence that needs to be acknowledged from the very outset, since it is intimately connected to the colonial and imperial roots of international law but also to the resistance against it.[8] The invocation of humanity is integral to the conception

[7] The same perspective is taken in Avishai Margalit, *The Decent Society*, trans. N. Goldblum (Cambridge, MA: Harvard University Press, 1995); Richard A. Wilson, 'When Humanity Sits in Judgment: Crimes against Humanity and the Conundrum of Race and Ethnicity at the International Criminal Tribunal for Rwanda', in *In the Name of Humanity: The Government of Threat and Care*, eds. I. Feldman and M. Ticktin (Durham, NC: Duke University Press, 2010), 27–57; Paulus Kaufmann, Hannes Kuch, Christian Neuhäuser and Elaine Webster, eds., *Humiliation, Degradation, Dehumanization: Human Dignity Violated* (Berlin: Springer, 2011); Andrea Sangiovanni, *Humanity without Dignity: Moral Equality, Respect, and Human Rights* (Cambridge, MA: Harvard University Press, 2017).

[8] Ilana Feldman and Miriam Ticktin, 'Introduction: Government and Humanity', in *In the Name of Humanity: The Government of Threat and Care*, eds. Ilana Feldman and Miriam Ticktin (Durham, NC: Duke University Press, 2010), 1–26, at 8 and 10.

of international law that played a crucial part in the *mission civilisatrice* of Europe. To this purpose, international law – a particular European tradition – was interpreted as possessing a universal scope and validity.[9] While laying down a so-called universal idea of legal order in the name of progress, colonisers also deliberately postponed the eradication of fundamental differences between themselves and the colonised, thus sustaining the dichotomy between the two.[10] Law was not just instrumental in the endeavour of colonialism, it played a constitutive role in conquering and suppressing indigenous peoples.[11] The colony often acted as a laboratory of some sort where new legal instruments could be tried out.[12]

The concept of sovereignty played a particularly significant role in this process. On a domestic level, it was easy to determine who the sovereign authority was. Since the Treaty of Westphalia of 1648, the state emerged as this authority, meaning that it had absolute power over its own territory and was in a relation of equality with other sovereign states.[13] This same doctrine posed, however, a serious question to the discipline of international law: 'how is legal order to be established among equal and sovereign states?'[14] For our purposes, the consequences of this question for the non-European world are of particular importance. For whereas it was taken as an unquestionable truth that the European states were sovereign, the possession of sovereignty by non-European states was not acknowledged. In this way, sovereignty was used to exclude the latter from power.[15] So, the driver of the doctrine of sovereignty has been this 'dynamic of difference', that is, the schism between the European and the non-European, making colonialism a central tenet of international law.[16]

One of the founding documents of the field, Francisco de Vitoria's 'On the Indians Lately Discovered', testifies to this. Arguing from natural law theory, de Vitoria tried to square the conquest and violence of the Spanish in the Americas with the Catholic faith. While he does speak more humanely of what he called 'the Indians' – that is, the indigenous peoples of the Americas, or Native Americans – than some of his contemporaries and acknowledges that their societies constitute a certain kind of order, he nevertheless assigns the Spaniards the task to act as their trustees, thus basically casting the Native Americans as children.[17] Whereas their humanity and duty of obedience to

[9] Martti Koskenniemi, 'International Law in Europe: Between Tradition and Renewal', *The European Journal of International Law* 16, no. 1 (2005): 113–24, at 117.

[10] John L. Comaroff, 'Colonialism, Culture, and the Law: A Foreword', *Law and Social Inquiry* 26, no. 2 (2001): 305–14, at 307–8.

[11] Comaroff, 'Colonialism, Culture, and the Law: A Foreword', 309.

[12] Comaroff, 'Colonialism, Culture, and the Law: A Foreword', 310–11. From a philosophical perspective, see also Achille Mbembe, 'Necropolitics', *Public Culture* 15, no. 1 (2003): 11–40.

[13] Antony Anghie, 'The Evolution of International Law: Colonial and Postcolonial Realities', *Third World Quarterly* 27, no. 5 (2006): 739–53, at 740.

[14] Anghie, 'The Evolution of International Law', 740.

[15] Anghie, 'The Evolution of International Law', 741.

[16] Anghie, 'The Evolution of International Law', 742.

[17] Anghie, 'The Evolution of International Law', 743.

natural law were recognised, this led to their infantilisation. For de Vitoria, in violating the natural law, the Native Americans show their true face as barbarians and, consequently, the Spaniards are allowed to wage a (virtually) perpetual war to tame them.[18]

When looking at the nineteenth century, when legal positivism was firmly established, the basic picture remains the same. With positivism, a whole range of formal doctrines and procedures that were explicitly based on the dichotomy between civilised and uncivilised states enters the scene.[19] Conquest was a legitimate way of obtaining land and through the doctrine of *terra nullius*, European countries essentially framed the original inhabitants as backward and inferior in order to get hold of territory.[20] When the era of colonisation ended, after the First World War, the ground structure underlying international law did not radically change, since by now European states had managed to put forward their particular standard as a universal one.[21] New was that the difference between the European and the non-European was now understood mainly in economic terms: the 'advanced' and the 'backward'.[22] The League of Nations was given the authority over the territories of the defeated countries and, when it found itself before the task of creating new self-governing and sovereign states, the interests of Western states were advanced.[23] In this way, economic subordination and sovereignty became two sides of the same coin.[24] In many respects, this is part of the explanation of the dominance of the Global North over the Global South.

The violence of the presumably universal category of humanity is born from the practical need to draw distinctions *within* this category.[25] Simultaneously, humanity was also invoked as a species in order to distinguish it from animality, thus inscribing this anthropocentric norm into Western thinking and politics.[26] As Ilana Feldman and Miriam Ticktin convincingly argue, humanity appears in modern legal, political and social theory as both an object of care and sympathy (think of humanitarianism) and a source of threat and insecurity (think of global war and environmental catastrophe).[27] Humanity seems at the same

[18] Francisco de Vitoria, 'Lecture on the American Indians', in *Political Writings*, eds. Anthony Pagden and Jeremy Lawrance (Cambridge: Cambridge University Press, 1991), 231–92, at 270–71.

[19] Anghie, 'The Evolution of International Law', 745. See also Brett Bowden, 'The Colonial Origins of International Law-European Expansion and the Classical Standard of Civilization', *Journal of the History of International Law* 7, no. 1 (2005): 1–24.

[20] Anghie, 'The Evolution of International Law', 745.

[21] Anghie, 'The Evolution of International Law', 746.

[22] Anghie, 'The Evolution of International Law', 746.

[23] Anghie, 'The Evolution of International Law', 746–47.

[24] Anghie, 'The Evolution of International Law', 747.

[25] Feldman and Ticktin, 'Introduction', 9.

[26] Allen Feldman, 'Inhumanitas: Political Speciation, Animality, Natality, Defacement', in *In the Name of Humanity: The Government of Threat and Care*, eds. Ilana Feldman and Miriam Ticktin (Durham, NC: Duke University Press, 2010), 115–49, at 117.

[27] Feldman and Ticktin, 'Introduction', 5–6.

time both necessary and impossible. Necessary, for governance within an ethical and political horizon that is faced with transnational and transgenerational problems requires the deployment of a universal category with proven effects upon individual lives.[28] Impossible, not only because the promise of universality is never fulfilled and one keeps encountering violent processes of in- and exclusion but also because humanity has many and often contradictory meanings and is invoked by many different actors.[29] In this cacophony, no final word can be said, no monopoly can be claimed.[30] Accordingly, this book will not attempt to formulate such a final word, either. It will, rather, try to attentively listen to this mesh of voices, trying to capture those that have received less attention.

A Note on Methodology

This is a work in the philosophy of law in at least two senses. On the one hand, it takes its cue from what lawyers say, write and think. While this book is not a study in the positive law of international atrocity crimes, it takes legal thought seriously as a fundamental and fine-grained manner of thinking and an obvious starting point for legal philosophy.[31] On the other hand, while this book is anchored in legal thought, it puts legal concepts in a wider philosophical context to lay bare fissures and cracks covered by what, at first sight, might appear as solid legal ground. Accordingly, the book aims to come to a philosophical understanding of the core or atrocity crimes from the specific perspective of the relationship between law and inhumanity.

Philosophically, the book approaches the relationship between law and inhumanity from a first-person perspective, that is, phenomenologically. A phenomenological approach is characterised by a specific stance or perspective. With Charles Taylor, one may speak of 'the radically reflexive stance': the first-person standpoint of an agent and their own experience of the world.[32] In other words, phenomenology studies the *concrete experiences* of a situated agent *from the standpoint of that agent itself*, that is, from a first-person perspective. That is how phenomenology got its name: it is 'the study of "phenomena": appearances of things, or things as they appear in our experience, or the ways we experience things, thus the meanings things have in our experience'.[33] Accordingly, what phenomenology provides is self-knowledge in the strong sense of 'self-attached

[28] Feldman and Ticktin, 'Introduction', 3. [29] Feldman and Ticktin, 'Introduction', 1–2.
[30] Feldman and Ticktin, 'Introduction', 1–2.
[31] For this perspective on legal scholarship, see Bert van Roermund, *Legal Thought and Philosophy: What Legal Scholarship Is About* (Cheltenham: Edward Elgar Publishing, 2013), especially Introduction.
[32] Charles Taylor, *Sources of the Self: The Making of the Modern Identity* (Cambridge: Cambridge University Press, 1989), 130–31.
[33] David Woodruff Smith, 'Phenomenology', in *The Stanford Encyclopedia of Philosophy* (Summer 2018 Edition), ed. Edward N. Zalta, accessed 23 March 2024, https://plato.stanford.edu/archives/sum2018/entries/phenomenology/.

knowledge', in contrast to mere 'knowledge of the person one happens to be'.[34] Accordingly, throughout this study, I will pay special attention to the experiences and affect of agents involved in atrocity crimes. Attention to experience allows me to focus on the pole of the self and the first-person perspective of humanity. The guiding hypothesis of this book is that referring to humanity is the invocation of a normative community. Any normative community, humanity, too, has its boundaries. Humanity appears under a negative guise in ICL because this legal field's main task is to respond when the normative boundaries of the community are violated. Attention to affect will help uncover the inhuman, for its appearance will always go hand in hand with a disruption of the order, an affective questioning that forces the order to respond.[35]

A normative community in the field of ICL expresses both that a certain behaviour is below a minimum threshold or norm and that this norm is established, enforced and violations are punished on behalf of a community, or public.[36] When that community is a 'we, humanity', what is excluded is both the non-human and the inhuman. ICL, as it exists today, is usually not directly concerned with the non-human (e.g., non-human animals, the environment). Environmental law is. Only in the crime of ecocide do the two fields converge, however this is not (yet) considered one of the core crimes.[37] This book does not deal with the legal relationship between the human and the non-human. It is a study about humanity and inhumanity.[38] If violence is done and legitimised in the name of humanity, resistance takes the form of the inhuman questioning of the boundaries of the order of humanity. Note that the latter comes in two guises.[39] Inhuman is the behaviour that violates the norm. Inhuman is also the suffering that transgresses the legal order of humanity. Both forms of inhumanity question the boundaries of humanity, but the latter in a more fundamental way, for it confronts the legal order of humanity with the inhumanity at its very core.[40] In short, in all its different guises, 'humanity' appears as a bounded concept; that is, as a notion that is not all-encompassing but rather in- and

[34] John Perry, 'Myself and I', in *Philosophie in synthetischer Absicht – Synthesis in Mind*, ed. Marcelo Stamm (Stuttgart: Klett-Cotta, 1998), 83–103.

[35] This is a recurring theme in the work of Bernhard Waldenfels, see Bernhard Waldenfels, *Phenomenology of the Alien: Basic Concepts*, trans. Tanja Stähler and Alexander Kozin (Evanston, IL: Northwestern University Press, 2011).

[36] For a concise version of this more general theory of criminal law in an international context, see Anthony Duff, 'Authority and Responsibility in International Criminal Law', in *The Philosophy of International Law*, eds. Samantha Besson and John Tasioulas (Oxford: Oxford University Press, 2010), 589–604.

[37] See Chapter 6 for a brief discussion of ecocide.

[38] Interestingly, one may argue that in the Anthropocene, the non-human increasingly presents itself as inhuman, thus questioning the boundaries of humanity. This fascinating theme falls outside the scope of this book. I hope to come back to it in future work.

[39] Here, I am inspired by the double reading of inhumanity developed in Jean-François Lyotard, *The Inhuman: Reflections on Time* (Redwood City, CA: Stanford University Press, 1991).

[40] For this formulation, I am indebted to the work of Hans Lindahl and especially his notion of a-legality; see Hans Lindahl, *Fault Lines of Globalization: Legal Order and a Politics of A-Legality* (Oxford: Oxford University Press, 2013).

exclusive. It is because of these boundaries, and their transgressions, that one may say that humanity is both inside and outside ICL.[41]

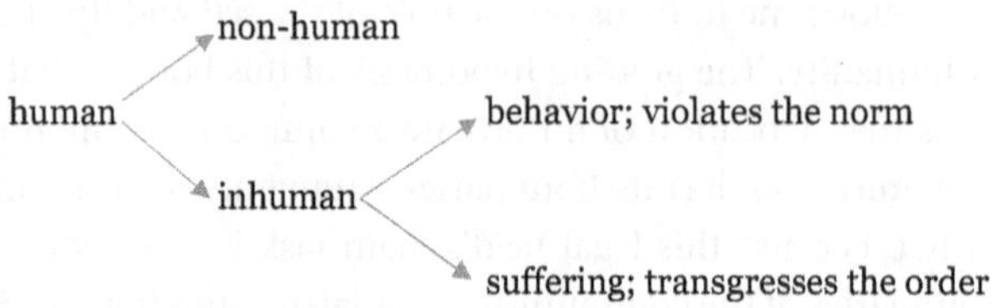

Overview of the Chapters

This book consists of six chapters. The first two chapters develop my account of the first-person plural. In Chapter 1, I start by critically engaging with existing academic work that either emphatically argues in favour of or radically dismisses the appeal to humanity within international law. The important critique on the invocation of humanity notwithstanding, I argue that a concept of humanity as a collective subject is necessary to grasp what is at stake in dehumanisation. Chapter 2 delves into the constitution of humanity as a collective subject. Drawing on the debate between ICL scholars about the we-talk in relation to the ICC and their engagement with the work of Durkheim, I develop the thesis that humanity should be understood as a collective subject that is represented as a symbolic order. Moreover, as with any order, the order of humanity is brought about by the process of self-inclusion of a first-person plural. Finally, I turn to the case of Ongwen to show how the inhuman questions the order of humanity.

Chapters 3 and 4 examine the experience of dehumanisation from a first-person singular perspective of the perpetrator and subsequently from that of the victim. Chapter 3 is a close reading of key documents and transcripts of the case of Duch of the Cambodia Tribunal. Interestingly, notions of humanity and inhumanity were used by several parties: prosecutors, attorneys for civil parties but also the defendant's lawyer, and Duch himself declared that the latter was dehumanised. Subsequently, I will put these findings in a philosophical context by bringing them in conversation with the work of Hannah Arendt, thus showing the structure of dehumanisation and rehumanisation. Chapter 4 explores the normative challenge of the experience of dehumanisation. It starts from a paradigmatic case of dehumanisation, as it was described from a first-person perspective, the torture of Jean Améry. This description offers a phenomenology of dehumanisation. To deepen the analysis, the experience of dehumanisation is subsequently confronted with recent work on alienation. This opens the critical potential of the experience of dehumanisation challenging important concepts that figure prominently in debates on (the aftermath) of atrocities.

[41] On humanity and global law, see Hans Lindahl, *Authority and the Globalisation of Inclusion and Exclusion* (Cambridge: Cambridge University Press, 2018).

Finally, Chapters 5 and 6 of the book take up normative questions from the first-person plural perspective. Both start from the observation that a political community is never done with inhumanity. Chapter 5 discusses the various timelines involved in the question of the imprescriptibility of atrocity crimes. I distinguish between four timelines involved in imprescriptibility and assess these from the viewpoint of philosophical debates on forgiveness and legal values. Taking the perspective of the judge, the chapter ends by spelling out what is at stake in the judgement on an imprescriptible international crime. Chapter 6 starts from the insight that, despite ICL's focus on individual responsibility, atrocity crimes are often the result of structural violence and ditto injustices: discrimination, social exclusion, exploitation and so on. If the violence is structural, the suffering becomes social, that is, inherent in societal structures. The question remains how the legal order can respond to structural injustice and social suffering. The chapter argues that these forms of injustice register as 'silent claims' at the brink of the legal order, questioning its boundaries. The Epilogue brings together the main themes of the book and sketches some avenues for further research.

1

Atrocity Crimes, the Community of Humanity and the Experience of Inhumanity

1.1 Introduction

International criminal tribunals have frequently referred to humanity, as have prosecutors.[1] Reflecting on this type of references, legal anthropologist Richard A. Wilson points out both the necessity and the problematic nature of the invocation of humanity in international criminal law (ICL).[2] In the eighteenth century, humanity appears as a secular political construct aimed at sustaining republican governance. Wilson argues that the concept can play this role because humanity appears, primarily, as a negative concept, which means that it is used to refer to what constitutes a breach of humanity. In other words, there is a primacy of inhumanity:

> In eighteenth-century European legal and political thought, humanity was largely a negative category. It was created by acts that repel and were considered odious, repugnant, and disgraceful, rather than by human behaviors deemed beautiful or intellectually or morally edifying. 'Humanity' materializes when there is an offense against natural law, the legal and moral basis of human rights in the eighteenth century. From the outset, laws of humanity have been a mirror for human cruelty that can seemingly be applied in any setting. These ideas retain an influence to this day, as evidenced by the category of 'crimes against humanity.' Humanity is still constructed in its breach.[3]

Law plays a vital role in this shift to secular humanity. In their work, scholars divorced the notion of humanity from any religious origins in order to have it act as an alternative ground for international law.[4] This gave rise to secular ideas of human rights, ICL and an ethos of humanitarian intervention.[5]

[1] For examples and an analysis, see: Luigi Corrias and Geoffrey M. Gordon, 'Judging in the Name of Humanity: International Criminal Tribunals and the Representation of a Global Public', *Journal of International Criminal Justice* 13, no. 1 (2015): 97–112.

[2] Richard A. Wilson, 'When Humanity Sits in Judgment: Crimes against Humanity and the Conundrum of Race and Ethnicity at the International Criminal Tribunal for Rwanda', in *In the Name of Humanity: The Government of Threat and Care*, eds. I. Feldman and M. Ticktin (Durham, NC: Duke University Press, 2010), 27–57.

[3] Wilson, 'When Humanity Sits in Judgment', 28.

[4] Wilson, 'When Humanity Sits in Judgment', 27–28.

[5] Wilson, 'When Humanity Sits in Judgment', 28–29.

Accordingly, the notion had the potential to get rid of political boundaries, or so it was presented, making it indispensable for formulating crimes that have *ius cogens* status, claiming universal jurisdiction to prosecute and pass judgement on them, but also to intervene (with military means) whenever these norms were transgressed.[6]

And yet, from the beginning there was also the suspicion that humanity was a political subject fabricated only to serve the interests of 'civilisation' and its 'privileged bearers', as became obvious in the imperial projects of Great Britain and the United States, among others.[7] In the nineteenth century, humanity was mostly mobilised through the distinction between 'civilised' nations and 'uncivilised' ones. Linking law with civilisation meant that law could be used as a powerful instrument for conquest, empire and colonisation – the means to pursue the *mission civilisatrice*.[8] It can be traced back to the very origins of international law in the writings of Francisco de Vitoria.[9] It can also be found in the work of the controversial legal theorists and political philosopher Carl Schmitt, who wrote that 'whoever invokes humanity wants to cheat', since, as he explains, 'To confiscate the word humanity, to invoke and monopolize such a term probably has certain incalculable effects, such as denying the enemy the quality of being human and declaring him to be an outlaw of humanity; and a war can thereby be driven to the most extreme inhumanity'.[10]

In this chapter, my aim is to show the leading role of the notion of humanity understood as a collective subject in the discourse on atrocity crimes and dehumanisation. I argue that the concept of humanity as a collective subject is crucial to understand dehumanisation, because dehumanisation cannot be adequately captured in terms of inclusion-exclusion only. Accordingly, the concept of humanity is a necessary background to grasp what is at stake in dehumanisation. More precisely, without humanity as a collective subject, no understanding is possible of either the constitutive role that law plays in making dehumanisation possible nor of the pleas of victims to reverse this process. These pleas, I argue, can be understood in terms of rehumanisation. The chapter sketches both the more positive appraisals of humanity within international (criminal) law and critical stances. It inquires specifically into the presuppositions of invoking humanity in legal and political discourses

[6] Wilson, 'When Humanity Sits in Judgment', 29–30.

[7] Wilson, 'When Humanity Sits in Judgment', 30.

[8] Brett Bowden, 'The Colonial Origins of International Law-European Expansion and the Classical Standard of Civilization', *Journal of the History of International Law* 7 (2005): 1–24, at 1–3.

[9] Bowden, 'The Colonial Origins of International Law', 23; Antony Anghie, 'Francisco de Vitoria and the Colonial Origins of International Law', *Social & Legal Studies* 5, no. 3 (1996): 321–36.

[10] Carl Schmitt, *The Concept of the Political* (Chicago: Chicago University Press, 2007), 54. For a reflection on this critique, see Luigi Corrias, 'The Inhuman Stain: Representing Humanity in International Criminal Law', in *Humanity across International Law and Biolaw*, eds. B. van Beers, L. Corrias and W. Werner (Cambridge: Cambridge University Press, 2013), 67–86.

related to the atrocity crimes. Section 1.2 sets out an influential understanding of key fields within international law that stipulates how humanity takes central stage, thus marking a paradigmatic shift in international law. The problem with this view, I argue, is that it only focuses on humanity understood as an *individual* and gives no attention to humanity as a collective subject. Section 1.3 discusses the work of several scholars who have pointed out how humanity's invocation within international law has never been neutral but has actually been used as a powerful instrument in the pursuit of colonial and imperial goals. In the work of this second group of scholars, humanity is analysed as a *collective* subject, albeit their appraisal of the invocation of this concept is negative. Some of these authors even go as far as to argue that we ought to get rid of 'humanity' in legal and political contexts. In Section 1.4, I take issue with the argument that humanity should be rejected altogether by showing how it plays a crucial role in understanding instances of dehumanisation. Capturing dehumanisation and the resistance to it in terms of 'inhumanity', I argue that we should retain the notion of humanity as a collective subject, while being sensitive to its excluding and including violence, making space for the challenge of inhumanity to humanity. This challenge cannot be grasped well through the binary inclusion–exclusion, for inhumanity is a category that does not fit easily on either side.

1.2 Humanity's Norms

Lawyers have argued that the twentieth century has shown how the international legal order with the nation-state as the prime legal subject and the centrality of the notion of state sovereignty has played a crucial role in colonialism and imperialism.[11] Some scholars have insisted that the individual human being should take over this central position from the state. Some of them found developments within international law and politics to support the claim that the system is actually moving in that direction. They point to the increasing role of 'human(e)' considerations in international law[12] or argue that humanity constitutes a founding principle of the international legal order.[13] The ubiquity of notions as 'humanity' or '(hu)mankind' in international law is reflected in a more general trend in scholarship that has been called the 'law of humanity-project'.[14] It puts forward the claim that the individual understood as the

[11] Antony Anghie, *Imperialism, Sovereignty and the Making of International Law*. Vol. 37 (Cambridge: Cambridge University Press, 2007).

[12] Robin Coupland, 'Humanity: What Is It and How Does It Influence International Law?' *International Review of the Red Cross* 83, no. 844 (2001): 969–89; Theodor Meron, *The Humanization of International Law* (Leiden: Brill Nijhoff, 2006).

[13] Anne Peters, 'Humanity as the A and Ω of Sovereignty', *European Journal of International Law* 20, no. 3 (2009): 513–44.

[14] Ukri Soirila, 'Persons and Things in International Law and "Law of Humanity"', *German Law Journal* 18 (2017): 1163–82, at 1170–75.

primary legal person stands at the centre of the global law of humanity.[15] A diverse group of scholars engaged in this debate, each with their own perspective, relying on both descriptive and normative arguments. Notwithstanding their differences, they share the conviction that the humanisation of international relations through law is something good, a form of progress. Instead of reconstructing this whole debate, I will discuss Ruti Teitel's work that I take as exemplary for this position.

Ruti Teitel argues that the 'Law of Humanity', or simply 'Humanity's Law', is a new framework of international law – encompassing international human rights law, ICL and the law of war – in which, crucially, the emphasis has shifted from state security to the security of individuals and peoples.[16] At play in this new interpretation are the agents, sources, content and institutions of international public law. State sovereignty does no longer constitute the fundamental norm for state action but has been replaced by the protection of humanity.[17] The result is an 'extended reach of legality' on humanitarian grounds, and a shift to human security.[18] 'Humanity's law' has the aspiration to protect all and bring a universal global society closer.[19] As a consequence, conflicts are, Teitel submits, better grasped as battles over the multiple meanings of humanity.[20]

Humanity's law posits the human person as the subject and orientation of international law, and as its standard of treatment: the very preservation of humanity is the new *telos* of international law.[21] Accordingly, 'Humanity's Law' pivots on the human being as both subject and standard of state action.[22] As a normative endeavour, humanity's law takes up such (historical) distinctions as between just and unjust wars, civilised and uncivilised nations,[23] civilisation and barbarians,[24] the universal morality of compassion and inhumane treatment.[25] Teitel's contention is that this framework can accommodate 'new and diverse *claims*, on the part of diverse voices that are new to international law and politics'.[26]

One way to understand this primacy of the individual human being is through crimes against humanity: the fact that these can be prosecuted universally signals the inviolability of 'humanity's rights'.[27] Thus, they form a kind of accountability mechanism and even a measure of justice.[28] The 'turn to international criminal justice', as Teitel calls it, is exemplary for the fact that the individual human person has taken central stage within international law, for the emphasis on the protected individual is mirrored by the prosecution

[15] Soirila, 'Persons and Things in International Law and "Law of Humanity"', 1170–71; Ruti Teitel, *Humanity's Law* (Oxford: Oxford University Press, 2011).

[16] Teitel, *Humanity's Law*, 4.

[17] Teitel, *Humanity's Law*, 8–10.

[18] Teitel, *Humanity's Law*, 8–9.

[19] Teitel, *Humanity's Law*, 232.

[20] Teitel, *Humanity's Law*, 13.

[21] Teitel, *Humanity's Law*, 19.

[22] Teitel, *Humanity's Law*, 20.

[23] Teitel, *Humanity's Law*, 22.

[24] Teitel, *Humanity's Law*, 24.

[25] Teitel, *Humanity's Law*, 25–26.

[26] Teitel, *Humanity's Law*, 31.

[27] Teitel, *Humanity's Law*, 58–59.

[28] Teitel, *Humanity's Law*, 72.

of individual perpetrators. As Teitel writes: 'International criminal law sets one party, the prosecutor, on behalf of international society against another, the defendant. In so doing, it gets beyond the approaches that are traditionally associated with the field of international human rights, where the respondent is the state. Human rights law sets down protected rights – whereas international criminal law sets down offenses'.[29]

Since the protected rights are *human* rights, the question becomes: On whose behalf are these offenses prosecuted? While the concept of international society remains ambiguous, later Teitel is more explicit on how to name the community at stake. She quotes Nuremberg Justice Robert Jackson who spoke of the International Military Tribunal (IMT) as 'the court of humanity', and, even more clearly, asserted: 'Humanity need not plead for justice with sobs, tears, and piteous weeping. It has been demonstrated here that the inalienable and fundamental rights of common man need not lack for a court to proclaim them and for a marshal to execute the court's judgments. *Humanity can assert itself by law. It has taken on the robe of authority*'.[30]

As we have seen, the core idea of humanity's law is the *individual* human being at the centre of the legal order. Yet, I argue that humanity's law cannot do without a reference to a *plural* perspective. This reference to a collective subject or normative community is implied in its dependence upon ICL to enforce norms. In claiming authority to speak on behalf of humanity, international criminal courts do not simply refer to individual human rights but identify crimes as instances in which humanity's norms are infringed. Thus, distinguishing between humanity and inhumanity, international tribunals cannot but refer to a first person plural. What is inhuman is behaviour that is not in accordance with humanity's law. This is because the distinction between humanity and inhumanity is not a neutral one but one in which humanity is preferred over inhumanity. Teitel is aware of the normativity of ICL and its influence on the norms of humanity. The distinct role of ICL is that it is constitutive for community: 'processes of condemnation and punishment can create a source of community'.[31] This fits expressive theories of punishment that emphasise how punishment, or even prosecution, are expressive of establishing unlawful behaviour, thus drawing the boundaries of the normative community of humanity.[32] Despite this attention to ICL, humanity understood as a collective subject remains underdeveloped in Teitel's work.

1.3 The Dark Side of Humanity

Whereas the project of 'the Law of Humanity' sees in the ubiquity of humanity within international (criminal) law a positive development, other scholars are much more critical. These critics emphasise the dark side of humanity

[29] Teitel, *Humanity's Law*, 75. [30] Robert Jackson quoted in Teitel, *Humanity's Law*, 77.
[31] Teitel, *Humanity's Law*, 93. [32] Teitel, *Humanity's Law*, 93.

as a construct or ideal that stands for a normative community that says who is counted as fully human and who is not. They show how humanity goes together with (colonial) hierarchies and violence. For this reason, it ought to be abandoned. Due to its influence on other scholars, the work of Talal Asad occupies a principal place here. Asad's aim in investigating concepts such as humanism and humanitarianism is to lay bare how grand Enlightenment ideals – compassion, civilisation, universal benevolence and concern – are intertwined with cruelty and violence.[33] Asad takes humanity to refer to (the claim of) a collective subject with members sharing a single essence and a singular human experience.[34] Humanity was a notion that internalised a secular form of the idea of a 'chain of being' that introduced a hierarchy within humankind itself between 'full' humans on the one hand and 'potential' humans on the other hand.[35] Violence and compassion interrelate in the idea that one could (help) reach one's full humanity through charity and chastisement – something that becomes even clearer in modern colonialism.[36] Here, a fundamental and pivotal a-symmetry is at work between the suffering, colonised subject and the sympathising coloniser.[37] Accordingly, subjectivation and domination go hand in hand with the violence of imperial exploitation.

Emerging in the nineteenth century, humanitarianism finds its origin in Christian theology, more specifically in the notion of redemption.[38] The modern legal doctrine that corresponds with this is the responsibility to protect (R2P). It is grounded in an understanding of sovereignty as *de facto* control.[39] Its twin is the project of international criminal justice and, more particularly, the ICC. The juridification of public life in general and this domain in particular goes hand in hand with an increase in (potential) violence.[40] The notion of humanity can function within this discourse because of its underlying metaphysical concept of life.[41] This notion pivots on the distinction between human and inhuman ways of killing. The former are those that fall within and are warranted by a legal framework of modern warfare that is built around notions such as intentionality and collateral damage.[42] Inhuman modes of killing lie outside of this framework and are, as a consequence, considered to be savage and barbaric.[43] Asad, however, points out that the result of both ways of killing is equally shocking; hence, what transpires here is that some manners of dying and killing are constitutive of the human being.[44] Only those acts that take place outside of the legal framework are deemed cruel and provoke horror.[45]

[33] Talal Asad, 'Reflections on Violence, Law, and Humanitarianism', *Critical Inquiry* 41 (Winter 2015): 390–427, at 390–94.
[34] Asad, 'Reflections on Violence', 395–96.
[35] Asad, 'Reflections on Violence', 397–98.
[36] Asad, 'Reflections on Violence', 398.
[37] Asad, 'Reflections on Violence', 400.
[38] Asad, 'Reflections on Violence', 401–2.
[39] Asad, 'Reflections on Violence', 408.
[40] Asad, 'Reflections on Violence', 410.
[41] Asad, 'Reflections on Violence', 411.
[42] Asad, 'Reflections on Violence', 412.
[43] Asad, 'Reflections on Violence', 411.
[44] Asad, 'Reflections on Violence', 412.
[45] Asad, 'Reflections on Violence', 413–14.

In their respective projects, Samera Esmeir, Ayça Çubukçu and Sinja Graf take issue with the liberal goal of understanding violence as exclusion (from humanity). Starting from constitutive documents of human rights law, Esmeir argues that the view underlying these documents stipulates that the world is split between sovereign states with strong citizens on the one hand and failed or developing states with 'yet-to-be humans' on the other hand.[46] Being fully human has become a matter of legal status, something that can be bestowed upon and also be taken away by law.[47] Here, status refers to 'the legal standing or position of a person as determined by her or his membership in some class of persons who are entitled, under the law, to a set of rights and obligated to certain duties'.[48] Hence, through this status – legal personhood – humanisation and, crucially, dehumanisation become possible.[49]

It was exactly this logic that underpinned the humanising mission of the colonial project, with at its core the aim to alleviate the suffering of the colonised subject and ensure that she could become fully human.[50] Esmeir's point is, however, that even humanist critics of violence keep using the same terms, thus continuing the same logic. Aside from the violence of this discourse, these critics effectually deny the agency of those they would like to help.[51] The danger, in short, is that 'the more we think of humanity as a juridical status, the more dehumanization becomes possible'.[52] Accordingly, Esmeir calls upon us to drop the language of (de)humanisation in terms of legal status.[53]

Çubukçu aims to criticise the liberal conception of human rights that is founded on two related doctrines. The first says that one is born a human being and therewith a bearer of rights, while the second stipulates that there are specific qualities associated with the notion of a human person.[54] Far from simply a member of the human species, the human person is the proper or full human and a holder of rights, this in sharp distinction with those who are merely *potential* humans and only potential bearers of rights.[55] Çubukçu argues that this potential or capacity for humanity underlies the modern humanist tradition: what humans have in common needs developing.[56] The project of human rights may then be grasped as a redemptive project aimed at cultivating humanity into a new and more moral version of itself.[57] The very scope of this project, and its

[46] Samera Esmeir, 'On Making Dehumanization Possible', *PMLA* 121, no. 5 (2006): 1544–51, at 1546.
[47] Esmeir, 'On Making Dehumanization Possible', 1547.
[48] Esmeir, 'On Making Dehumanization Possible', 1547.
[49] Esmeir, 'On Making Dehumanization Possible', 1547.
[50] Esmeir, 'On Making Dehumanization Possible', 1547–49.
[51] Esmeir, 'On Making Dehumanization Possible', 1549.
[52] Esmeir, 'On Making Dehumanization Possible', 1549.
[53] Esmeir, 'On Making Dehumanization Possible', 1550.
[54] Ayça Çubukçu, 'Thinking against Humanity', *London Review of International Law* 5, no. 2 (2017): 251–67, at 255.
[55] Çubukçu, 'Thinking against Humanity', 255–56.
[56] Çubukçu, 'Thinking against Humanity', 256.
[57] Çubukçu, 'Thinking against Humanity', 257.

link to (state) violence, transpires once one acknowledges that it has been the prerogative of the state to protect the rights and security of its citizens – a prerogative that can be traced back to the natural law of self-preservation.[58]

Accordingly, inclusion in humanity as a *potential* human being went hand in hand with exclusion from humanity as having the status of a human person.[59] One should therefore understand the problem in terms of *inclusion*, not simply in terms of exclusion, and this is a major philosophical critique of liberalism. The ideas of evolution and hierarchy *within* humanity are intrinsic to it.[60] This double nature of humanity – both species encompassing all and collective subject to be cultivated, both fact and ideal – has been made possible through the ideas of a common human essence and a common human experience.[61] Since speaking of humanity always involves speaking of sub-humanity – included within humanity but only as potentially human – Çubukçu rejects the discourse altogether and opts instead for a way of thinking of potential action, solidarity and justice across species.[62] Whoever still aims to take the risk of speaking about humanity has the burden, Çubukçu submits, to take seriously the violence brought about by humanism.[63]

The immense value of Graf's work is that she connects the notion of humanity with that of a universal crime, thus showing that humanity as a collective subject is always involved.[64] Her starting point is the notion of crime against humanity, not in its ethical or legal but rather in its profoundly political sense. From this perspective, a crime against humanity is the paradigmatic example of a universal crime: a crime that presupposes humanity as a collective concept or subject. Importantly, all are included within humanity. However, Graff stresses, what matters is the capacity in which all are included, namely as potential offenders against humankind. The notion of universal crime thus has 'injured humanity' at its core.[65] Universal crime typically distinguishes between two groups.[66] On the one hand, we have the non-Europeans as the offenders or criminals against humanity. On the other hand, there are the Europeans who function as guardians of humanity. Hence, through the notion of universal crime, colonial violence was legitimised and made possible.

58 Çubukçu, 'Thinking against Humanity', 260. On the way in which self-preservation as modern rationality underlies present understandings of security, see Michiel Besters, '*A Politics of (In)Security: A Philosophical Analysis of Collective Security*' (PhD diss., Tilburg University, 2016).

59 Çubukçu, 'Thinking against Humanity', 262.

60 Çubukçu, 'Thinking against Humanity', 262.

61 Çubukçu, 'Thinking against Humanity', 263–64.

62 Çubukçu, 'Thinking against Humanity', 265–66.

63 Çubukçu, 'Thinking against Humanity', 267. In her book *For the Love of Humanity: The World Tribunal on Iraq*, Çubukçu explores possibilities for political action in the name of humanity. I will discuss this work in Chapter 6.

64 Sinja Graf, *The Humanity of Universal Crime. Inclusion, Inequality, and Intervention in International Political Thought* (Oxford: Oxford University Press, 2021), 2–3.

65 Graf, *The Humanity of Universal Crime*, 8.

66 Graf, *The Humanity of Universal Crime*, 36–40.

By taking humanity as a collective notion, Graf argues against the liberal reduction of humankind to individual human rights and against the typical liberal argument that regards only exclusion as problematic. By stressing how criminality actually entails inclusion into humanity, Graf also rejects the well-known argument of Carl Schmitt regarding 'the enemy of humanity'.[67] For Graf, humanity is not only a collective but also a normative, hierarchical and transcendent subject.[68] It is normative in that it posits who/what 'ought' to count as part of humanity. It is hierarchical because the inclusion into humanity goes hand in hand with a strict dichotomy between Europeans and non-Europeans, making military interventions of the former into the latter's states possible. Humanity is transcendent since its invocation has the discursive power of a kind of secular religion.

Graf takes up the normative inclusion via criminal law in more detail. She holds that the criminal against humanity, unlike the enemy of humanity, has a status *internal* to the law's symbolic universe because casting someone as a criminal is an act of juridical recognition or legal inclusion. In the case of a universal crime, this inclusion goes together with a hierarchical notion of humanity, thus inscribing inequality *within* humanity. In this respect, Graf speaks of a 'corrective inclusion': since as a human being everyone falls under the law of humanity, everyone may also be punished when infringing this natural law.[69] Vitoria's famous argument that the Indigenous peoples of the Americas were subject to this natural law is a good example of 'inclusion via liability'.[70] This then is a key point for Graf: how infringement of the law of humanity could be found outside of Europe, giving Europeans the authority to punish non-Europeans. While a related problem is the Eurocentrism inherent in the idea of international law, leading to 'the coloniality of power', which is still at work in some parts of the world.[71]

These critical authors are acutely aware of the colonial and imperial undertones of the notion of humanity as used in modern international law. Despite their important critique, these scholars seem to ignore some other aspects of the concept of humanity within legal and moral discourse. First, whereas the critical authors have shown that the legal inclusion within humanity can be a form of violence, this in itself does not mean that the legal *exclusion* from humanity is not also violent. My point is that the exclusion from humanity by means of law remains a way to inflict violence and this should be acknowledged. Such dehumanisation by law was practiced by the Nazis, for example. The Jews were not included within humanity as potential human beings. They were simply

[67] Graf, *The Humanity of Universal Crime*, 11–17. On this concept and its potential value for ICL, see David Luban, 'The Enemy of All Humanity', *Netherlands Journal of Legal Philosophy* 47, no. 2 (2018): 112–37.

[68] Graf, *The Humanity of Universal Crime*, 15–19.

[69] Graf, *The Humanity of Universal Crime*, 36.

[70] Graf, *The Humanity of Universal Crime*, 37.

[71] Anibal Quijano, 'Coloniality of Power and Eurocentrism in Latin America', *International Sociology* 15, no. 2 (2000): 215–32.

regarded as sub-humans not worthy of living. As such, they do not fit the analysis of the critical authors. Second, the experience of victims of atrocity crimes is often described by themselves by referring to humanity and inhumanity. This experience of inhumanity, as I will call it, seems to escape the binary logic of either inclusion or exclusion and presents humanity instead with a claim. Third, it is an undeniable fact that humanity remains ubiquitous within international legal discourse. This might be due to its important symbolic effects, something also Wilson points out. These effects are, however, largely ignored by the critical authors. I will take some of these points up in Section 1.4.[72]

1.4 Dehumanisation and the Experience of Inhumanity

Against the suggestion made by some of the critical scholars discussed in Section 1.3 that one ought to get rid of the concept of humanity in legal and political contexts altogether, I argue that the concept of humanity as a collective subject is valuable and necessary to understand the notion of dehumanisation central to discourses on atrocity crimes. Without a concept of humanity, there can be no concept of dehumanisation and no understanding of either the constitutive role that law plays in making these atrocities possible nor of the pleas of victims to reverse this process. These pleas, I argue, may be understood in terms of rehumanisation: pleas to be acknowledged in one's humanity in view of dehumanising practices and experiences, to be recognised as a full member of humanity. In the following, I will discuss three cases to show how mass atrocities and dehumanisation relate and how a plea to end dehumanisation follows the same logic of relying on a concept of humanity that refers to a normative community. These cases are slavery, genocide, and state violence against political opponents.

ICL now recognises slavery as a crime against humanity.[73] Apart from the legal qualification of this injustice, it is important to grasp the nature of this wrong. For this we need to appeal to a notion of dehumanisation. With Stanley Cavell, I characterise dehumanisation inherent within slavery as a denial of an internal relation between owners of enslaved persons and the enslaved persons.[74] Cavell speaks here of soul-blindness, a concept developed through a reading of the work of Ludwig Wittgenstein. The latter wrote on aspect blindness as 'lacking in the capacity to see something as something'.[75] Recall how someone can see Jastrow's famous image of the duck-rabbit as an image of

[72] I will discuss the symbolic effects of invoking humanity in Chapter 2.

[73] For a reflection and references to the sources, see Mahmoud Cherif Bassiouni, 'Enslavement as an International Crime', *New York University Journal of International Law and Politics* 23 (1990): 445–517.

[74] Stanley Cavell, *The Claim of Reason: Wittgenstein, Skepticism, Morality, and Tragedy* (Oxford: Oxford University Press, 1999), 376. My reading of Cavell and Wittgenstein is indebted to Jonathan Havercroft and David Owen, 'Soul-Blindness, Police Orders and Black Lives Matter: Wittgenstein, Cavell, and Rancière', *Political Theory* 44, no. 6 (2016): 739–63.

[75] Ludwig Wittgenstein, *Philosophical Investigations*, trans. G. E. M. Anscombe (Oxford: Basil Blackwell, 1967), 213.

only one of the two animals. This may change, Wittgenstein writes, when someone is struck by another aspect and an 'aspect change' occurs.[76] Such dawning of a new aspect is a change in one's practical attitude towards the picture.[77] Cavell argues that three activities are involved in aspect dawning: '(1) connecting together different things; (2) realising the significance that grows out of these connections; (3) making the behavior real to myself'.[78] It is the last activity that Cavell describes as 'bearing the right internal relation to others'.[79] Thus, soul-blindness captures the denial of another's humanity, 'as en-souled, where the concept of "soul" draws attention to the character of human beings as beings whose conduct gives expression to the inner lives that they have'.[80]

Four aspects are important in this regard.[81] First, analogous to Wittgenstein's view on aspects, in the case of soul-blindness, one fails to be struck by another's humanity. Second, since the injustice here involves the denial of an internal relationship, overcoming this requires establishing this internal relationship. This involves an act of acknowledgement, which is a practical attitude involving one's response and relationship towards others. More precisely, soul-blindness constitutes 'a failure to see the suffering of another as making a claim on our sympathy of the same kind that our own suffering would do so'.[82] The third aspect concerns the fundamental difference in worldview between the one who is and the one who is not soul-blind. In this difference in *Weltanschauung*, one realises how soul-blindness has not just to do with one's attitude towards a particular individual but is interrelated with one's relationship towards society and social institutions. The soul-blind person and the person who is not soul-blind – the owner of enslaved persons and the individual for whom enslaving others is out of the question – inhibit a different world.

Fourth and finally, to overcome this chasm and get rid of soul-blindness, one needs an experience of soul dawning, leading to a new practical relationship with oneself and the world. This happens through a politics that sensitises a soul-blind person to the claims to equal humanity of those who are not considered human, in the words of Cavell:

> It is sometimes imperative to say that women or children or Black people or criminals are human beings. This is a call for justice. For justice to be done, a change of perception, a modification of seeing, may be called for. But does it follow that those whose perceptions, or whose natural reactions, must suffer change have until that time been seeing women or children or Black people or criminals as something *other* than human beings?[83]

[76] Wittgenstein, *Philosophical Investigations*, 197.
[77] Wittgenstein, *Philosophical Investigations*, 205.
[78] Havercroft and Owen, 'Soul-Blindness, Police Orders and Black Lives Matter', 742.
[79] Cavell, *The Claim of Reason*, 378.
[80] Havercroft and Owen, 'Soul-Blindness, Police Orders and Black Lives Matter', 742.
[81] Havercroft and Owen, 'Soul-Blindness, Police Orders and Black Lives Matter', 742–45.
[82] Havercroft and Owen, 'Soul-Blindness, Police Orders and Black Lives Matter', 744.
[83] Cavell, *The Claim of Reason*, 372.

In a similar vein, the motive of racism or racist discrimination as a leading thread in the history of Western philosophy is at the heart of the work of Emmanuel Chukwudi Eze. Interestingly, also in his argument, the concept of humanity functions prominently. Discrimination on racial grounds 'manifests itself as a refusal to love others – those who are considered, literally or metaphorically nonbrothers and nonsisters'.[84] Eze's book – *Achieving Our Humanity* – ends with the defence of a 'postracial idea of humanity' that does not deny the importance of race in understanding injustices, nor strives for some kind of colourless community, but rather consists of 'those moments, in thought and practice, where we acknowledge and work to overcome the explicit and the implicit racial social mechanisms operating to thwart opportunities for some and enhance opportunities for others. To transcend race in this modest sense of both recognition and sublation requires that disabling racial labels may no longer be forced upon individuals or groups'.[85]

Dehumanisation also occurred during the Second World War. In trying to unearth the philosophical underpinnings of the process of dehumanisation and what is needed to counter it, Raimond Gaita takes his bearings from the work of Holocaust survivor Primo Levi, among others. Primo Levi's testimony is one of the gateways to grasp the relationship between morality and the notion of humanity. Gaita emphatically defends the notions of a common humanity and the preciousness of each unique human being and their inner life. Gaita submits that we cannot get rid of the notion of humanity, if we want to grasp the moral wrong of the Holocaust and how to come to terms with it, if that is ever possible. The distinctive evil of the Holocaust, Gaita argues, resides not only in the death camps being places of industrial murder but also in the way in which the Jews were dehumanised in the camps.[86] For lawyers, the peculiar thing about Auschwitz is how it was made possible, not despite, but with the help of the positive law of Nazi Germany. Hence, law was always implicated: Auschwitz was the culmination of a legal genocide, a legal form of dehumanisation.[87] Furthermore, a specific discourse on human dignity was complicit as well: 'To ascribe the predicate "human" to another being can be a subtle way to deprive her of her alterity, to reduce her to what is already confirmed as, made akin to, or appropriated by the first-person agent: *his* concept of a person, *his* social contract, *his* culture, *his* world'.[88] This deprivation of human dignity in the name of human dignity has become associated with the

[84] Emmanuel C. Eze, *Achieving Our Humanity: The Idea of the Postracial Future* (Abingdon: Routledge, 2013), 179.

[85] Eze, *Achieving Our Humanity*, 223.

[86] Raimond Gaita, *A Common Humanity: Thinking about Love and Truth and Justice* (Abingdon: Routledge, 2013), 141.

[87] Luigi Corrias, 'Dehumanization by Law', in *The Routledge Handbook of Dehumanization*, ed. Maria Kronfeldner (Abingdon: Routledge, 2021), 201–13.

[88] Bert van Roermund, *Legal Thought and Philosophy: What Legal Scholarship Is about* (Cheltenham: Edward Elgar Publishing, 2013), 87.

name Auschwitz. For the final solution was a matter, not beyond, but squarely within the confines of (Nazi) law.[89]

What we conceptually need when dealing with this kind of injustices, Gaita argues, is a notion of justice that acknowledges the reintegration of victims within a common humanity.[90] This is already at play within intersubjective relationships, where a form of human acknowledgement after suffering injustice becomes crucial.[91] This struggle for the acknowledgement of one's full humanity, for being recognised as a full member of humanity understood as a collective subject, is the one for social justice.[92] It can only take off if we recognise the independent reality of the other as a limit to our will.[93] Notice how this call to social justice cannot be reduced to distributive justice in the sense of fairness.[94] Rather, fairness presupposes social justice because the latter answers the question of who is in the position to demand fairness in the first place.[95] Doing justice to these kinds of wrongs may therefore only proceed through the recognition of these wrongs that are irreducible to the harm.[96]

Finally, moving to another political context, the concept of dehumanisation is also necessary to capture the specific violence used by political regimes that do not allow any dissident voices. The 1981 massacre in Iran is an interesting, albeit understudied, example. The massacre formed part of the Cultural Revolution in Iran, which was organised by the rulers 'to "purify" higher education from undesirable non-Islamic, Western, liberal, or leftist elements'.[97] On 20 June 1981, the People's Mojahedin Organization of Iran organised the largest anti-government demonstration, where dozens of protestors were killed.[98] This massacre was a crucial moment in the establishment of a new legal order; the violence proved to be constitutive in creating and maintaining the new order.[99]

Islamic revolutionary courts have sentenced thousands of dissidents to death without a fair trial and proper legal procedure.[100] Many victims are buried in mass graves or remain unidentified. Nasiri and Faghfouri Azar argue that on a symbolic level, mass graves perform three functions for the Iranian regime.[101] First, by desecrating graves and creating mass graves, the state could consolidate its power. Second, the desecration of gravestones forms the

[89] Van Roermund, *Legal Thought and Philosophy*, 84–6. [90] Gaita, *A Common Humanity*, 72.
[91] Gaita, *A Common Humanity*, 51. [92] Gaita, *A Common Humanity*, xx–xxi.
[93] Gaita, *A Common Humanity*, 52. [94] Gaita, *A Common Humanity*, 81.
[95] Gaita, *A Common Humanity*, 81–2. [96] Gaita, *A Common Humanity*, 82.
[97] Shahin Nasiri and Leila Faghfouri Azar, 'Investigating the 1981 Massacre in Iran: On the Law-Constituting Force of Violence', *Journal of Genocide Research* 26, no. 2 (2024): 164–87, at 166.
[98] The 1981 massacre of political dissidents was an atrocity that was followed by death sentences by the Islamic Revolutionary Courts in 1988. The 1988 massacre was later qualified as a crime against humanity; see Nasiri and Faghfouri Azar, 'Investigating the 1981 Massacre in Iran', 168.
[99] Nasiri and Faghfouri Azar, 'Investigating the 1981 Massacre in Iran', 169–70.
[100] Nasiri and Faghfouri Azar, 'Investigating the 1981 Massacre in Iran', 171. Nasiri and Faghfouri Azar come to an estimation of a total of more than 3,400 victims, among whom many are minors.
[101] Nasiri and Faghfouri Azar, 'Investigating the 1981 Massacre in Iran', 183–85.

ultimate stage of dehumanisation for ideological enemies: in life they were already cast as 'evil forces' and by desecrating their graves, the regime could 'deny their humanity even long after their death'.[102] Finally, since ideological enemies stood for a different form of society, their presence in collective memory was a threat to the totalitarian state and needed to be eradicated.

To reverse this dehumanisation, concrete actions to treat the remains of the victims of the 1981 massacre as *human* remains are necessary: identifying victims, notifying their families, reburying the victims in proper graves, and so on. Since the process of dehumanisation was part of a campaign of state violence, rehumanisation should also be done by the state. Through apologies and public monuments, the state can keep the memories of the victims alive.[103] The state could acknowledge their full humanity by restoring them not as merely human but as legally and politically equal. Rehumanisation could, accordingly, only make sense if it restores the full humanity, legal personhood and citizenship to these victims.[104] From ideological enemies, they must be transformed into political opponents who had the right to protest and contest the regime. As long as this is not done, the 1981 massacre will remain the inhuman violence that it is today.

1.5 Conclusion

This chapter has given a non-exhaustive overview of the invocation of humanity within legal, political and philosophical discourses relating to the atrocity crimes. The overview was guided by the primacy of inhumanity: the idea that humanity shows itself in its breach. This primacy explains why humanity is frequently invoked by international courts judging cases of atrocities. Within legal scholarship, a focus on the individual human being within international law has been greeted with enthusiasm by some scholars, for it heralded a new era within international relations where state sovereignty has been curbed and the rights of the individual human being take central stage, or so they argued. I have shown that, despite these scholars paying little to no attention to this, an analysis in terms of 'humanity's norms' does not make sense without a notion of humanity as a normative community, or collective subject.

More critical scholars in the field of political theory are, on the other hand, acutely aware of humanity being invoked as a collective subject. Crucially, they showed how in colonial and imperial contexts, even though all were included within humanity, this did not lead to all being equal. Indeed, for the colonised subject, inclusion within humanity and a sub-human status were two sides of the same coin. Accordingly, one needs to remain sensitive as to how the inclusion within humanity can be a violent act – a critique that remains relevant

102 Nasiri and Faghfouri Azar, 'Investigating the 1981 Massacre in Iran', 185.

103 See for interesting reflections on this topic: Matt Howard, *Law's Memories* (London: Palgrave Macmillan, 2023).

104 Corrias, 'Dehumanization by Law'.

today. This important criticism notwithstanding, there are instances in which dehumanisation can lead to exclusion from humanity, which do not follow the logic as it plays out within colonialism. Philosophers and legal and political theorists have used the notions of humanity and dehumanisation in reflecting on contexts of mass atrocities. From these reflections, one can learn that 'treat me as a human being' can be a strong moral appeal with important legal and political repercussions. Furthermore, the experience of being treated as an inhuman, as someone with a sub-human status, cannot be understood in terms of unfairness only. Far from simply being a problem of distributive justice, the experience of inhumanity signalled a problem in terms of social justice. For a process of rehumanisation is often needed to reverse dehumanisation. Such a process is demanded in pleas that are voiced in terms of acknowledgement of one's humanity in view of dehumanising experiences, of one's recognition as a full member of humanity. Therefore, we need the concept of humanity as a collective subject in order to express what is at play in dehumanisation.

In Chapter 2, I will discuss the way in which humanity as a collective subject is concretely constituted from a first-person perspective and how the inhuman questions it. In the chapters that follow, the analysis of the experience of inhumanity will take central stage, showing how the figure of the inhuman, in different guises, plays an important but often neglected role in the discourse on the atrocity crimes. While the experience of inhumanity shows the normative limits of the community of humanity, the figure of the inhuman remains elusive, ungraspable for the legal order. Ultimately, trying to understand the inhuman entails taking seriously the temporal disruption and normative demand that the inhuman poses to the legal order.

2

'We' and Crimes against Humanity

2.1 Introduction

In Chapter 1, I discussed several instances in which humanity is invoked within debates on the atrocity crimes. There, I have argued that it is necessary to introduce the first-person plural perspective to grasp what is at stake in these invocations. This chapter turns to the notion of crime against humanity. The central question it tackles is: in what sense(s) is humanity invoked in the notion of crime against humanity? The concept of crime against humanity occupies a principal place in international criminal law (ICL).[1] It can be found in legal documents, policy statements and publications of non-governmental organisations. In the preamble of the Rome Statute of the International Criminal Court (ICC), a relation is drawn between certain crimes and humanity:

> Mindful that during this century millions of children, women and men have been victims of unimaginable atrocities that deeply shock the conscience of humanity; [...] Affirming that the most serious crimes of concern to the international community as a whole must not go unpunished and that their effective prosecution must be ensured by taking measures at the national level and by enhancing international cooperation.[2]

This statement raises several questions. First, how may ICL be understood, or even legitimised, with a reference to humanity? To tackle this problem, ICL scholars have turned to Emile Durkheim, one of the founding fathers of sociology. Section 2.2 rereads this work to lay bare an influential, albeit critically received, view on the legitimacy of ICL. Read against the background of the preamble and the link between specific crimes and humanity, crime against humanity may be understood as the paradigmatic case of atrocity crime.

Subsequently, the statement of the preamble triggers the question of what understanding of humanity is presupposed in ICL in general and the concept

[1] See for examples: Sinja Graf, *The Humanity of Universal Crime: Inclusion, Inequality, and Intervention in International Political Thought* (Oxford: Oxford University Press, 2021), 1–2.

[2] Text of the Rome Statute circulated as document A/CONF.183/9 of 17 July 1998 and corrected by process-verbaux of 10 November 1998, 12 July 1999, 30 November 1999, 8 May 2000, 17 January 2001 and 16 January 2002, preamble.

of crime against humanity in particular. Drawing on work in political theory and phenomenology, Section 2.3 puts forward the argument that within ICL, humanity is to be understood as a normative community. The unity of this community is to be established on a symbolic level. I argue that 'humanity' is the name for the symbolic construction from which international society can see and understand itself as one.

Drawing on phenomenology and speech act theory, Section 2.4 traces the genesis of the community of humanity. I argue that the normative community of humanity is the result of a process of self-constitution. Hence, judgements on crimes against humanity are always given from a first-person plural perspective, from the standpoint of 'we, humanity'. As I will argue, representation plays a crucial part here. International tribunals judge on behalf of humanity, thus acting as its representatives. Finally, what is in- and excluded in ICL's invocation of humanity? Taking the phenomenological analysis one step further, Section 2.5 starts from the premise that even a reference to humanity is not all-encompassing. Humanity appears as a bounded whole. What cannot be integrated is the inhuman. Yet, the inhuman does not simply disappear but lingers at the fringes of the ICL order, appearing at its twilight and confronting it with its blind spot. While the normative consequences of inhumanity are unfolded at a later stage of this book, Section 2.5 takes Dominic Ongwen as an exemplary inhuman, in the specific sense identified earlier. Ongwen is, quite literally, extra-ordinary. It is, I argue, exactly this nature that explains ICL's difficulty in coming to terms with him.

2.2 On the Use and Abuse of Durkheim for International Criminal Law

Several ICL scholars have explicitly posed the question of the 'we' within the field: on whose behalf are 'we' punishing the perpetrators of atrocity crimes?[3] In their work, Durkheim's writings figure prominently, albeit not without being criticised. To grasp this fascination with Durkheim and his work's relation to the question of the 'we' within ICL, I will discuss selected aspects of the work of Durkheim and its reception within ICL scholarship. The section is structured as follows. First, I will explain Durkheim's views on law. Then, I will turn to the way in which his thoughts have been applied to ICL. Finally, I will discuss the value and limitations of a Durkheimian approach to ICL.

For Durkheim, the most important question is what binds society together. His answer is the social solidarity that resulted from the division of labour in

[3] Immi Tallgren has, arguably, delved deepest into this question in many publications. See, for instance, Immi Tallgren, 'The Voice of the International: Who Is Speaking?', *Journal of International Criminal Justice* 13, no. 1 (2015): 135–55.

modern society.[4] Yet, here a problem arises, for one cannot study this solidarity directly, since it cannot appear as an object for observation.[5] Instead, one should study law because law is a social fact and, more specifically, the visible appearance of social solidarity.[6] Hence, law forms an object of sociological inquiry.[7] Here, the concept of the collective conscience plays a crucial role. Durkheim describes the *conscience collective* as follows: 'The totality of beliefs and sentiments common to the average members of a society forms a determinate system with a life of its own. It can be termed the collective or common consciousness'.[8] These beliefs are especially deeply rooted within society.[9] Durkheim also refers to the collective conscience as the sacred or transcendental dimension of law and social ordering.[10]

Law, in its repressive function, reflects this collective by protecting moral values and enhancing solidarity.[11] In this way, law ties different actors of

[4] Emile Durkheim, *The Division of Labour in Society*, trans. W. D. Halls (London: Palgrave Macmillan, 1984), 23: 'It is through the division of labour, or at least mainly through it, that the cohesion of societies would be ensured'.

[5] Durkheim, *Division* 24:

> Social solidarity is a wholly moral phenomenon which by itself is not amenable to exact observation and especially not to measurement. To arrive at this classification, as well as this comparison, we must therefore substitute for this internal datum, which escapes us, an external one which symbolises it, and then study the former through the latter. That visible symbol is the law.

[6] Durkheim, *Division* 25:

> In fact, social life, wherever it becomes lasting, inevitably tends to assume a definite form and become organised. Law is nothing more than this very organisation in its most stable and precise form. Life in general within a society cannot enlarge in scope without legal activity simultaneously increasing in proportion. Thus we may be sure to find reflected in the law all the essential varieties of social solidarity.

[7] Emile Durkheim, *The Rules of Sociological Method*, trans. W. D. Halls (New York City, NY: Free Press, 1982), 82:

> Apart from the individual acts to which they give rise, collective habits are expressed in definite forms such as legal or moral rules, popular sayings, or facts of social structure, etc. As these forms exist permanently and do not change with the various applications which are made of them, they constitute a fixed object, a constant standard which is always to hand for the observer, and which leaves no room for subjective impressions or personal observations. A legal rule is what it is and there are no two ways of perceiving it. Since, from another angle, these practices are no more than social life consolidated, it is legitimate, failing indications to the contrary, to study that life through these practices.

[8] Durkheim, *Division* 38–39.

[9] Durkheim, *Division* 37:

> Thus the collective sentiments to which a crime corresponds must be distinguished from other sentiments by some striking characteristic: they must be of a certain average intensity. Not only are they written upon the consciousness of everyone, but they are deeply written. They are in no way mere halting, superficial caprices of the will, but emotions and dispositions strongly rooted within us.

[10] Nikolas M. Rajkovic, 'What Is a "Grave" International Crime? The Rome Statute, Durkheim and the Sociology of Ruling Outrages', *Loyola University Chicago International Law Review* 16 (2020): 65–86, at 73.

[11] Immi Tallgren, 'The Durkheimian Spell of International Criminal Law?', *Revue interdisciplinaire d'études juridiques* 71, no. 2 (2013): 137–69, at 146.

society together. In Durkheim's view on law, criminal law takes a special place. A crime is a violation of collective sentiments.[12] Indeed, this is what makes an act criminal in the first place.[13] Durkheim even presents the condemnation of crime as a criterion for a 'healthy consciousness'.[14] For him, the *public* and *affective* nature of punishment is crucial. As an act of solidarity, punishment is a reaction to crimes aimed at protecting the *conscience collective*. In other words, punishment is an expression of those same sentiments and reinforces the collective beliefs.[15] Accordingly, punishment is a public affair because it regards not primarily the individual victims but rather society as a whole.[16] Durkheim also stresses the passionate nature of punishment.[17] For him, punishment is to be regarded as an affective response to a threat to social cohesion.[18]

12 Durkheim, *Division* 31:

> The bond of social solidarity to which repressive law corresponds is one the breaking of which constitutes the crime. We use the term 'crime' to designate any act which, regardless of degree, provokes against the perpetrator the characteristic reaction known as punishment. To investigate the nature of this bond is therefore to ask what is the cause of the punishment or, more precisely, what in essence the crime consists of.

13 Durkheim, *Division* 39: 'We may state that an act is criminal when it offends the strong, well-defined states of the collective consciousness'.

14 Durkheim, *Division* 33–34:

> Indeed, the only feature common to all crimes is that, saving some apparent exceptions to be examined later, they comprise acts universally condemned by the members of each society. (…) The real nature of the fact we have just established cannot be disputed, viz., that crime disturbs those feelings that in any one type of society are to be found in every healthy consciousness.

15 Durkheim, *Division* 62:

> The same holds good for collective emotions. Every act that disturbs them is not dangerous in itself, or at least is not so perilous as the condemnation it earns. However, the reprobation such acts incur is not without reason. For, whatever the origin of these sentiments, once they constitute a part of the collective type, and particularly if they are essential elements in it, everything that serves to undermine them at the same time undermines social cohesion and is prejudicial to society. In their origin they had no usefulness but, having survived, it becomes necessary for them to continue despite their irrationality. This is generally why it is good that acts that offend these sentiments should not be tolerated.

16 Durkheim, *Division* 48: 'If it is society alone that exerts repression, it is because it is harmed even when the harm done is to individuals, and it is the attack upon society that is repressed by punishment'.

17 Durkheim, *Division* 44: 'In the first place, punishment constitutes an emotional reaction'.

18 Durkheim, *Division* 62–63:

> The same is true of punishment. Although it proceeds from an entirely mechanical reaction and from an access of passionate emotion, for the most part unthinking, it continues to play a useful role. (…) Its real function is to maintain inviolate the cohesion of society by sustaining the common consciousness in all its vigour. If that consciousness were thwarted so categorically, it would necessarily lose some of its power, were an emotional reaction from the community not forthcoming to make good that loss. Thus there would result a relaxation in the bonds of social solidarity. The consciousness must therefore be conspicuously reinforced the moment it meets with opposition. The sole means of doing so is to give voice to the unanimous aversion that the crime continues to evoke, and this by an official act, which can only mean suffering inflicted upon the wrongdoer.

Punishment is ultimately about vengeance.[19] This view can be summarised in Durkheim's own words: 'Thus punishment constitutes essentially a reaction of passionate feeling, graduated in intensity, which society exerts through the mediation of an organised body over those of its members who have violated certain rules of conduct'.[20]

What does that mean for the judicial process? The criminal trial replaces private vengeance, and the criminal tribunal represents – acts on behalf of – society.[21] In this respect, Durkheim's views on religion are important. Religion plays an important social function. It expresses sentiments within a society and regulates social relations.[22] In modern, industrial societies, Durkheim argues, this function is taken over by law. Hence, punishment restores the sacred rule. Therefore, the trial takes on a communicative model addressing both the criminal and society.[23] Just as law takes over from religion, in modernity the human being has taken the place of God. Consequently, the individual is sacred for Durkheim.[24]

I will now discuss the attractiveness of Durkheim's views on law and society for the young field of ICL. There are at least three reasons why Durkheim is so interesting for ICL's quest for an ultimate ground, or justification.[25] First, his work – focusing primarily on the social ties constitutive for society – can be adapted to fit different social environments, including the field of ICL. Second, Durkheim's theory gives a moral ground for ICL in the collective representation of humanity. Finally, there are functional reasons to draw on Durkheim for ICL, for his theory can help explain how and why ICL operates as it does.

Within the 'international community', ICL is the repressive law reaffirming the '*conscience collective* of humanity' by prosecuting and punishing those responsible for the atrocities that 'shock its conscience'.[26] This would make the Rome Statute of the ICC into a symbolic text, wherein an 'international "we" is called into existence'.[27] Accordingly, one could underscore the relevance of Durkheim for ICL in that

[19] Durkheim, *Division* 47: 'Thus punishment has remained for us what it was for our predecessors. It is still an act of vengeance, since it is an expiation. What we are avenging, and what the criminal is expiating, is the outrage to morality'.

[20] Durkheim, *Division* 52.

[21] Salif Nimaga, 'An International Conscience Collective? A Durkheimian Analysis of International Criminal Law', *International Criminal Law Review* 7, no. 4 (2007): 561–619, at 569–71.

[22] Marina Aksenova, 'Solidarity as a Moral and Legal Basis for Crimes against Humanity: A Durkheimean Perspective', in *Breaking the Cycle of Mass Atrocities: Criminological and Socio-Legal Approaches in International Criminal Law*, eds. M. Aksenova, E. Van Sliedregt and S. Parmentier (London: Hart Publishing, 2019), 73–92, at 89.

[23] Nimaga, 'An International Conscience Collective?', 579.

[24] Nimaga, 'An International Conscience Collective?', 582.

[25] Aksenova, 'Solidarity as a Moral and Legal Basis for Crimes against Humanity', 75–77.

[26] Tallgren, 'The Durkheimian Spell of International Criminal Law?', 149–51.

[27] Rajkovic, 'What Is a "Grave" International Crime?', 86.

> criminal law responses carve out the moral boundaries of a community, while enhancing social cohesion within the group through regulated yet 'passionate' reactions to deviant behavior. Through its responses to criminal behavior, a collectivity (re)discovers its outer limits and identity; the moral boundaries that cannot be transgressed. Not only the injuries suffered by the direct victim are at stake in criminal law but also the integrity of the 'collective conscience' that needs to be defended against its enemies.[28]

International criminal law is seen as embodying a global consciousness and punishes attacks on 'the *jus cogens* core of international law'.[29] With the Nuremberg trials, a global culture was born that may be the basis for a collective conscience.[30] The development of ICL after the Second World War may then even be understood as explicating the *conscience collective*, which was implicitly already there.[31] Within ICL, punishment's key function would be upholding human dignity and integrating perpetrators into global society.[32] Here, Durkheim's insistence on the sacredness of the individual may also benefit the perpetrator, protecting him from being dehumanised.[33] Indeed, with the help of Durkheim, one could also stress the communicative or expressivist function of the ICC.[34] In short, ICL is portrayed as an expression of global solidarity. Accordingly, international criminal trials may be seen as religious rituals: 'in the aftermath of mass atrocities, the international community comes together to craft an institution that religiously follows legal procedure in creating a space between the perpetrators and the victims'.[35] In this process, victims appear as sacred because they play an important role in the containment of vengeance due to their distance from the perpetrators.[36]

Apart from the positive reception of his work, legal scholars have also pointed out the weak spots in a Durkheimian reading of ICL. One can discern several related forms of criticism. First, one may question how universal the international *conscience collective* of ICL is. The demarcation of the 'most serious crimes' leaves many forms of 'slow violence' outside of the ICC's reach.[37] Consequently, the indeterminacy and contingency of the

[28] Wouter Werner, *Repetition and International Law* (Cambridge: Cambridge University Press, 2022), 140.
[29] Aksenova, 'Solidarity as a Moral and Legal Basis for Crimes against Humanity', 84.
[30] Nimaga, 'An International Conscience Collective?', 588.
[31] Nimaga, 'An International Conscience Collective?', 603–4.
[32] Nimaga, 'An International Conscience Collective?', 593.
[33] Nimaga, 'An International Conscience Collective?', 600.
[34] Nimaga, 'An International Conscience Collective?', 617:

> The ICC is communicating to a global society messages of the legalisation of the international sphere and the importance of due process in the punishment of perpetrators in recognition of their humanity. Most importantly, however, the work of the court marks the vindication of the most blatant violations of the values resulting from the religion built around human dignity in order to prevent a dwindling belief in these values.

[35] Aksenova, 'Solidarity as a Moral and Legal Basis for Crimes against Humanity', 90.
[36] Aksenova, 'Solidarity as a Moral and Legal Basis for Crimes against Humanity', 90.
[37] Tallgren, 'The Durkheimian Spell of International Criminal Law?', 145.

so-called grave crimes cannot be acknowledged by Durkheim.[38] Notions such as 'gravity' and 'seriousness' function as gatekeepers ensuring that other kinds of violence remain 'invisible' and cannot be scrutinised.[39] ICL is far from universal, and it is difficult to speak of international solidarity.[40] The existence of an international collective consciousness is therefore highly questionable. Moreover, the enforcement of ICL is not obvious.[41] Much depends on the willingness of individual nation-states and enforcement often cannot avoid being a violent act, itself. Finally, Durkheim's ideas of collective consciousness and sacredness remain reified and a-historical.[42] Durkheim leaves no room for social change or conflict about the values inherent in society.[43] In a Durkheimian perspective, law appears as neutral, hiding political and ideological choices within the ICL architecture from view.[44] In short, what is hidden from view in Durkheim are the genealogical aspects of ICL, that is, how law is always the contingent outcome of a power struggle, or contest.[45]

2.3 Humanity as Symbolic Order

Notwithstanding the important criticisms of Durkheim's views, I submit that there are valuable elements in his work that need to be retained, notably his theory regarding 'the constitution' of ICL.[46] Indeed, this aspect is crucial in order to grasp the practice of ICL from the perspective of the tribunals involved. These, typically, invoke humanity when judging atrocities. Going beyond a purely formal view on law, Durkheim points to law's transcendental dimension that is called upon in the solidarity triggered by outrages making a sum of individuals into a collective.[47] The sacred, represented as situated outside of us, is a necessary illusion for it constitutes us as a unity.[48] Another way of saying that is that the sacred for Durkheim has a strong symbolic power.[49] Allow me to cite Durkheim in full on this crucial point:

[38] Rajkovic, 'What Is a "Grave" International Crime?', 79–84.
[39] Rajkovic, 'What Is a "Grave" International Crime?', 77–81. I will return to this problem in Chapter 6.
[40] Tallgren, 'The Durkheimian Spell of International Criminal Law?', 155.
[41] Tallgren, 'The Durkheimian Spell of International Criminal Law?', 159.
[42] Rajkovic, 'What Is a "Grave" International Crime?', 74.
[43] Tallgren, 'The Durkheimian Spell of International Criminal Law?', 151–52.
[44] Tallgren, 'The Durkheimian Spell of International Criminal Law?', 153–55.
[45] Rajkovic, 'What Is a "Grave" International Crime?', 73.
[46] Rajkovic, 'What Is a "Grave" International Crime?', 71–72, and 85.
[47] Rajkovic, 'What Is a "Grave" International Crime?', 73–74. In a related argument, Nimaga defends Durkheim against the criticism that his notion of *conscience collective* is static and does not take into account the political dimension of law and society, by pointing out that the collective conscience is what makes debate within society possible, in the first place. See Nimaga, 'An International Conscience Collective?', 576–77.
[48] Rajkovic, 'What Is a "Grave" International Crime?', 74.
[49] Rajkovic, 'What Is a "Grave" International Crime?', 76, and 85–86.

> Thus it is always to the collective consciousness that we must return. From it, directly or indirectly, all criminality flows. Crime is not only injury done to interests which may be serious; it is also an offence against an authority which is in some way transcendent. (…) When we demand the repression of crime it is not because we are seeking a personal vengeance, but rather vengeance for something sacred which we vaguely feel is more or less *outside and above us.* Depending upon time and place, we conceive of this object in different ways. Occasionally it is a simple idea, such as morality or duty. Very often we represent it to ourselves in the form of one or several concrete beings: ancestors, or a divinity. This is why penal law is not only of essentially religious origin, but continues always to bear a certain stamp of religiosity. This is because the acts that it punishes always appear as attacks upon something which is transcendent, whether this is a being or a concept. It is for this same reason that we explain to ourselves how such attacks appear to require from us a higher sanction than the mere reparation we content ourselves with in the sphere of purely human interests. *Such a representation is assuredly an illusion.* In one sense it is indeed ourselves that we are avenging, and ourselves to whom we afford satisfaction, since it is within us, and within us alone, that are to be found the feelings that have been offended. *But this illusion is necessary.* Since these sentiments, because of their collective origin, their universality, their permanence over time, and their intrinsic intensity, are exceptionally strong, they stand radically apart from the rest of our consciousness, where other states are much weaker. They dominate us, they possess, so to speak, something superhuman about them.[50]

A Durkheimian perspective on ICL reveals something that is not visible from a purely doctrinal view, namely that ICL is instituted and legitimised as a symbolic order, made up of representations outside of us. I argue that this symbolic dimension is necessary in ICL. The challenge is hence to keep what is valuable in the Durkheimian reading of ICL – his insights regarding the symbolic constitution of international society – while avoiding its pitfalls. For this purpose, I suggest reading Durkheim's work concerning the symbolic through the lens of Claude Lefort's work on the symbolic institution of society. In his exploration of the theological-political aspect of modern political regimes, Lefort acknowledges a similarity between religion and politics regarding the unity of society.[51] Indeed, this unity or order is the fruit of

> a primal division which is constitutive of the space we call society. And the fact that this space is organized as one despite (or because of) its multiple divisions and that it is organized as *the same* in all its multiple dimensions implies a reference to a place from which it can be seen, read and named. Even before we examine it in its empirical determinations, this symbolic pole proves to be

[50] Durkheim, *Division* 43 and 56. My italics, LC. See also Rajkovic, 'What Is a "Grave" International Crime?', 74.

[51] Claude Lefort, *Democracy and Political Theory*, trans. D. Macey (Hoboken, NJ: Wiley, 1991), 222–23: 'Every religion *states* in its own way that human society can only open on to itself by being held in an opening it did not create. Philosophy says the same thing, but religion said it first, albeit in terms which philosophy cannot accept'.

power; it manifests society's self-externality, and ensures that society can achieve a quasi-representation of itself. We must of course be careful not to project this externality on to the real; if we did so it would no longer have any meaning for society. It would be more accurate to say that power makes a gesture towards something *outside*, and that it defines itself in terms of that outside. Whatever its form, it always refers to the same enigma: that of an internal–external articulation, of a division which institutes a common space, of a break which establishes relations, of a movement of the externalization of the social which goes hand in hand with its internalization.[52]

I argue that what ought to be retained from Durkheim is his connection between criminal law and the symbolic pole of power, as I have interpreted it with the help of Lefort. The collective conscience of ICL as it appears in the reference to humanity is the symbolic pole of power from which international society appears as a unity, or bounded whole. The symbolic nature of the collective conscience refers to it being an imaginative point from which to give meaning to ICL as one legal order enacted in the name of humanity. The notion of power speaks to the representational nature of this symbolic dimension. It highlights how also (international) courts and tribunals – the ICC is a case in point – are political actors in the specific sense that they act on behalf of, indeed represent, the normative community of humanity.[53]

Using Lefort's work makes it possible to shed more light on the type of international society that is called into being by ICL's claim, as voiced by (international) courts and tribunals, to embody a normative community of humanity. Focusing on the forming principles of society, one may draw a distinction between various kinds of regimes, in the sense of specific forms in which a society exists in time and space and the ways in which relations within society are structured. Every type of regime is a specific way of giving form to society (*mise-en-forme*), which both gives meaning to social relationships within society (*mise-en-sense*) and provides them with a stage (*mise-en-scène*).[54] With the instituting principles, one may capture the markers that order the experience within society.

Accordingly, ICL entails a specific form to international society that offers the ICC, together with other tribunals, as the stage where individuals are called to account for 'the most serious crimes of concern to the international community as a whole'. ICL provides a list of what is most serious, casting what is not on the list as less serious and, hence, not of concern to the international community. This is how it gives meaning to relations within international

[52] Lefort, *Democracy and Political Theory*, 225.

[53] Luigi Corrias, and Geoffrey M. Gordon, 'Judging in the Name of Humanity: International Criminal Tribunals and the Representation of a Global Public', *Journal of International Criminal Justice* 13, no. 1 (2015): 97–112.

[54] Lefort, *Democracy and Political Theory*, 217–19. Strictly speaking, for Lefort this is the dimension of 'the political' as distinguished from 'politics'.

society: curbing state sovereignty, juridifying (depoliticising) relations and seeking individual criminal responsibility.[55] Furthermore, it gives meaning by offering a legal language to make sense of this juridified world. In this world, strict dichotomies, such as the one between victim and perpetrator, take centre stage. Finally, it casts the legal solution of universal ICL above other local or political solutions, thus legitimising the ICC and other international courts and tribunals.

Reading Durkheim through the lens of Lefort also reveals that what is at stake here is a process of *self*-constitution. This is the function of humanity within ICL: it is the name of the collective subject of self-constitution. It is important to stress that mine is a phenomenological and non-normative analysis, that is, it describes the practice of ICL from the first-person perspective of the tribunals involved. Accordingly, my claim is solely that in judging atrocity crimes, tribunals pose as if representing the global public or acting on behalf of the normative community of humanity. This in itself does not say anything about whether they are legitimated to do so, nor is it an apology for this practice. I will return to this type of question in Section 2.4.

2.4 The Self-Constitution of Humanity within International Criminal Law

What needs to be done now is to show how the normative community of humanity is constituted: how does 'we, humanity' come about in the context of ICL? While Durkheim and Lefort have put us on track with the symbolic nature of humanity as a collective subject invoked by international tribunals, an analysis of its constitution from a first-person perspective requires looking into the specific speech acts that call humanity into being. In a pioneering article, Immi Tallgren has exactly posed the question under which condition the use of 'we' in ICL is warranted. With the phenomenologist Herbert Spiegelberg, she distinguishes between the '"we of co-presence" and the "absentee-we"'.[56] In this section, I will critically reconstruct Spiegelberg's argument, paying special attention to its potential application in legal-political contexts, before developing an alternative view on we-talk in ICL.

[55] Compare this with Bruce Rosenstock, 'Against Sovereign Impunity: The Political Theology of the International Criminal Court', in *After Secular Law*, eds. Winnifred Sullivan, Robert A. Yelle, and Mateo Taussig-Rubbo (Redwood City, CA: Stanford University Press, 2011), 160–79 at 163–75. Rosenstock also points out that ICL should be seen within a larger framework that is meant to put limits on the power of sovereign states. Accordingly, what the ICC represents – 'the international community as a whole' – is something else than merely the collection of sovereign states. What is shocking to 'the conscience of mankind' is the impunity by which sovereign states could commit crimes. Ending impunity is thus central to ICL and, consequently, the procedure is less about the protection of the rights of the suspect than it is about recording the memory of the victims, Rosenstock argues.

[56] Tallgren, 'The Voice of the International', 140.

In everyday discourse, there are two basic ways in which 'we' occurs.[57] In the case of the 'we of co-presence', the speaker stands in a direct face-to-face relationship with those she includes. In this case, saying 'we' involves a claim to unanimity.[58] In contrast to this situation, in the case of the 'absentee we', the speaker acts as a representative of absent contemporaries. The speaker necessarily refers to an exclusive 'we' but may also include unborn others.[59] Spiegelberg speaks here of an act of 'sheer arrogance' because there is no way of knowing the future intentions of the collective.[60] One of the most important functions of we-talk is that it aligns others into joining the speaker in their camp and claims them as partners or associates.[61] When discussing this aligning function of we-talk, Spiegelberg makes a statement that is particularly important for the argument in this chapter: 'clearly it presupposes some prior authorization or subsequent ratification. In this sense all the we-talk in the absence of the committed is on credit, as it were. The decisive question is whether or not the speaker has some kind of a proxy for them. Without it, all we-talk in the absence of the we-partners is clearly false pretense'.[62]

I will return to this claim and whether it can make sense of legal and political speech acts in the first-person plural. This is related to the legitimacy of we-talk. Is there a moral right to say 'we'? Spiegelberg proves to be critical.[63] Since it is basically impossible to receive the consent of all present in an audience, saying 'we' is often a usurpation. Yet, Spiegelberg does seem to allow for a limited right under the condition that the proposed partner is actually present and allows for the use of the first-person plural. In other words, this actual presence is a condition for rejection, because in such a case, the lack of rejection, or explicit consent, would give a speaker a right to say 'we'.[64] This condition is, however, hardly ever satisfied in politics. Indeed, Spiegelberg's sparse remarks on the 'we' in politics relate solely to dictators or demagogues abusing the first-person plural.[65] When analysing the 'absentee-we', Spiegelberg

[57] Herbert Spiegelberg, '"We": A Linguistic and Phenomenological Analysis', in *Doing Phenomenology. Essays on and in Phenomenology* (The Hague: Martinus Nijhoff, 1975), 215–45, at 218.

[58] Spiegelberg, '"We": A Linguistic and Phenomenological Analysis', 219.

[59] Spiegelberg, '"We": A Linguistic and Phenomenological Analysis', 224.

[60] Spiegelberg, '"We": A Linguistic and Phenomenological Analysis', 224.

[61] Spiegelberg, '"We": A Linguistic and Phenomenological Analysis', 222–23.

[62] Spiegelberg, '"We": A Linguistic and Phenomenological Analysis', 224.

[63] Spiegelberg, '"We": A Linguistic and Phenomenological Analysis', 241: 'Whenever I claim to speak in your name as well as in my own without your consent and especially over your protest, I have violated your moral right to the respect I owe you as a person'.

[64] Spiegelberg, '"We": A Linguistic and Phenomenological Analysis', 243:

> The very fact that I say so in your presence puts my claim to the test and gives you a chance to protest, thus giving me the lie. The 'we' is then merely an invitation to accept my 'we' formulation and an attempt to simplify matters for you by way of a rejectable offer. Your very presence at my speaking constitutes your protection against my usurpation.

[65] Spiegelberg, '"We": A Linguistic and Phenomenological Analysis', 243.

does acknowledge that the speaker acts as a representative.[66] Here is the crucial passage:

> To say 'we, the people' and even more so 'we, the United Nations' is a bold claim indeed, which can all too easily turn out to be a rhetorical fiction invalidated by the fact that none of the we-partners even knew that he was included by his representatives. (…) In short, in the case of the absentee we one's right depends on the existence of live credentials testifying to the support of the absentees. Ultimately even the absentee we points back to the conditions for the legitimate use of the we of copresence.[67]

Spiegelberg, as noted, presupposes the actual presence of a 'we' to legitimise the use of we-talk. This legitimisation may occur either by prior explicit consent, or by post facto silent support. In a similar vein, Tallgren stresses the highly problematic nature of we-talk in ICL. Failing to form a genuine 'we-union' because of the lack of reciprocity between the parties, the 'we' of ICL remains defective.[68] This leads to an abuse of 'we-talk', not acknowledging 'unequal conditions of discourse' within ICL.[69] As a result, the 'we' of ICL is expansive, excludes subaltern voices and fails to do proper justice to victims.[70] Yet, at the same time, Tallgren admits that 'we-talk' might be part and parcel of legal rationality, making it unavoidable.[71] The fundamental question, already posed by Spiegelberg, becomes 'the move from "you and I" to "we"'.[72]

Indeed, the philosophical problem cuts deeper than that of the factual presence of the partners. This points to the necessity of representation. Using the very same example as Spiegelberg – 'We, the People' – Jacques Derrida shows how representation is not only necessary but also constitutive for the 'we': paradoxically, it is the representative act that calls 'we' into being.[73] In a seminal article, Bert van Roermund offers a fine-grained theory of first-person plural speech acts in legal and political contexts that tackles exactly this problem. Concisely, the argument highlights political reflexivity in showing how legislation in modernity has the canonical form of an act of collective self-legislation and can be rephrased as a first-person plural speech act. In other

[66] Spiegelberg, '"We": A Linguistic and Phenomenological Analysis', 244.
[67] Spiegelberg, '"We": A Linguistic and Phenomenological Analysis', 244.
[68] Tallgren, 'The Voice of the International', 150–52.
[69] Tallgren, 'The Voice of the International', 153.
[70] Tallgren, 'The Voice of the International', 136–38, and 143.
[71] Tallgren, 'The Voice of the International', 138.
[72] Tallgren, 'The Voice of the International', 142.
[73] Jacques Derrida, 'Declarations of Independence', *New Political Science* 7, no. 1 (1986): 7–15, at 10:

> The 'we' of the declaration speaks 'in the name of the people'. But this people does not exist. They do not exist as an entity, it does not exist, before this declaration, not as such. If it gives birth to itself, as free and independent subject, as possible signer, this can hold only in the act of signature. The signature invents the signer. This signer can only authorize him- or herself to sign once he or she has come to the end [parvenu au vout], if one can say this, of his or her own signature, in a sort of fabulous retroactivity.

words, legislation is *self*-legislation and can be understood as a collective ruling over themselves, or formulated as a speech act from the perspective of this collective: 'we rule over ourselves'. Van Roermund and Hans Lindahl developed the approach to law that undergirds this theory distinguishing between different we-positions. In discussing this theory, I will refer to the passage from the Preamble of the Rome Statute of the ICC that was discussed earlier:

> Mindful that during this century millions of children, women and men have been victims of unimaginable atrocities that deeply shock the conscience of humanity; [...] Affirming that the most serious crimes of concern to the international community as a whole must not go unpunished and that their effective prosecution must be ensured by taking measures at the national level and by enhancing international cooperation.[74]

First, there is a 'we' speaking.[75] 'We' is always uttered by singular individuals, the spokespersons. These function as representatives of a collective. *Pace* Spiegelberg, representation is not a contingent but a necessary element of first-person plural speech acts: since a plurality of speakers cannot speak with one voice, representation is indispensable.[76] Here, the paradox of representation applies. There is no collective, no 'we' before representation. It is the representative who calls the collective into being in saying 'we'. Representation is, in other words, constitutive for unity. Yet, if there is no collective before the representation, there is also no prior permission to represent. This marks the act of representation with a moment of illegitimacy. Indeed, every representation is necessarily partial and provisional, so there is no such thing as an all-encompassing community or agent. Also, 'humanity' is necessarily bounded.[77]

In the case of the preamble, there are different speakers saying 'we': heads of state, ministers, negotiators, civil servants and so on. These speakers represent a collective subject agent – humanity – in the double sense that representation takes in these practices: while they claim to substitute the agent (i.e., humanity), at the very same time they will need to depict this agent as a unity of which they are already part. To reformulate this from the perspective of the representatives: only if they assert that they are already mandated by the collective they claim to represent will they be able to paint a credible collective subject. Their success as a representative depends on this depiction, as it is taken up

[74] Text of the Rome Statute circulated as document A/CONF.183/9 of 17 July 1998 and corrected by process-verbaux of 10 November 1998, 12 July 1999, 30 November 1999, 8 May 2000, 17 January 2001 and 16 January 2002, preamble.

[75] Hans Lindahl, *Authority and the Globalisation of Inclusion and Exclusion* (Cambridge: Cambridge University Press, 2018), 99–102 and Bert van Roermund, *Law in the First Person Plural: Roots, Concepts, Topics* (Cheltenham: Edward Elgar Publishing, 2020), 102–4.

[76] Or, in Bernhard Waldenfels's apt formulation, 'a we cannot say we'. See Bernhard Waldenfels, *Verfremdung der Moderne: Phänomenologische Grenzgänge*, Vol. 10 (Göttingen: Wallstein Verlag, 2001), 39.

[77] For a defence of this thesis in the context of global law, see Lindahl, *Authority and the Globalisation of Inclusion and Exclusion.*

and followed and/or acted upon by others.[78] However, because of the lack of a prior existing collective, there can also be no permission to represent. The success of a representative claim can, accordingly, be determined in hindsight only. If and only if uptake actually occurs is the act of representation seen as legitimate. Only in hindsight may the legitimacy of uttering 'we, humanity' be determined.

Second, the speech act involves a 'we' deciding.[79] Here, one encounters the underlying author of the preamble, as Hobbes would put it, the collective that is represented.[80] In the case of the Rome Statute, the collective comes under the name 'humanity'. Indeed, humanity – understood as a collective subject – is the presumed author of the Rome Statute who decides to end impunity for the gravest crimes of concern to the international community by establishing the ICC.

Third, there is a 'we' acting.[81] This aspect emphasises that the preamble is a collective intention, where a collective self is thought of as the entity that performs the action. The key point to keep in mind is that 'in intentions one pictures *oneself* doing something. Thus, the "self" is what one thinks about and what is about to act'.[82] One is dealing here with reflexivity, or identity in the sense of selfhood.[83] Again, one encounters here 'humanity', but this time under the specific aspect of the actor of the intention, in this context the end of impunity. Linking this to the preamble: it is humanity that 'takes measures' and 'enhances cooperation' to end impunity.

Fourth and finally, in the speech act, there is a reference to a 'we' at stake.[84] The question then becomes: whose interests are being protected by the Rome Statute? The answer must be humanity, or that is the claim. It is in the interest of humanity itself that 'unimaginable atrocities' or 'the most serious crimes of concern to the international community as a whole' are prosecuted and punished. Crucially, speakers of the speech act can only be successful if they credibly consider the interests of the collective they claim to represent. In other words, speakers should, in depicting the interests of

[78] For more on this necessity of uptake, see Luigi Corrias, *The Passivity of Law: Competence and Constitution in the European Court of Justice* (Berlin: Springer Science & Business Media, 2011) and Luigi Corrias, 'The Legal Theory of the Juridical Coup: Constituent Power Now', *German Law Journal* 12, no. 8 (2011): 1553–72.

[79] Lindahl, *Authority and the Globalisation of Inclusion and Exclusion*, 106–8 and Van Roermund, *Law in the First Person Plural*, 104–6.

[80] Thomas Hobbes, *Leviathan* (London: Penguin Press, 1968), 217–22. See on this view of Hobbes and its value for ICL, also Luigi D. A. Corrias and Geoffrey M. Gordon, 'Judging in the Name of Humanity: International Criminal Tribunals and the Representation of a Global Public', *Journal of International Criminal Justice* 13, no. 1 (2015): 97–112.

[81] Van Roermund, *Law in the First Person Plural*, 106–8.

[82] Van Roermund, *Law in the First Person Plural*, 106.

[83] Paul Ricoeur, *Oneself as Another*, trans. K. Blamey (Chicago and London: The University of Chicago Press, 1992), 118–25.

[84] Lindahl, *Authority and the Globalisation of Inclusion and Exclusion*, 103–6 and Van Roermund, *Law in the First Person Plural*, 108–10.

the collective, reckon with their audience and how this audience sees its own interests. Protests take the form of 'not in our name', thus rejecting the representational act.[85]

In sum, one could read the preamble of the ICC as the narrative institution of a specific regime in the sense of Lefort: a specific way of giving form to society that gives meaning to social relationships and provides them with a stage. Which story does the preamble tell? It depicts humanity as a collective subject in a narrative that focuses on unimaginable atrocities, as they have occurred in the twentieth century. As a result, humanity is shocked and this shock takes up the metaphor of a conscience, a moral category par excellence. Thus, signalling how the transgression of the boundaries of humanity captured under the international core crimes does not only involve legal boundaries but also other normative registers. This ties in well with what we have seen in a Durkheimian analysis: ICL is represented as a reaction to the violation of global consciousness by an atrocity crime.[86] Moving beyond Durkheim: the boundaries of the normative community of humanity are triggered by what remains irreducible to the categories of its order. This is the inhuman.

2.5 Inhumanity: Ongwen as a Strange Figure

Interestingly, the act of constituting 'we, humanity' is an act of self-constitution that draws boundaries around what belongs to the 'own'. What is deemed inhuman resists integration in this order as strange. Yet, it does not simply disappear but remains at the margins of the order and may question the very boundaries of humanity. These encounters between human and inhuman take place within concrete (legal and political) practices, embedded within forms of life. This entails that humanity as a political agent is neither a fact nor an ideal. It is, rather, an order brought about by representation and self-constitution. It is an order in the sense of a bounded whole. I start with a quote from Bernhard Waldenfels to illustrate what this would entail for the invocation of humanity within ICL:

[85] For the analysis of an example, see Luigi Corrias, 'Environmental Law and Youth Protests: Future Generations between Speech Acts and Political Representation', *International Journal for the Semiotics of Law-Revue internationale de Sémiotique juridique* 36, no. 2 (2023): 893–906.

[86] See also the summary in Elies van Sliedregt, 'International Criminal Law: Over-Studied and Underachieving?', *Leiden Journal of International Law* 29 no. 1 (2016): 1–12, at 3–4:

> International crimes are the most serious violations of international law. The increasingly popular label 'mass atrocity crimes' signals the abhorrent and systemic nature of international crimes, with genocide, regarded as the 'crime of crimes', at the apex of international criminality. The grave nature and scale of international crimes, and the fact that they impact upon international peace and security, magnifies many of the issues at stake. International trials are framed as historical moments and the trials themselves are regarded as contributing to a historical narrative. It is no surprise that ICL captures the imagination. The story is simple and has classic ingredients: evil, justice and a hero.

> But it is not so easy with humanity. It cannot be equated with a limitless We that would be able to represent itself and speak in its own name. We cannot get rid of strangeness by relying on humanity; because it is always a particular authority that claims to speak 'for all of us' and to fight 'for all of us' without obtaining our consent. The lived humanity is polyphonic, a unanimous humanity is nothing more than an idée fixe, but an effective one. In this way, the globalization of the 'free world' remains a source of hostility, regardless of the interests behind it. It is questioned by a strangeness that resists integration.[87]

Waldenfels puts us on track for grasping the relationship between humanity and inhumanity. Invocations of humanity may be understood as particular enactments of the humanity/inhumanity distinction in concrete practices and always from a first-person perspective. When the community incorporates some understandings of humanity while casting others aside, it is claiming a power to create designations of humanity and inhumanity. There is no neutral third position from where the line between human and inhuman can be drawn. Humanity is always the result of a process of self-inclusion by drawing boundaries around a preferred inside, an own time, space and normativity of humanity as distinct from inhumanity. Because the 'humanity' of ICL only represents a particular conscience shocked by selective crimes, it pushes other forms of suffering to the margins as strange to it. Accordingly, inhumanity must be understood under the heading of the strange or the alien: hiding in the twilight of humanity, lurking in its shadows but always ready to appear, present its demand and question humanity's self-understanding.[88]

A legal-philosophical theory of the way in which the inhuman appears in ICL remains to be developed. In this section, I turn to the case of Dominic Ongwen to make a beginning with this. Ongwen is certainly not the only but an exemplary case of what one may call a strange, alien or extra-ordinary figure in ICL. Instead of giving a legal analysis, I will analyse how the case of Ongwen was received by the academic community, focusing on Ongwen's double nature of both victim and perpetrator. I will first briefly sketch the background of Ongwen and his trial before giving an overview of the reception of the trial within academic literature. After that, I will argue that the way in which Ongwen is described affirms his strangeness, or inhumanity. Finally, I explain what this tells us about the constitution of humanity.

Ongwen was most probably born in 1980 under the name of Dominic Okumu Savio.[89] He came to life in an age of turmoil in Uganda, a country with

87 Bernhard Waldenfels, *Fremdheit, Gastfreundschaft und Feindschaft*, www.information-philosophie.de/?a=1&t=219&n=2&y=1&c=1 (accessed 8 March 2024) aus: Heft 5/2006, S. 7–18. My translation, LC.

88 I will discuss the issue of selectivity and the specific structure of the inhuman demand, or 'silent claim' in Chapter 6.

89 Erin K. Baines, 'Complex Political Perpetrators: Reflections on Dominic Ongwen', *The Journal of Modern African Studies* 47, no. 2 (2009): 163–91, at 168–69.

a complex and often violent history.[90] Ongwen was abducted and forced to join the Lord's Resistance Army (LRA), when he was approximately ten years old.[91] He quickly rose in the LRA's ranks, because he was an obedient and good fighter.[92] At the same time, people who knew him described him as a conflicted man who could be both empathic and cruel.[93] He stood trial for the ICC on several counts, among which was the conscription of child soldiers. Thus, Ongwen became the first suspect who was also a victim to be tried by the ICC.

When it comes to the academic literature, scholars agree that the case against Ongwen is marked by several paradoxes. First and most importantly, the neat categories of ICL seem not to fit Ongwen.[94] In this way, also the core objectives of ICL were at play: protecting the vulnerable and punishing the guilty.[95] Furthermore, Ongwen was portrayed as both sick and healthy, a mentally unstable killer and as a perpetrator who was not traumatised because of his previous victimhood. Ongwen appears as a transitional figure, somewhere between angel and demon, while it remains unclear how the threshold between the summum of innocence and the top point of evil is passed. Someone who does not 'fit the script' and provokes 'unease'.[96] In sum, Ongwen appears as extra-ordinary.

Ongwen has the 'dual status' of child-adult and victim-perpetrator.[97] Nevertheless, the trial judges do not take this into consideration. In the case of Lubanga, the ICC Trial Chamber stressed the long-term detrimental effects on child soldiers. Yet, in the Ongwen case, these effects were not considered when judging a child soldier turned commander. It seems unfair to hold someone who lacks 'ordinary moral perception' responsible.[98] ICL's categories proved too rigid to capture Ongwen's case. Since the ICC has failed to address Ongwen's double nature, clinging to clear-cut legal dichotomies instead, it has

90 For a concise explanation and references to other sources, see Filip Strandberg Hassellind, 'The International Criminal Trial as a Site for Contesting Historical and Political Narratives: The Case of Dominic Ongwen', *Social and Legal Studies* 30, no. 5 (2021): 790–809 at 793.

91 Baines, 'Complex Political Perpetrators', 168–69.

92 Baines, 'Complex Political Perpetrators', 171–73.

93 Baines, 'Complex Political Perpetrators', 172–73.

94 Thijs B. Bouwknegt and Barbora Holá, '*Dominic Ongwen: The ICC's Poster and Problem Child*' (16 March 2020), www.justiceinfo.net/en/44014-dominic-ongwen-icc-poster-and-problem-child.html (accessed 11 March 2024): 'In all the complexities of their social realities and experiences, child soldiers escape easy qualifications. They do not neatly fit the legal binaries of childhood or adulthood, guilt or innocence, victim or perpetrator, even more so when former child soldiers continue or even aggravate their crimes into adulthood, like Ongwen'.

95 Bouwknegt, and Holá, '*Dominic Ongwen*'.

96 Bouwknegt, and Holá. '*Dominic Ongwen*'.

97 Nini Els Pieters and Tonny Raymond Kirabira, '*The Ongwen Judgement at the ICC: A Missed Opportunity for Former Child Soldiers?*' (22 June 2021), https://internationallaw.blog/2021/06/22/the-ongwen-judgement-at-the-icc-a-missed-opportunity-for-former-child-soldiers/ (accessed 11 March 2024).

98 For this argument, see Renée Nicole Souris, 'Virtue Ethics, Criminal Responsibility, and Dominic Ongwen', *International Criminal Law Review* 19, no. 3 (2019): 475–504.

missed an important opportunity to develop more subtle views on legal and moral responsibility.

Ongwen has also been called a 'complex political perpetrator'; a victim who has turned perpetrator by using violence as a tool to thrive and regain some control over their life.[99] He is neither to be regarded as a scapegoat nor as a monster.[100] Rather, Ongwen shows the limitations of (international) criminal law in the aftermath of mass atrocities.[101] While ICL is ultimately interested in the guilt question of individual suspects, the trial of Ongwen could have been used as a site to introduce alternatives to this traditional liberal approach.[102] Ongwen, in being presented as a new critical subject beyond the simple dichotomy of victim and perpetrator, ruptures the official narrative of ICL and presents it with its 'blind spots'.[103]

One of the big problems when judging this case arises because there is no universal conception of childhood.[104] Legally, it seems obvious to find the answer in the official legal age of adulthood. Yet, rather than giving a solution, this strict line marks a problem.[105] It denies the conundrum of time, as pointed out by Jean Améry, amongst others.[106] Furthermore, it hides the responsibility of adults from view.[107] Pitting innocence, passivity and vulnerability against guilt, agency and cruelty is too simple.[108] The same goes for saying that 'time' is the key to choosing between these two families of categories.[109] It would be equally unfair to blame the law or the legal system.[110] What does seem to be clear is that the case of Ongwen raises a number of difficult legal and moral issues that give rise to a multiplicity of stories. We should ensure that these stories are heard.[111]

Perhaps a trial is not the best place for these stories. Primo Levi is someone who in his writings kept searching for subtler languages to capture the dilemma of what to make of 'victims who victimise'.[112] Levi reserves the concept of

[99] Baines, 'Complex Political Perpetrators', 180.
[100] Baines, 'Complex Political Perpetrators', 181.
[101] Baines, 'Complex Political Perpetrators', 182–83.
[102] Hassellind, 'The International Criminal Trial as a Site for Contesting Historical and Political Narratives', 791–94.
[103] Hassellind, 'The International Criminal Trial as a Site for Contesting Historical and Political Narratives', 803–4.
[104] Jill Stauffer, 'Law, Politics, the Age of Responsibility, and the Problem of Child Soldiers', *Law, Culture and the Humanities* 16, no. 1 (2020): 42–52, at 44.
[105] Stauffer, 'Law, Politics, the Age of Responsibility, and the Problem of Child Soldiers', 47.
[106] Stauffer, 'Law, Politics, the Age of Responsibility, and the Problem of Child Soldiers', 48–49. For an analysis of Améry, see Chapter 4.
[107] Stauffer, 'Law, Politics, the Age of Responsibility, and the Problem of Child Soldiers', 51.
[108] Stauffer, 'Law, Politics, the Age of Responsibility, and the Problem of Child Soldiers', 46.
[109] Stauffer, 'Law, Politics, the Age of Responsibility, and the Problem of Child Soldiers', 52.
[110] Stauffer, 'Law, Politics, the Age of Responsibility, and the Problem of Child Soldiers', 50: 'It is not law's fault if it can't fix the whole problem. It is our fault if we think law can or should do that on its own'.
[111] Stauffer, 'Law, Politics, the Age of Responsibility, and the Problem of Child Soldiers', 47.
[112] Mark A. Drumbl, 'Victims Who Victimize', *London Review of International Law* 4, no. 2 (2016): 217–46.

'grey zone' to understand the morality of inmates of concentration camps who, in procuring their own survival, take another person's demise for granted.[113] From this perspective, it makes little sense to prosecute 'a former child soldier as an enemy of humankind'.[114] This victim-perpetrator provokes discomfort.[115] This discomfort, a characteristic affect provoked by the strange phenomenon of inhumanity, questions, ultimately, ICL's claim to be regarded as a response to a shocked collective consciousness of humanity.

2.6 Conclusion

Taking the concept of crime against humanity as my starting point, I have developed a first-person plural reading of humanity in this chapter. In the wake of a number of ICL scholars, I have first analysed the work of Durkheim, more specifically his notion of *conscience collective*. Durkheim develops a theory that helps us make sense of the constitution of ICL. Yet, as several ICL scholars have also pointed out, his theory falls prey to hypostatising law and denying its contingency and historicity. I developed a genetic reading of humanity within ICL to leave these deficiencies behind. Regarding humanity *in statu nascendi* meant taking into account how humanity is always invoked by representatives – typically international tribunals – giving judgement in its name. Humanity appears as a normative community. Approaching the act of representation from a first-person perspective of 'We, humanity' revealed how in this act in- and exclusions take place. In Section 2.5, I turned to these.

Interpreting Dominic Ongwen as an exemplary case, I argued that he is a strange figure: vis-à-vis the order of humanity, Ongwen appears as extraordinary, or inhuman, and his inclusion within the ICL order is a problem. Starting with the latter, ICL has indicted and finally judged Ongwen, finding him guilty on several counts and sentencing him to twenty-five years of imprisonment.[116] This is ICL's inclusion of Ongwen within its categories and as a suspect in a criminal procedure, he is entitled to a range of procedural rights. As we have seen, the literature is critical as to whether Ongwen fits these categories and the dichotomies underlying them. These categories form part of the vocabulary of a court that claims to speak on behalf of 'We, humanity', a normative community. With each judgement, the ICC redraws the boundaries of this community of humanity. While included within ICL, Ongwen also remains outside of it. Thus, he shows that (even) the community of humanity cannot be all-encompassing. It gives rise to its inhumanity, which provokes an affective response: unease. This unease underlines how inclusion in this case

[113] Drumbl, 'Victims Who Victimize', 223 and 227. The chapter on the 'grey zone' can be found in Primo Levi, *The Drowned and the Saved* (New York City, NY: Simon and Schuster, 2017).

[114] Drumbl, 'Victims Who Victimize', 234.

[115] Drumbl, 'Victims Who Victimize', 242.

[116] On 6 May 2021, Ongwen was sentenced to twenty-five years of imprisonment by Trial Chamber IX. On 15 December 2022, the Appeals Chamber confirmed the decisions, both those on Ongwen's guilt and on the sentence.

is not a solution but rather a problem.[117] Against the liberal tendency to cast problems in terms of exclusion and present inclusion as the solution, my analysis of Ongwen shows how his inclusion within the normative community of humanity proved problematic.

Child – adult, innocent – guilty, vulnerable – cruel, passive – active, victim – perpetrator, angel – demon, human – monster, traumatised – mentally stable, suffering – abusing, peaceful – violent, civilian – soldier: Ongwen does not only fall in-between (legal) categories or unite opposite categories in one and the same person. Moreover, he also questions the way in which the boundaries of ICL, the boundaries of the normative community of humanity, are drawn. Questioning these elemental categorisations of the normative community of humanity, Ongwen is inhuman: a figure who appears to the order of humanity as its extra-ordinary.

As I will argue in more detail in Chapter 6, the inhuman also presents the order with a claim. This is a claim that cannot be captured in the categories of the law, yet still registers as a claim to the legal order. In the case of Ongwen, it might be formulated as the claim to see the child behind the soldier. Against the prosecutor's strategy to make the former disappear and only paint Ongwen as the latter and the ICC's failure to address the issue – even if Ongwen was charged and found guilty of the crime of which he was first a victim, that is, the conscription of child soldiers – Ongwen's claim is: let me be a child, allow me to return home, let me pay for my deeds in a different way.[118] Ongwen is an emblematic inhuman figure but not the only one. In the remaining chapters of the book, I will further develop the notion of inhumanity and its claim to the order of humanity.

117 I will explicitly return to this topic in Chapter 6.

118 In formulating this claim, I was helped by the reflections on childhood and criminal responsibility in Stauffer, 'Law, Politics, the Age of Responsibility, and the Problem of Child Soldiers'.

3

Crimes against Humanity, Dehumanisation and Rehumanisation

The Case of Duch

3.1 Introduction

Ever since its introduction at the Nuremberg trials, lawyers, philosophers and political theorists have been engaged in a discussion on the meaning and scope of the concept of crime against humanity, what kind of harm and to whom it postulates and whether or not it is supposed to capture a new kind of evil, among many other aspects.[1] This chapter does not directly participate in that debate. Rather, it takes up the concept of crime against humanity and its repercussions for the identity of different actors within the context of a specific case. The main question driving this chapter is how the concept of humanity and the related notions of dehumanisation and rehumanisation are employed in the case of Duch and what that says about the boundaries of humanity, understood as a normative community or order. I have chosen this specific case because it is a relatively recent case in which the defendant was accused and ultimately found guilty of crimes against humanity. Interestingly, notions of humanity and inhumanity were used by several parties: prosecutors, attorneys for civil parties but also – and herein lies the true value of this case for our purposes – the defendant's lawyer and Duch himself declared that the latter was dehumanised.

The first part of the chapter aims at mapping the different guises of humanity in the case of Duch. In a second move, I will put these findings in a philosophical context. For this part of the chapter, I will mainly build on the work of Hannah Arendt. Her work has become a *topos* in the debate on crime against humanity, without, however, offering a magical formula to answer all questions. Her interpretation of crimes against humanity as crimes against

[1] See, for example, Richard Vernon, 'What Is Crime against Humanity?', *Journal of Political Philosophy* 10, no. 3 (2002): 231–49; David Luban, 'A Theory of Crimes against Humanity', *The Yale Journal of International Law* 29, no. 1 (2004): 85–167; Larry May, *Crimes against Humanity: A Normative Account* (Cambridge: Cambridge University Press, 2005); Christopher Macleod, 'Towards a Philosophical Account of Crimes against Humanity', *European Journal of International Law* 21, no. 2 (2010): 281–302; Luigi Corrias, 'The Inhuman Stain: Representing Humanity in International Criminal Law', in *Humanity across International Law and Biolaw*, eds. Britta van Beers, Luigi Corrias and Wouter Werner (Cambridge: Cambridge University Press, 2014), 67–86.

the human status is, nevertheless, still very influential.[2] Yet, I rely on Arendt's oeuvre not only because of the continuous relevance of her reflections on evil,[3] and the crucial place her oeuvre has occupied in the philosophy of international criminal law.[4] Another reason to make use of Arendt's work to analyse the discourse on humanity in the case of Duch is given by several parties of the case, for they themselves refer to her work. I would like to stress that I do not intend to contribute to the already expansive literature on *Eichmann in Jerusalem*. Rather, I will draw on Arendt to devise a conceptual framework to analyse humanity, dehumanisation and rehumanisation in the case of Duch. This chapter proceeds with a brief introduction of the facts of the case of Duch (Section 3.2). Then, I will outline the discourse on dehumanisation (Section 3.3) and on rehumanisation (Section 3.4). In Sections 3.5 and 3.6, I will use an Arendtian framework to analyse the discourse in order to grasp what is at stake in the concept of humanity in international criminal law as it appears in the case of Duch.

3.2 Case 001: Duch

Before introducing the facts of the case, it might be useful to say something about the court that issued the decision.[5] The Extraordinary Chambers in the Court of Cambodia (ECCC) is officially an *ad hoc* Cambodian tribunal with the international assistance of the United Nations. Practically, this means that the tribunal's staff (e.g., the judges) consists of both Cambodians and foreigners. It was established in 2006 for the purpose of bringing to trial major suspects of crimes committed during the reign of the Democratic Kampuchea regime, more commonly known as the Khmer Rouge. This lasted from 17 April 1975 to 6 January 1979. During this period, 1.7 million people died as a result of the acts of the regime. Instituted under Cambodian law but with international assistance, the ECCC is a hybrid court. Its jurisdiction is temporally limited to the period of the Khmer Rouge regime. Its personal jurisdiction covers 'senior leaders of Democratic Kampuchea and those who were most responsible' for crimes committed during the period between 17 April 1975 and 6 January 1979. Regarding the subject matter, the tribunal's jurisdiction covers both national

[2] See, for example, Hannah Arendt, *Eichmann in Jerusalem: Report on the Banality of Evil* (London: Faber and Faber, 1963) and Robert Fine, 'Crimes against Humanity: Hannah Arendt and the Nuremberg Debates', *European Journal of Social Theory* 3, no. 3 (2000): 293–311.

[3] See, for example, Patrick Hayden, 'The Relevance of Hannah Arendt's Reflections on Evil: Globalization and Rightlessness', *Human Rights Review* 11, no. 4 (2010): 451–67 and Patrick Hayden, 'Systemic Evil and the International Political Imagination', *International Politics* 51, no. 4 (2014): 424–40.

[4] See David Luban, 'Hannah Arendt as a Theorist of International Criminal Law', *International Criminal Law Review* 11, no. 3 (2011): 621–41.

[5] Based chiefly on the information on the official webpages of the ECCC: www.eccc.gov.kh/en (consulted 8 March 2016).

and international crimes, such as genocide, crimes against humanity and breaches of the Geneva Conventions.[6]

The defendant in the very first case before the court was Kaing Guek Eav alias Duch. Starting from 1975 until he was forced to flee from the Vietnamese army in 1979, Duch took up several positions within S-21, Taul Sleng. This was 'the Khmer Rouge's most important interrogation, detention, torture and extermination centre'.[7] Most notably, Duch was the chairperson of S-21 from March 1976 until January 1979. At least 12,380 people, the majority of whom were Cambodians, were killed in S-21. Duch was charged with and ultimately found guilty of crimes against humanity and breaches of the Geneva Convention.

S-21 played a pivotal role in Democratic Kampuchea. As chairperson of the prison, Duch fell directly under and had immediate contact with the Central Committee, the highest executive organ of the Khmer Rouge. Furthermore, when the internal purges started, Communist Party of Kampuchea (CPK) cadres were sent to S-21.[8] The overall purpose of S-21 was to kill everyone who entered.[9] This is something Duch has admitted.[10] Moreover, it was the aim of S-21 to uncover as many traitors as possible.[11] Here, torture played a crucial role.[12] While he admits that he has ordered the systematic torture of detainees at S-21, Duch denies having tortured himself.[13] It was, however, only Duch who could decide when a prisoner would be executed.[14] Even besides

[6] Law on the Establishment of Extraordinary Chambers in the Courts of Cambodia for the Prosecution of Crimes Committed during the Period of Democratic Kampuchea with inclusion of amendments as promulgated on 27 October 2004, art 1–8.

[7] Will Fitzgibbon, 'Visions of Justice: Shakespeare and Duch's Proposed "Return to Humanity"', *ANU College of Law Research Paper*, no. 11–32 (2010) Electronic copy available at: http://ssrn.com/abstract=1948272 (consulted 8 March 2016), 14. See also David Chandler, *Voices from S-21: Terror and History in Pol Pot's Secret Prison* (Berkeley: University of California Press, 1999).

[8] Transcript of Proceedings, 'Duch' Trial Public, Trial Chamber of the Extraordinary Chambers in the Courts of Cambodia, 30 March 2009, Trial Day 1, at 12: 'S21 was unique in the network of security centres given its direct link to the Central Committee and its role in the detention and execution of CPK cadre'.

[9] Transcript of Proceedings, 'Duch' Trial Public, Trial Day 1, at 16: 'The primary role of S21 was to implement "[t]he Party political line regarding the enemy" according to which prisoners "absolutely had to be smashed." The term "smash" was used and widely understood at the relevant time to mean "kill." Every prisoner who arrived at S21 was destined for execution'.

[10] Transcript of Proceedings, 'Duch' Trial Public, Trial Day 1, at 19: 'Duch recognized that his role as Chairman of S21 was to focus the office on smashing purported traitors within the ranks of the revolution itself'.

[11] Transcript of Proceedings, 'Duch' Trial Public, Trial Day 1, at 22: 'In addition to executing prisoners condemned in advance as traitors, an overriding purpose of S21 was to extract confessions from prisoners in order to uncover further networks of possible traitors'.

[12] Transcript of Proceedings, 'Duch' Trial Public, Trial Day 1, at 40: 'Duch confirmed that the use of torture within S21 was systematic and noted that "anyone taken for interrogation mostly could not avoid torture"'.

[13] Transcript of Proceedings, 'Duch' Trial Public, Trial Day 1, at 43 and 44–45.

[14] Transcript of Proceedings, 'Duch' Trial Public, Trial Day 1, at 51–52:

> following an incident where a prisoner was killed before the completion of his interrogation, Son Sen required Duch to sign off on every execution. Thereafter, Duch necessarily decided how long a prisoner would live, since he ordered their execution based on a personal

the torture and the killing, life for the detainees was very hard.[15] Also, '[e]vidence suggests that S21 personnel performed medical experimentation on prisoners'.[16]

Regarding the life of Duch, the following aspects are of interest for our purposes. Duch was born in the province of Kampong Thom on 17 November 1942. His parents were poor peasants of Chinese origin. He was a particularly good student and ultimately became a math teacher in 1965, working in a small village called Skoun. Learning about communism as a schoolchild, Duch was a devoted Maoist by the time he became a teacher. His students later described him as 'a sincere, devoted man, always seeking to help the impoverished'.[17] In 1967, Duch joined the Khmer Rouge in hiding from the authorities. He was, however, arrested in January 1968 and sentenced to twenty years imprisonment for breaching state security. As part of a general amnesty for political prisoners, Duch was freed on 18 March 1970. Five years later, the Khmer Rouge took power. Duch married his wife in 1976 and had four children with her.[18] Before coming to S-21, Duch worked as the chairperson of another security prison, M-13. He did this from July 1971 until January 1975. Here, he already worked under the orders of Son Sen, an appointed chairperson of the General Staff.[19]

After the capitulation of 1979, Duch fled with the Khmer Rouge for more than ten years. He says that he was basically their prisoner. He was mainly ordered to teach; for example, his superior Son Sen sent him to China to teach Khmer. Only in 1992 did Duch lose contact with his commanders.[20] He was now in Phkoâm village, where he continued to teach but also traded in rice and bred pigs. He lost his wife in a mysterious burglary in 1995, for which he blames Pol Pot as Duch believes it to have been an attempt to assassinate him. In 1996, he converted to Christianity and had his children baptised. From 1997 onwards, Duch worked as a humanitarian aid worker for the American Refugee Committee, amongst others, and became a respected person in the camps. In 1999, Duch was discovered and between 1999 and 31 July 2007, he was held without a charge at the Cambodian Military Prison in Phnom Penh.[21]

The psychological examination before the trial concluded that Duch was fully responsible for his acts, that he was highly intelligent and possessed a

determination of whether a prisoner had fully confessed. As there was no right to release, there was an implicit standing order from Duch, as Chairman, to kill prisoners according to the system created at S21.

15 Transcript of Proceedings, 'Duch' Trial Public, Trial Day 1, at 33: 'Prisoners were kept in restraints nearly twenty-four hours a day. (…) Stringent rules governed the lives of prisoners and deprived them of the most basic human needs'.

16 Transcript of Proceedings, 'Duch' Trial Public, Trial Day 1, at 35. See also at 57: 'Some prisoners were killed by having large quantities of blood withdrawn by medics'.

17 ECCC, Office of the Co-Investigating Judges, Closing Order Indicting Kaing Geuk Eav alias Duch (8 August 2008), at 40 (paragraph 164).

18 Closing Order Indicting Kaing Geuk Eav alias Duch, at 41 (paragraph 165).

19 Closing Order Indicting Kaing Geuk Eav alias Duch, at 2 (paragraph 2).

20 Closing Order Indicting Kaing Geuk Eav alias Duch, at 41 (paragraph 166).

21 Fitzgibbon, 'Visions of Justice: Shakespeare and Duch's Proposed "Return to Humanity"', 17.

good memory.[22] Indeed, 'Duch has consistently recognised his responsibility for the crimes committed at S21 under his command'.[23] His regret notwithstanding, the experts observed that Duch suffered from what they call 'disempathy', that is, 'Duch's imagination is limited in scope, as is his ability to put himself in other people's shoes'.[24] Unlike other defendants at the ECCC, Duch confessed his crimes, cooperated with the court and showed remorse.[25] Duch was first convicted to thirty-five years, and in higher instance to forty years imprisonment for the crimes of which he was found guilty.

3.3 Dehumanisation in the Case of Duch

In this section of the chapter, I will analyse the discourse on dehumanisation in the case of Duch. If we ask the question 'who was dehumanized?', then we find three answers, three 'objects of dehumanization'. First, Duch's victims were dehumanised. The people who were tortured and killed under the responsibility of Duch were dehumanised. Second, as the concept of crime *against humanity* seems to imply, not only the direct victims of Duch but also humanity itself is dehumanised because of the atrocities committed in S-21. These first two acts of dehumanisation appear in the closing statement of the prosecutor Smith and of two attorneys for the victims. The third answer to the question who was dehumanised is, surprisingly perhaps, Duch himself. In all these instances, it is Duch who does the dehumanisation. In other words, Duch is both the subject and the object of dehumanisation. I will now discuss these three 'objects of dehumanization' in the sequence in which they were mentioned.

The closing statement of international prosecutor William Smith addresses two issues. The first is the legal interpretation of Duch's individual criminal responsibility. The second issue regards sentencing. Regarding the former, it is important for our purposes that Smith wants the Court to find Duch guilty for Joint Criminal Enterprise (JCE), a specific form of commission. In this way, Smith links Duch's behaviour and the 'horrific efficiency of S-21'[26] with deeds tried by other international criminal courts, including Nuremberg.[27] Without getting into the legal technicalities, this means that Smith wants Duch to be

22 Closing Order Indicting Kaing Geuk Eav alias Duch, at 42 (paragraph 171).
23 Closing Order Indicting Kaing Geuk Eav alias Duch, at 41 (paragraph 167).
24 Closing Order Indicting Kaing Geuk Eav alias Duch, at 43 (paragraph 171).
25 Duch's apologies can even be found in a separate document ('Compilation of statements of apology made by Kaing Guek Eav alias Duch during the proceedings') at the website of the ECCC. Note that there is more than one version of this document. I relied on the one which may be found at www.eccc.gov.kh/sites/default/files/publications/Case001Apology_En_low_res.pdf (consulted 8 March 2016).
26 Transcript of Proceedings, 'Duch' Trial Public, Trial Chamber of the Extraordinary Chambers in the Courts of Cambodia, 25 November 2009, Trial Day 75, at 4.
27 Transcript of Proceedings, 'Duch' Trial Public, Trial Day 75, at 18. It is in this context that Smith quotes the work of Hannah Arendt: 'As the philosopher and Holocaust survivor, Hannah Arendt states: "Terror turns not only against its enemies but against its friends and

seen as completely in charge of the well-planned murders in S-21.[28] Regarding the sentencing, Smith mentions that the acts committed within S-21 were 'heinous and shocking',[29] to the extent that they are 'rarely matched in modern history in terms of their combined barbarity, scope, duration, premeditation and callousness'.[30] Furthermore, the way in which Duch committed the crimes is telling, according to Smith: 'Taken together, the evidence does not show a fearful man. To the contrary, it demonstrates a confident man who spreads terror across Cambodia through his work at S-21; a man who was irreplaceable in his position'.[31] Smith described Duch as 'an experienced, hardened torturer and killer well before arriving at S-21',[32] as someone who 'committed his crimes as a devoted man with the enthusiasm and zeal of an ardent revolutionary'.[33]

Asking for a severe punishment and doubting the extent and truth of Duch's remorse, Smith pleads punishment for the sake of humanity: 'We believe that to take the first step in righting the wrongs of S-21, humanity must be made whole by sternly punishing one of its own for ignoring it so gravely. Doing so will do far more for humanity, and even the accused's humanity, than giving in to a misguided notion that a disproportionately low sentence somehow facilitates reconciliation'.[34] Due to the fair trial he received, Duch was already treated with more humanity than he ever showed to his victims.[35] In forgetting the dignity of his victims, Duch also forgot his very own conscience.[36] Finally,

supporters as well. The climax of terror is reached when the police state begins to devour its own children; when yesterday's executioner becomes today's victim."'

28 Transcript of Proceedings, 'Duch' Trial Public, Trial Day 75, at 5: 'The essence of committing a crime via JCE is that individuals in positions of power must be held accountable for the full extent of their criminal responsibility. The gravity of their criminality comes from their grand criminal vision. It comes from the abuse of their power and authority through which they employ others as tools to achieve their criminal objectives'. See also at 35, where Smith describes Duch as the 'loyal and dedicated agent' of the system, because 'he engineered, perfected and meticulously managed the CPK's most effective killing machine'.

29 Transcript of Proceedings, 'Duch' Trial Public, Trial Day 75, at 8.

30 Transcript of Proceedings, 'Duch' Trial Public, Trial Day 75, at 12.

31 Transcript of Proceedings, 'Duch' Trial Public, Trial Day 75, at 18.

32 Transcript of Proceedings, 'Duch' Trial Public, Trial Day 75, at 23.

33 Transcript of Proceedings, 'Duch' Trial Public, Trial Day 75, at 29–30.

34 Transcript of Proceedings, 'Duch' Trial Public, Trial Day 75, at 31–32.

35 Transcript of Proceedings, 'Duch' Trial Public, Trial Day 75, at 34:

> Let's recall that unlike his prisoners at S-21 to whom this accused denied even the slightest shred of humanity, he has been met with open even-handed justice in this Court. He has received a fair trial in accordance with the law and a bench of independent and impartial judges. If convicted, he will be sentenced to a punishment proportionate to those crimes. Although he belonged to one of the most murderous and barbarous regimes in the history of mankind, he will be sentenced only for the crimes he committed. At S-21, prisoners never received such treatment. (…) On the contrary, the accused insured they were treated as animals. To him, they were enemies of the state who deserved no mercy and no compassion.

36 Transcript of Proceedings, 'Duch' Trial Public, Trial Day 75, at 35–36:

> Mr. President, allow me to refer to a quote which encapsulates the dilemma that human dignity would have put before the accused when he perpetrated these crimes. William Shawcross, the leading British prosecutor at the Nuremburg War Crimes Trial, said: 'There

after arguing that Duch should be punished with forty years of imprisonment, Smith submits that also this is for the sake of humanity:

> Not just the victims and their families, but the whole of humanity demands a just and proportionate response to these crimes and this Court must speak on behalf of that humanity. It must punish the accused justly and send a clear message that crimes like these must never be perpetrated again. Cambodians have come to this Court from their towns and villages from around the country. Many have come from overseas and millions of others are watching intently on TV. They are waiting for a justice that tells us how humanity will be protected. They are waiting for a justice that tells them and tells those distant voices from S-21 that this justice was done in their name, every single one of them. Mr. President, Your Honours, let your judgement speak for justice in finding this accused guilty and imposing the sentence we have recommended; a sentence which reflects criminal responsibility for more than 12,000 crimes. In imposing this penalty, you are not taking away the accused's humanity, but you are giving it back; back to the victims of S-21.[37]

When we analyse this closing statement of Smith, we can see that humanity appears in several veins. It appears as humaneness in the sense of the way in which Duch is treated by giving him a fair trial, and this humaneness he denied to his victims. Then, humanity appears as human dignity, that is, as an impersonal norm or ideal that should have urged Duch to follow his conscience. Furthermore, humanity is invoked in the meaning of the whole community of mankind, which demands a severe punishment, and Smith even holds that the Court represents that humanity and should protect it. Finally, humanity appears as an attribute that can be taken away and given back. Duch has taken the humanity from his victims, the Court, so Smith argues, is to give it back to them, and perhaps even to Duch himself.

In their final statements, two attorneys for the civil parties also referred to humanity. First, Ms. Jacquin denies that Duch has genuinely asked for forgiveness because there were no 'words of deep contrition, of apology, of forgiveness, and of humanity, vis-a-vis the victims'.[38] She also speaks of Duch failing 'to preserve the fundamental humanitarian values such as everyone's right to life'.[39] Humanity thus appears here in the sense of humaneness and the values inherent in human rights and humanitarian law. The other attorney of the victims, Mr. Cannone, does not explicitly mention humanity, save for pointing to the 'humanism' in Roux's final statement. Expressing his disappointment with Duch's absence of true remorse, he submits 'Mr. Kaing Guek Eav only for a very

comes a point when a man must refuse to answer to his leader if he is also to answer to his own conscience'. Your Honours, in committing these crimes, the accused abandoned his conscience. In fact, he abandoned every duty we, as human beings, owe to one another.

37 Transcript of Proceedings, 'Duch' Trial Public, Trial Day 75, at 37–38.

38 Transcript of Proceedings, 'Duch' Trial Public, Trial Chamber of the Extraordinary Chambers in the Courts of Cambodia, 26 November 2009, Trial Day 76, at 102.

39 Transcript of Proceedings, 'Duch' Trial Public, Trial Day 76, at 103.

fleeing moment conferred upon them the status of a human being so that victims could transcend hatred and turn towards the future'.[40] He ends on the following note: 'This is most troubling. This is most troubling because perhaps this gentleman has not understood a single thing. Perhaps he is still in his methodical mindset. He is still lost in his footnotes. He is still ensconced in the most absurd bureaucracy where reasoning, contemplation and sensitivity were completely absent'.[41] This lack of understanding and overall bureaucratic attitude of which Duch is accused here is something we will return to in Section 3.4.

Recall that Duch himself was also an 'object of dehumanization'. Duch is dehumanised, and even in two ways. On the one hand, 'Duch has been widely described inside and outside the courtroom as a "monster"'.[42] It is important to acknowledge that what is referred to here is a 'moral monster' as distinguished from the purely 'scientific monster':

> While the monster in the scientific sense represents a maximal divergence with regards to normality (…) and is thus neutrally definable in statistical terms, things are seen quite differently from the moral point of view: (…) we loathe it because of its crimes, its appalling cruelty and its 'inhumanity'. What does this mean? The corruption of a free being, the surrender to evil for the sake of evil. What does humanity then become? It degenerates, as if seized by a sort of regressive fever. (…) Moral monstrousness is an insane squandering of the possibilities of freedom.[43]

François Roux, Duch's international defence lawyer, firmly rejects this characterisation.[44] In this respect, Roux submits that depicting Duch as a monster would make his client into a scapegoat.[45] Later, Roux explains exactly what he means by this latter notion:

> I would like it to be clearly understood what is meant when I use the expression 'scapegoat'. As you well know, scapegoats in societies, including societies of old, was loaded with all the evils, with all the suffering of a society. All of this was loaded onto the head of a goat. Amongst the Hebrews, the goat was sent into the desert so that the social group could be reformed because they would say, 'This goat bears all our wrongdoings'. That is the scapegoat.[46]

Duch is, however, also dehumanised in another way. By committing the crimes he has confessed, by dehumanising his victims and humanity, Duch

40 Transcript of Proceedings, 'Duch' Trial Public, Trial Day 76, at 104–5.
41 Transcript of Proceedings, 'Duch' Trial Public, Trial Day 76, at 105.
42 Fitzgibbon, 'Visions of Justice: Shakespeare and Duch's Proposed "Return to Humanity"', 10.
43 Dominique Janicaud, *On the Human Condition* (Abingdon: Routledge, 2005), 20–21.
44 Transcript of Proceedings, 'Duch' Trial Public, Trial Day 76, at 18.
45 Transcript of Proceedings, 'Duch' Trial Public, Trial Day 76, at 19. See also Transcript of Proceedings, 'Duch' Trial Public, Trial Chamber of the Extraordinary Chambers in the Courts of Cambodia, 31 March 2009, Trial Day 2, at 78 and 80, where Kar Savuth, Duch's Cambodian defence lawyer, uses the same expression to criticise the fact that Duch alone of 196 prison heads under the Khmer Rouge regime is brought to trial.
46 Transcript of Proceedings, 'Duch' Trial Public, Trial Day 76, at 19.

has dehumanised *himself* in the sense that he has made himself an outcast of humanity (inhuman, or an outsider of humanity). This category does not coincide with that of a monster. This can be derived from the fact that whereas the latter category was firmly rejected by Roux, the one of Duch as 'an outcast of humanity' is upheld by both Roux and Duch himself. Interestingly, both Duch and his attorney understand the effects of the crimes committed by Duch to be as such. Already in his very first statement, Duch says 'I am sure that the general public now regards me as a cowardly and inhumane person'.[47] On 2 September 2009, he states that 'I asked them [i.e., two psychological experts involved in the trial] to counsel me about what I could do to make the world see me as a human being once again. For that is where my remorse lies'.[48] Duch returns to this problem fourteen days later: 'Lastly, I asked the psychologists what I should do so that humankind might know and accept me as a person again. I am still questioning myself about this issue. I am grappling with it constantly'.[49] When back at Tuol Sleng for a crime scene re-enactment, Duch remembers 'the wretched victims and their families who were subjected to suffering, torture, disgrace and countless inhumane acts before they lost their lives'.[50] He then comes to 'the inevitable acknowledgment that in the role of S-21 director I participated in crimes against humanity within the entire framework of S-21'.[51] He ends his final statement saying:

> I have made a genuine request to the psychological experts to help me with the ideas on what I can do to make people recognise me as part of humankind again. In order to contribute to relieving the great sorrow of the Cambodian people, I promise I will do everything for my people, should they need me in the future in whatever circumstances. I pray the Court consider this additional point when it makes its decision.[52]

Duch thus calls the acts committed within S-21 'inhumane' and acknowledges that he is guilty of crimes against humanity. This has made him into

[47] 'Compilation of statements of apology', at 3. (The text refers to Transcript of Proceedings, 'Duch' Trial Public, Trial Chamber of the Extraordinary Chambers in the Courts of Cambodia, 31 March 2009, Trial Day 2, at 68.)

[48] 'Compilation of statements of apology', at 13. (The text refers to Duch, Transcript of Proceedings, 'Duch' Trial Public, Trial Chamber of the Extraordinary Chambers in the Courts of Cambodia, 2 September 2009, Trial Day 69, at 84.)

[49] 'Compilation of statements of apology', at 13 (The text refers to Transcript of Proceedings, 'Duch' Trial Public, Trial Chamber of the Extraordinary Chambers in the Courts of Cambodia, 16 September 2009, Trial Day 72, at 41.)

[50] 'Compilation of statements of apology', at 14. (The text refers to Transcript of Proceedings, 'Duch' Trial Public, Trial Chamber of the Extraordinary Chambers in the Courts of Cambodia, 16 September 2009, Trial Day 72, at 48. The visit to Tuol Sleng and Duch's statement were made on 27 February 2008.)

[51] 'Compilation of statements of apology', at 14 (The text refers to Transcript of Proceedings, 'Duch' Trial Public, Trial Chamber of the Extraordinary Chambers in the Courts of Cambodia, 16 September 2009, at 49.)

[52] 'Compilation of statements of apology', at 15. (The text refers to Transcript of Proceedings, 'Duch' Trial Public, Trial Chamber of the Extraordinary Chambers in the Courts of Cambodia, 25 November 2009, Trial Day 75, at 69.)

someone who stands outside of humankind, or humanity. Through his remorse, his apologies and the forgiveness of the survivors, he hopes to be part of mankind again.

3.4 Rehumanisation in the Case of Duch

François Roux, Duch's international defence lawyer, also acknowledged that Duch's acts have cast him outside of humanity. Indeed, his whole plea consists of a proposal to return Duch to humanity.[53] In his opening statement, Roux phrases it as follows:

> What allows a man who is confronting all of this, what allows him to remain today alive? If it is not because he is convinced that he still has a role to play in humanity? By requesting, by asking for forgiveness from the victims, by address[ing] himself to his people. By addressing himself to young people. By telling them 'this is it, this is what we have done, this is what we fell into, this is what you should never repeat'.[54]

And at the end of the statement, Roux formulates the stakes of the whole trial:

> I am not sure that Duch on his own has the answer to this tragic question: why all of this? Why these scenes? These unthinkable scenes, these unbearable scenes at S-21? Why these scenes that de-humanise the victims? But who also de-humanise at the same time those that perpetrated these atrocities. Will we be able at the end of these hearings to have, to be able to return to the victims all of the humanity? But to also be able to allow those or the one who, had exited humanity to return to humanity. This is the stake, for our court.[55]

Not only does Roux explicitly say that victims and perpetrators of atrocities are dehumanised, he also makes the reversal of the process – the rehumanisation of both groups – the ultimate goal of the trial.

How can we understand this plea for rehumanisation? If we analyse the closing statement of Roux, it becomes evident that for him it forms the opposite of a monsterisation of Duch. Roux states that even though Duch admitted his moral and legal responsibility from the very first day, 'the prosecutor decided to submit a conventional, traditional argument whose underlying philosophy is as follows. This man is a monster, even though they said "I am not saying this man is a monster." In fact, the attempt was made to portray him as such'.[56] Instead, the task that lies ahead is that 'we must try to understand the mechanisms that lead a man, who is a decent man by all accounts, to become a torturer'.[57] Depicting Duch as a monster would make him into a scapegoat, yet one 'will not advance by so much as a millimetre in the

53 See Fitzgibbon, 'Visions of Justice: Shakespeare and Duch's Proposed "Return to Humanity"'.
54 Transcript of Proceedings, 'Duch' Trial Public, Trial Day 2, at 90.
55 Transcript of Proceedings, 'Duch' Trial Public, Trial Day 2, at 91–92.
56 Transcript of Proceedings, 'Duch' Trial Public, Trial Day 76, at 18.
57 Transcript of Proceedings, 'Duch' Trial Public, Trial Day 76, at 18.

development of humanity'.[58] In contrast, the alternative of Roux does serve this aim. Hence, we may already distinguish between two subjects of rehumanisation: Duch and humanity itself. It is striking that one dehumanised group is missing: the victims and survivors. This seems to be no omission but a deliberate choice. In the context of a legal trial, there is no place for a (full) rehumanisation of the victims because the task of the judge is to render justice, as Roux tells the Court:

> the best way forward for a tribunal is that at the end of the day justice is rendered. You are not in charge of effecting reconciliation. It is not your obligation to impose upon the victims a duty of forgiveness. That is not your work. Nobody can force the victims to forgive. This is a matter for them alone, but you must and you should render justice.[59]

As an attorney, Roux specialised in defending people who performed acts of civil disobedience.[60] For Duch, Roux makes use of what he considers the opposite category. Referring to the famous Milgram experiment, he states that Duch's crimes were crimes of obedience.[61] This resonates in Duch's own final statement that he was merely 'a cog in an unstoppable machine'.[62] Indeed, Roux argues, making Duch into a monster is far too simple and easy a solution, for it would prevent us from asking the difficult question: '"This will not happen again," they say. Well, let me tell you it will happen as long as we haven't brought up with lucidity the phenomena that lead a normal man to become one day an executioner'.[63] As an attorney of people who consciously and deliberately disobeyed the law, he knows about their difficulties in court and his most powerful argument in this regard throws us back upon ourselves:

> if we do not learn how to disobey in a democratic system, what will we do in a dictatorship? However, speaking about disobedience, that sends us so much back to ourselves, sends us back to what we live through every day. How – how in any democratic state, how do all the armies operate? Or more simply, all of the administrations, how do they function? And even more simply, all of our

[58] Transcript of Proceedings, 'Duch' Trial Public, Trial Day 76, at 20.

[59] Transcript of Proceedings, 'Duch' Trial Public, Trial Day 76, at 5.

[60] Transcript of Proceedings, 'Duch' Trial Public, Trial Day 76, at 65 where, interestingly, Roux also refers to the work of Arendt. Speaking of civil disobedience, he states:

> It is a practice that you know very well in Cambodia because you're not so far from India. It is the practice, or let's say the strategy even, that has been perfected by Mahatma Gandhi. It is the practice that is so well described by Hannah Arendt. Yes, indeed, Hannah Arendt. She didn't only write about Eichmann; she also asked herself the right questions by stating that when situations are blocked, well then the citizens must rise and must revolt in a non-violent way and disobey the laws. Then we have to learn how to disobey.

[61] Transcript of Proceedings, 'Duch' Trial Public, Trial Day 76, at 65.

[62] 'Compilation of statements of apology', at 15. (The text refers to Transcript of Proceedings, 'Duch' Trial Public, Trial Chamber of the Extraordinary Chambers in the Courts of Cambodia, 25 November 2009, Trial Day 75, at 68.)

[63] Transcript of Proceedings, 'Duch' Trial Public, Trial Day 76, at 64.

> societies? At all levels you have a boss receiving orders and a boss giving orders to his subordinates. You know this very well. I even heard that in this courtroom, people saying to the Chamber, 'I cannot answer you. I must ask my superior for his permission.' Yes, indeed. That's how we all operate; all of us. We all operate in this way.[64]

Roux's plea for Duch's rehumanisation is thus based on the bridging of the gap between Duch and us. In other words, the difficulty of the question lies exactly in the fact that it puts us in front of the mirror, so to say: 'To find the source of evil that was implemented each and every single day in S-21, we didn't have to look any further than ourselves. This is terrifying, but this is far removed from the very easy explanation of identifying a scapegoat'.[65] The challenge is to see the man behind the torturer.[66] Given that the main purpose of sentencing is rehabilitation,[67] the issue is: 'can Duch still be useful to humanity? That is the question that you will ask yourselves'.[68]

Two attorneys for the civil parties take the opportunity to directly react to Roux's plea. Both Kong Pisey[69] and Pierre-Olivier Sur[70] refer to Arendt's statements regarding Eichmann to refute Roux's argument for Duch only obeying orders. More interesting still, Sur directly takes issue with Roux's attempt at a rehumanisation of Duch by casting doubts on the precise meaning of such a process. He states that

64 Transcript of Proceedings, 'Duch' Trial Public, Trial Day 76, at 67.

65 Transcript of Proceedings, 'Duch' Trial Public, Trial Day 76, at 69.

66 Transcript of Proceedings, 'Duch' Trial Public, Trial Day 76, at 69.

67 Transcript of Proceedings, 'Duch' Trial Public, Trial Day 76, at 77.

68 Transcript of Proceedings, 'Duch' Trial Public, Trial Day 76, at 79. See also at 82, where Roux, at the very end of his statement, addresses both the judges and Duch:

> Duch, all your victims were your brothers and sisters in humanity. You said that you had been cowardly and that you did not go to see them while they were in detention. In human eyes, you will never be absolved of these crimes and the eyes of those you did not wish to meet will remain on you forever. But what about us, Your Honours? Are we prepared to look Duch in the eye and see him for the fellow human that he is? And the final question; through your ruling will you bring back Duch into the fold of humanity?

69 Transcript of Proceedings, 'Duch' Trial Public, Trial Chamber of the Extraordinary Chambers in the Courts of Cambodia, 23 November 2009, Trial Day 73, at 66–67:

> Therefore, his [i.e., Duch's] self-depiction as a simple recipient of orders who was obliged to obey is refuted. At this point we would like to quote Hannah Arendt, from her book 'Eichmann in Jerusalem: A Report on the Banality of Evil' where she suggests that the Court should have told the accused, Eichmann, who as well referred to having obeyed orders, the following which I want to address to the accused. 'There still remains the fact that you have carried out and therefore actively supported a policy of mass murder. For politics it is not like the nursery. In politics, obedience and support is the same'.

70 Transcript of Proceedings, 'Duch' Trial Public, Trial Day 73, at 117–18:

> Furthermore, Mr. President, Your Honours, there is a third emotion that transpires from these hearings when we speak together. It is Duch's argument, telling us that he was just a pawn, just a pawn in the Khmer Rouge machinery. Then if somebody else had been at the head of S-21, he would have done the job a bit as Eichmann has pleaded when he was in Jerusalem. This argument is not admissible.

> Duch finally is seeking through his counsel to be rehumanised. Indeed, it is important that the Chamber treat him as he was treated during these proceedings; that is to say, with respect to the defence and with respect to the person he is, but if he has to be rehumanised, what does this mean? What does it mean to be rehumanised? It means that if we have to bring him back to our community of human beings, this means that we have to consider that he is part of our social group, that he is a member of the social contract that unites us all and that generates our society. So he must be judged in his role; that is to say, the role of a criminal, a criminal against humanity.[71]

Thus, according to this statement of Sur, recognising the humanity of Duch implies taking him seriously as a fellow human being who wronged the very community of mankind and ought to be punished for that.[72]

3.5 Reading the Case of Duch with Hannah Arendt

It is time to retrace our steps. In Sections 3.3 and 3.4, we have seen that humanity is referred to in Duch's statements and in the plea of Roux in the following contexts: inhumane acts or behaviour (crimes against humanity), the community of mankind (the normative community of humanity), an outcast of humanity (inhuman) and a monster. In this section and Section 3.6, I will take up several aspects of this discourse and analyse them with the help of an Arendtian framework. More specifically, from this perspective, three issues can be raised in connection with the case of Duch: the purpose of the trial, the nature of a crime against humanity and the question of (the banality of) evil.

When it comes to the purpose of the trial, recall Roux underlined that a trial ought to render justice. For him, this entailed the rehumanisation of Duch. Here, Arendt seems to be in agreement with Roux, for in *Eichmann in Jerusalem* she writes: 'The purpose of a trial is to render justice and nothing else (…) to weigh the charges brought against the accused, to render judgment, and to mete out due punishment'.[73] In this respect, Arendt stresses the importance of distinguishing the civil lawsuit, which centres on the concept of (individual) harm from a criminal trial:

> Criminal proceedings, since they are mandatory and thus initiated even if the victim would prefer to forgive and forget, rest on laws whose 'essence' (…) 'is that a crime is not committed only against the victim but primarily against the community whose law is violated'. The wrongdoer is brought to justice because his act has disturbed and gravely endangered the community as a whole, (…) it is

[71] Transcript of Proceedings, 'Duch' Trial Public, Trial Day 73, at 119.

[72] In this respect, one ought to complement the conclusions reached by Fitzgibbon, 'Visions of Justice: Shakespeare and Duch's proposed "return to humanity"': if Roux's attempt at a rehumanisation of Duch does not succeed it is not only because of the latter's 'twisting character' but also because it remains unclear what rehumanisation exactly entails and because of the one-sided breach of the 'contract of humanity'.

[73] Arendt, *Eichmann in Jerusalem: Report on the Banality of Evil*, 232.

> the body politic itself that stands in need of being 'repaired', and it is the general public order that has been thrown out of gear and must be restored, as it were.[74]

We might want to understand Arendt as a forerunner of the theory of criminal trials as advocated by Anthony Duff.[75] He stresses that trials are communicative enterprises in which a criminal is taken to be responsible (i.e., answerable) for his crimes and is called to account by a prosecution acting on behalf of a public, for crimes are public wrongs. This means that the next question becomes: which public is wronged in the case of Duch, where the suspect is eventually convicted for crimes against humanity?

This brings us to the second issue I would like to discuss here: the nature of a crime against humanity. Arendt defends a specific interpretation: crimes against humanity are crimes against the human status. She traces this phrase back to François de Menthon, the French prosecutor at the Nuremberg trials.[76] Arendt argues that also Eichmann ought to have been indicted for committing crimes against the human status. Instead, he was charged with crimes against the Jewish people. While Arendt does regret this fact, she acknowledges that '[i]t was the great advantage of a trial centered on the crime against the Jewish people (…) that the difference between "inhuman acts" (which were undertaken for some known, though criminal, purpose, such as expansion through colonisation) and the "crime against humanity," whose intent and purpose were unprecedented, was clarified'.[77] Arendt is very critical of a confusion of crimes against humanity and inhumane acts: 'I have mentioned before the Nuremberg Charter's definition of "crimes against humanity" as "inhuman acts," which were translated into German as *Verbrechen gegen die Menschlichkeit* – as though the Nazis had simply been lacking in human kindness, certainly the understatement of the century'.[78] Understanding them as 'inhuman(e) acts' does not capture what is at stake in the unprecedented and completely new crimes of the Nazis. It was especially difficult for Jewish people to come to terms with this newness, because they tended to understand the crimes of the Nazis as the latest in a long line of pogroms.[79]

Yet, Arendt stresses that the crimes of the Nazis were 'different not only in degree of seriousness but in essence'.[80] The essence of these crimes was

[74] Arendt, *Eichmann in Jerusalem: Report on the Banality of Evil*, 239–40.

[75] See for a statement of this theory in the context of ICL: Antony Duff, 'Authority and Responsibility in International Criminal Law', in *The Philosophy of International Law*, eds. Samantha Besson and John Tasioulas (Oxford: Oxford University Press, 2010), 589–604.

[76] Arendt, *Eichmann in Jerusalem: Report on the Banality of Evil*, 236.

[77] Arendt, *Eichmann in Jerusalem: Report on the Banality of Evil*, 252.

[78] Arendt, *Eichmann in Jerusalem: Report on the Banality of Evil*, 252.

[79] Arendt, *Eichmann in Jerusalem: Report on the Banality of Evil*, 245–46. This issue is related to her views on anti-Semitism. In its most extensive form, these can be found in the first part of Hannah Arendt, *The Origins of Totalitarianism* (New York: Harcourt Brace, 1973). See also David M. Seymour, 'The Autonomy of the Political and the Dissolution of the Jews', *International Journal of Law in Context* 3, no. 4 (2007): 373–87, at 373.

[80] Arendt, *Eichmann in Jerusalem: Report on the Banality of Evil*, 246.

genocide: 'an attack upon human diversity as such, that is, upon a characteristic of the "human status" without which the very words "mankind" or "humanity" would be devoid of meaning'.[81] For this reason, Arendt criticises the Jerusalem court:

> At no point, however, either in the proceedings or in the judgment, did the Jerusalem trial ever mention even the possibility that extermination of whole ethnic groups – the Jews, or the Poles, or the Gypsies – might be more than a crime against the Jewish or the Polish or the Gypsy people, that the international order, and mankind in its entirety, might have been grievously hurt and endangered.[82]

Here we can find an answer to the question which public is at issue in these crimes:

> these modern, state-employed mass murderers must be prosecuted because they violated the order of mankind, and not because they killed millions of people. Nothing is more pernicious to an understanding of these new crimes, or stands more in the way of the emergence of an international penal code that could take care of them, than the common illusion that the crime of murder and the crime of genocide are essentially the same. The point of the latter is that an altogether different order is broken and an altogether different community is violated.[83]

Arendt seems to suggest that the community of mankind (humanity), or what one might call a global public, is wronged. Therefore, justice ought to be done in the name of humanity.[84]

When we now return to what we have seen in the case of Duch, we can observe that Duch was accused of inhumaneness. Notwithstanding Arendt's efforts, the confusion between crimes against humanity and inhuman(e) acts still exists and it seems likely that it will continue to exist.[85] This is only a

81 Arendt, *Eichmann in Jerusalem: Report on the Banality of Evil*, 247.

82 Arendt, *Eichmann in Jerusalem: Report on the Banality of Evil*, 252. See also Thomas Mertens, 'The Eichmann Trial: Hannah Arendt's View on the Jerusalem Court's Competence', *German LJ* 6, no. 2 (2005): 407–24.

83 Arendt, *Eichmann in Jerusalem: Report on the Banality of Evil*, 249.

84 See for a critical reflection on this type of claim: Luigi Corrias and Geoff Gordon, 'Judging in the Name of Humanity: International Criminal Tribunals and the Representation of a Global Public', *Journal of International Criminal Justice* 13, no. 1 (2015): 97–112.

85 Indeed, article 5 of the Law on the Establishment of the ECCC describes crimes against humanity as follows: 'Crimes against humanity, which have no statute of limitations, are any acts committed as part of a widespread or systematic attack directed against any civilian population, on national, political, ethnical, racial or religious grounds, such as: murder; extermination; enslavement; deportation; imprisonment; torture; rape; persecutions on political, racial, and religious grounds; other inhumane acts'. Moreover, 'inhumane acts' form one aspect of the definition of crimes against humanity contained in the 2019 Fourth Report of the Special Rapporteur on Crimes against Humanity. See Sean D. Murphy, 'Fourth Report of the Special Rapporteur on Crimes against Humanity' (2019) United Nations International Law Commission, A/CN.4/725; where in draft article 3, section 1 sub k it mentions: 'Other inhumane acts of a similar character intentionally causing great suffering, or serious injury to body or to mental or physical health'.

problem when one believes that the two notions of a crime against the human status and an inhumane act contradict one another, or if a quest for the essence of a crime against humanity demands a single definition. I believe that neither is the case, so the two understandings may work as complementary in elucidating what is at play in crimes against humanity. What speaks in favour of Arendt's interpretation is Smith's statement that the ECCC should do justice for humanity and even Roux's statement that with the case of Duch there was a lesson to be learned for the whole of mankind.

Of more interest might be the question of whether we can also understand the dehumanisation of Duch from an Arendtian perspective. I believe this to be the case and for this purpose, we should turn to what Arendt says about the punishment of Eichmann. Having committed crimes against the human status marks Eichmann, according to Arendt, as 'in actual fact *hostis generis humani*'.[86] Because his purpose was 'to "liberate" mankind from the "rule of subhumans"',[87] for Arendt this justifies the death penalty: 'Because he had been implicated and had played a central role in an enterprise whose open purpose was to eliminate forever certain "races" from the surface of the earth, he had to be eliminated'.[88] In her fictitious speech to Eichmann, Arendt is even more explicit:

> Let us assume, for the sake of argument, that it was nothing more than misfortune that made you a willing instrument in the organization of mass murder; there still remains the fact that you have carried out, a policy of mass murder. For politics is not like the nursery; in politics obedience and support are the same. And just as you supported and carried out a policy of not wanting to share the Earth with the Jewish people and the people of a number of other nations – as though you and your superiors had any right to determine who should and who should not inhabit the earth – we find that no one, that is, no member of the human race, can be expected to want to share the earth with you. This is the reason, and the only reason, you must hang.[89]

From these statements, it is hard to understand the attempt at a rehumanisation of Duch as pursued by Roux. According to Arendt, someone guilty of crimes against the human status has lost their place in the order of mankind. However, at this point the analogy between Duch and Eichmann seems to reach its limits. First, speaking purely legally, only Duch was charged with and found guilty of crimes against humanity, Eichmann was not. Second, and more importantly, Arendt makes no distinction between genocide and crimes against humanity. This distinction does, however, count legally.

If we want to understand Roux's plea for a rehumanisation of Duch from an Arendtian perspective, it might be more interesting to look into another aspect

[86] Arendt, *Eichmann in Jerusalem: Report on the Banality of Evil*, 253.
[87] Arendt, *Eichmann in Jerusalem: Report on the Banality of Evil*, 254.
[88] Arendt, *Eichmann in Jerusalem: Report on the Banality of Evil*, 254.
[89] Arendt, *Eichmann in Jerusalem: Report on the Banality of Evil*, 255–56.

of her work: her phrase 'the banality of evil', which she coined in her report on the Eichmann case. Faced with the task of understanding Eichmann's character, the judges

> knew, of course, that it would have been very comforting indeed to believe that Eichmann was a monster, (...) The trouble with Eichmann was precisely that so many were like him, and that the many were neither perverted nor sadistic, that they were, and still are, terribly and terrifyingly normal. From the viewpoint of our legal institutions and of our moral standards of judgment, this normality was much more terrifying than all the atrocities put together.[90]

In a letter to Gershom Scholem, she would later write that evil 'possesses neither depth nor any demonic dimension'.[91]

In *The Life of the Mind*, Arendt returns to the expression 'the banality of evil': 'Behind that phrase, I held no thesis or doctrine, although I was dimly aware of the fact that it went counter to our tradition of thought – literary, theological, or philosophic – about the phenomenon of evil. Evil, we have learned, is something demonic'.[92] Before attending the Eichmann trial, Arendt herself spoke of the Nazi crimes in terms of radical or absolute evil, descriptions that occur on several pages of *The Origins of Totalitarianism*.[93] The phenomenon of evil is, however, not a major theme of the book (it is not even included in the index of the book). It was Eichmann's character that made Arendt use this specific phrase and more accurately it was his 'absence of thinking':

> I was struck by a manifest shallowness in the doer that made it impossible to trace the uncontestable evil of his deeds to any deeper level of roots or motives. The deeds were monstrous, but the doer – at least the very effective one now on trial – was quite ordinary, commonplace, and neither demonic nor monstrous. There was no sign in him of firm ideological convictions or of specific evil motives, and the only notable characteristic one could detect in his past behavior as well as in his behavior during the trial and throughout the pre-trial police examination was something entirely negative: it was not stupidity but *thoughtlessness*.[94]

As a description of Eichmann's character, Arendt's phrase has been severely criticised.[95] That does not directly concern me here. What is of interest to me is

[90] Arendt, *Eichmann in Jerusalem: Report on the Banality of Evil*, 253.

[91] Hannah Arendt, 'The Eichmann Controversy: A Letter to Gershom Scholem', in *Hannah Arendt: The Jewish Writings*, eds. Jerome Kohn and Ron H. Feldman (New York: Schocken Books, 2007), 465–71, at 471.

[92] Hannah Arendt, *The Life of the Mind.* Part One: *Thinking* (New York: Harcourt Brace, 1978), 3.

[93] See, for example, Arendt, *The Origins of Totalitarianism*, ix, 443 and 459.

[94] Arendt, *The Life of the Mind.* Part One: *Thinking*, 4. For a concise overview of Arendt's reflections on thinking, see Wout Cornelissen, 'Arendt on the Activity of Thinking', in *The Bloomsbury Companion to Arendt*, eds. Yasemin Sari and Peter Gratton (London: Bloomsbury, 2020), 291–301.

[95] For an overview of the severe criticism when *Eichmann in Jerusalem* was just published, see Michael Ezra, 'The Eichmann Polemics: Hannah Arendt and Her

whether Duch (or, more specifically, his character) is banal in the specific sense described by Arendt. Here, there is simply too little evidence to conclude that he was. On one occasion, Duch was accused of being 'lost in his footnotes'.[96] Furthermore, Duch's disempathy as diagnosed by the psychological experts and his lack of imagination may be understood in the specific Arendtian interpretation of thoughtlessness, since for her thinking has to do with imagination in the sense of the ability to take (absent) others into account.[97] On the other hand, Duch completely lacked the cliché-like behaviour of Eichmann, which was so shocking to Arendt.[98]

3.6 Duch, Arendt and We

There is, however, another way of understanding the phrase 'the banality of evil': not so much as the description of the character of Eichmann but rather as an alternative view on the nature of the phenomenon of evil. There is also evidence for this reading in the work of Arendt. We can find it already in a text of 1945, which was reissued in her collection *Essays in Understanding*, where she writes that there are men who reject 'the hypocritical confession "God be thanked, I am not like that"', and '[r]ather, in fear and trembling, have they finally realized of what man is capable – and this is indeed the precondition of any modern political thinking'.[99] Robert Fine captures the significance of this view well:

> In short, what was at issue for Arendt in this seemingly arcane distinction between 'radical evil' and 'banality of evil' was not only the character of the accused, not only the justice of the trial itself, but also a struggle between two philosophies: one rooted in sheer alterity, the other in a politics of recognition that understands the value for ourselves of not dehumanising the dehumaniser.[100]

Fine summarises the value by using the notion of reflexivity, a notion Roux could agree with. For reflexivity denotes that something concerns or affects *us*: we ourselves are being affected. Even the most hideous atrocities committed on earth are done not by non-human monsters but by fellow human beings. Acknowledging this may also help us to exercise prudence

Critics', *Democratiya* 9 (2007): 141–69. For a summary of the debate sparked by the film *Hannah Arendt* and an alternative interpretation of the 'banality of evil', see Roger Berkowitz, 'Misreading "Eichmann in Jerusalem"' 7 July *New York Times* 2013, accessed 8 March 2016, http://opinionator.blogs.nytimes.com/2013/07/07/misreading-hannah-arendts-eichmann-in-jerusalem/?_php=true&_type=blogs&_r=1.

96 Transcript of Proceedings, 'Duch' Trial Public, Trial Day 76, at 105.

97 Hannah Arendt, 'Thinking and Moral Considerations', in *Responsibility and Judgment*, ed. Jerome Kohn (New York: Schocken Books, 2003), 159–65, at 165.

98 Arendt, *The Life of the Mind. Part One: Thinking*, 4.

99 Hannah Arendt, 'Organized Guilt and Universal Responsibility', in *Essays in Understanding, 1930–1954*, ed. Jerome Kohn (New York: Schocken Books, 1994), 121–32, at 132.

100 Robert Fine, 'Dehumanising the Dehumanisers: Reversal in Human Rights Discourse', *Journal of Global Ethics* 6, no. 2 (2010): 179–87, at 187.

when judging the perpetrators of even the most terrible crimes. It might be this that Roux had in mind when he spoke of 'the development of humanity',[101] of seeing 'the man behind the torturer',[102] of recognising Duch as a fellow human being, indeed a brother.[103] Perhaps this is one of the lessons humankind, not just the Cambodian people but the whole international community, has to learn.[104]

In a powerful way, we are confronted with ourselves as human beings in the moving testimony of François Bizot. He was a prisoner of Duch at M-13, the prison where Duch was a chairperson before he was transferred to S-21. Bizot was the only Westerner to survive imprisonment by the Khmer Rouge and he wrote a book on it ('Le Portail' – The Gate). During his imprisonment, Bizot developed 'some kind of familiarity' with Duch, especially during a longer talk he had with his captor the day before his release, the evening of Christmas Day.[105] As Bizot recalls

> I had expected to encounter a monster, an inhumane person, but I realized then that things were much more tragic, much more frightening. I realized that in front of me there was a man who looked very much like many friends of mine, a Marxist, a human being who was a Marxist who was prepared to surrender his life for his country for the revolution.[106]

A certain understanding even results from this encounter:

> So speaking of the monster in front of me, in a way it was his duty. It was his duty to be the interrogator, the questioner. (…) And then I truly realized that this monster was indeed endowed with human characteristics and this was extremely disturbing. I myself was no longer sheltered and it would be the greatest possible mistake to turn such monsters into a different category of people, a different species. (…) I then figured that it was necessary to make known that this kind of danger was not due to a person who was a monster, a different category of person; that this person was a human being like any other human being. Consequently, it is necessary to make a distinction between what humans do from what humans are.[107]

The full significance of his ambiguous feelings towards Duch comes to the fore when Bizot is asked to answer the last question on a specific passage in his book, where he writes about a certain Duong who arrested him in 1971 but for

[101] Transcript of Proceedings, 'Duch' Trial Public, Trial Day 76, at 20.

[102] Transcript of Proceedings, 'Duch' Trial Public, Trial Day 76, at 69.

[103] Transcript of Proceedings, 'Duch' Trial Public, Trial Day 76, at 82.

[104] Transcript of Proceedings, 'Duch' Trial Public, Trial Day 2, at 82–83, where Kar Savuth states: 'Madame Co-Prosecutor this morning said this prosecution is for humankind to learn as a lesson, but the humankind is not only for the Cambodian people but also for the international community'.

[105] Transcript of Proceedings, 'Duch' Trial Public, Trial Chamber of the Extraordinary Chambers in the Courts of Cambodia, 8 April 2009, Trial Day 6, at 64.

[106] Transcript of Proceedings, 'Duch' Trial Public, Trial Day 6, at 71.

[107] Transcript of Proceedings, 'Duch' Trial Public, Trial Day 6, at 72–73.

whom he nevertheless feels affection. At this point, the whole internal struggle of Bizot shines through his answer:

> And, now, you referred to a specific point, this point, this idea of affection, that you can have affection for something even if it has been a source of evil. I must say that my encounter with Duch left a print on my destiny and conditioned the entirety of what I am today for a very simple reason and for a tragic reason as well. It is that I owe – I must come to terms with what's in me in relation to a double reality, the reality of a man who was the vector, the force of massive killing, state institutionalised massive killing, I should say, and I cannot imagine being in his shoes today with so much horror behind – left behind; and on the other hand, the recollection that I have of a young man who committed his life and his existence to a cause and to a purpose that was based on the idea that crime was not only legitimate but that it was deserved. I do not know what I can make of this, Your Honour. (…) And that's where things are particularly difficult for me. I felt that these crimes were the crimes of a man and in order to understand its horror – their horror, it was certainly not by transforming Duch into some kind of monster, but rather it was by acknowledging in him his humanity as ours, and that is – and that was obviously not an obstacle, unfortunately, to the massive killings that were perpetrated. And it is this awareness of this ambiguity of – this ambiguity in his humanity, inhumanity, that causes my tragedy, my personal tragedy today, Your Honour.[108]

Duch should not be turned into a monster. No, the truth is much more frightening, almost unbearably so for Bizot: Duch's inhuman humanity, his human inhumanity is also ours.

The truth of Bizot might also contain a lesson for international (criminal) law: 'in our world international law should not be conceived as a reconstituted form of transcendent authority, at once criminalising the Other and idealising Oneself. It should rather be conceived as a material resource we have for confronting anew the problems of living together and constituting ourselves as a collectivity'.[109] Hence, the plea for a rehumanisation of Duch may be considered in another Arendtian light. If Duch himself asks to become a member of the community of humanity once again, in order, hopefully, to play a role in it, we might want to understand this plea as one of befriending humanity. For Arendt, action is always intricately linked to speech, for '[i]n acting and speaking, men show who they are, reveal actively their unique personal identities and thus make their appearance in the human world. (…) This revelatory quality of speech and action comes to the fore where people are *with* others and neither for nor against them – that is, in sheer human togetherness'.[110] Hence, humanisation, and by the same token rehumanisation, takes place through speech: 'We humanize what is going on in the world and in

[108] Transcript of Proceedings, 'Duch' Trial Public, Trial Day 6, at 96–98.
[109] Fine, 'Dehumanising the Dehumanisers: Reversal in Human Rights Discourse', 188.
[110] Hannah Arendt, *The Human Condition*, 2nd ed. (Chicago: University of Chicago Press, 1998), 179–80.

ourselves only by speaking of it, and in the course of speaking of it we learn to be human'.[111] Here, the notion of friendship becomes relevant in the specific Arendtian sense of a friendship that 'is not intimately personal but makes political demands and preserves reference to the world'.[112] And 'world' should be understood as the intersubjective realm, the ethico-political background and the constitutive horizon of our being: the common context in which friendship takes place and which may even become the object of friendship.[113] Thus, the rehumanisation of Duch is only achieved when we keep open for him the opportunity for speech and action with his fellow human beings. Only in this way may he be able to play a role for humanity and for the world.

3.7 Conclusion

So, where does this leave us when it comes to the boundaries of humanity in ICL? Our in-depth analysis of one case may not give more than the contours of an answer. Our inquiry has, nonetheless, shown several key features of an invocation of humanity. First, the case of Duch does show how 'humanity' itself comes in different guises (e.g., as the community of humanity, which is the victim of atrocities, as the community in whose name justice ought to be done, as an abstract ethical ideal). Second, it shows how 'humanity' is intimately connected with related notions, such as dehumanisation and rehumanisation. The case of Duch shows how both perpetrators and victims can be dehumanised, in the sense that they are excluded from the normative community of humanity. Two distinct categories of inhumanity can be discerned. Victims are treated as inhuman, since their dignity is violated. Duch, the perpetrator, is the inhuman because he has placed himself outside of humanity.

Let me stress, however, that the case also shows how both groups of inhuman are related to the normative community of humanity: they do not exist completely outside of humanity but retain a constitutive relationship with the normative community. Their inclusion in the symbolic universe of the legal case shows this. Moreover, the very possibility of rehumanisation already demonstrates how humanity and inhumanity are interrelated. It is important to stress that one can only speak here of a *possibility*; there are no guarantees and failure remains a real risk. Furthermore, I by no means want to imply that the legal setting of the trial is the only, or the first, site where processes of rehumanisation ought to take place. Boundaries between humanity and inhumanity are not fixed once and for all but appear as permeable and open to change. This, in turn, bears on all of us, every time we (all too easily) want to construe a normative gap between the human and the inhuman. Rather, inhumanity is a threshold experience.

111 Hannah Arendt, 'On Humanity in Dark Times: Thoughts about Lessing', in *Men in Dark Times*, ed. Hannah Arendt (New York: Harcourt Brace, 1968), 3–25, 25.

112 Hannah Arendt, 'On Humanity in Dark Times: Thoughts about Lessing', 25.

113 See Patrick Hayden, 'From Political Friendship to Befriending the World', *The European Legacy* 20, no. 7 (2015): 745–64.

Finally, with the help of the work of Hannah Arendt, these concepts were put in a larger conceptual framework. This framework is, I believe, valuable not as much for the answers it provides as for the questions it allows us to ask: What is, or what are, the purpose(s) of international criminal trials? What does it mean to do justice on behalf of humanity? What is the relationship between international crimes and evil? Most fundamentally perhaps, the work of Arendt may allow us to take our cue from legal and political documents to ask one of the most fundamental questions human beings can ask themselves: What does it mean to be human? Indeed, behind the many different purposes for which the concept of humanity is used and the many different meanings it takes, we are ultimately confronted with ourselves and our own (in)humanity.

4

Estranged from the World

The Experience of Dehumanisation and Its Normative Implications

4.1 Introduction

In Chapter 3, we have seen how processes of dehumanisation and rehumanisation play out in a legal case. The chapter showed how one needs to presuppose the notion of a normative community, or order of humanity, to grasp the logic of these processes. In this chapter, I will analyse the experience of dehumanisation. Dehumanisation is increasingly used to both describe and evaluate grave injustices. The notion regularly occurs in media outlets, and it is the object of scholarly work. Important work on dehumanisation has been done by psychologists,[1] scholars in genocide studies[2] and philosophers,[3] among others.[4]

At first sight, it might seem that dehumanisation does not occupy a leading role in legal doctrine, legal theory or legal practice. However, I submit that dehumanisation plays an important but often implicit role in law. To understand dehumanisation, one implicitly already presupposes a legal framework because it is difficult to make sense of dehumanisation without an infringement of fundamental rights. In other words, from a legal perspective, dehumanisation is a process that appears as the infringement of the fundamental rights of the victim, that is, the one who is dehumanised. Yet, not every infringement of fundamental rights amounts to dehumanisation. For our purposes, we can define dehumanisation as the process that by infringing someone's fundamental rights allows one to treat someone as sub-human, that is, not human to the same extent or on the same footing as the dehumaniser. When understood in this vein, one could argue that lawyers have developed a broad

[1] Examples include Nour Kteily and Emile Bruneau, 'Darker Demons of Our Nature: The Need to (Re)Focus Attention on Blatant Forms of Dehumanization', *Current Directions in Psychological Science* 26, no. 6 (2017): 487–94; Maria. D. Morera, Maria N. Quiles, Ana D. Correa, Naira N. Delgado, and Jacques-Phillipe Leyens, 'Perception of Mind and Dehumanization: Human, Animal, or Machine?', *International Journal of Psychology* 53, no. 4 (2018): 253–60.

[2] Gregory. H. Stanton, 'The 10 Stages of Genocide', Human Rights Watch 2006–2013, available at http://genocidewatch.net/genocide-2/8-stages-of-genocide/. Accessed 2 March 2021.

[3] David L. Smith, 'Paradoxes of Dehumanization', *Social Theory and Practice* 42, no. 2 (2016): 416–43.

[4] See also the various contributions to: Maria E. Kronfeldner, *Routledge Research Handbook of Dehumanization* (Abingdon: Routledge, 2021).

range of legal documents and case law as a reaction to instances of dehumanisation. The intrinsically fragile nature of human beings came to the fore, for instance, in the mass atrocities of the twentieth century, those 'barbarous acts which have outraged the conscience of mankind' and to which the Universal Declaration of Human Rights of 1948 was a direct response.[5]

The aim of this chapter is to contribute to the debate on dehumanisation by addressing the question of what characterises the experience of dehumanisation and the relation of this experience to international legal discourse. More specifically, I focus on the lived experience of dehumanisation as it occurs within a concrete and paradigmatic case to grasp what is at stake in those legal and political documents referring to humanity as a response to its violation. Starting from a situation of dehumanisation as described by the victim, this chapter seeks to shed light on what constitutes this experience. This will be a first and necessary step in understanding why it forms a violation of humanity. Inquiring into the experience of dehumanisation helps one to better understand the specific harm or wrong involved.[6] Furthermore, as I will argue in more detail later in this chapter, the experience of dehumanisation poses an important normative challenge to central concepts within debates on (the aftermath of) atrocities. Section 4.2 takes the experience of Jean Améry as a paradigmatic case of dehumanisation that describes it from a first-person perspective, to grasp what is characteristic of this experience. Section 4.3 deepens this analysis by confronting it with recent work on the phenomenon of alienation. Section 4.4 will draw the normative conclusions from this exercise.

4.2 The *Conditio Inhumana*: A Phenomenology of Dehumanisation

What characterises the experience of dehumanisation? While dehumanisation is undoubtedly a multifaceted phenomenon, Jean Améry provides us with a description of the *conditio inhumana* as a paradigmatic case of dehumanisation.[7] Améry was born in Austria in 1912 as Hans Mayer. The *nom de plume* that he took was an anagram. He was the son of a Catholic mother and a Jewish father. The latter died in the First World War. After the *Anschluss* in 1938, Améry fled first to France and then to Flanders, where he worked for a resistance group. The event that altered his life took place in 1943 when Améry was arrested and tortured by the Gestapo. Subsequently, he was sent to various

[5] Arnd Pollmann, 'Embodied Self-Respect and the Fragility of Human Dignity: A Human Rights Approach', in *Humiliation, Degradation, Dehumanization: Human Dignity Violated*, eds. Paulus Kaufmann, Hannes Kuch, Christian Neuhäuser and Elaine Webster (Berlin: Springer, 2011), 243–61, at 246–47.

[6] Andreas Maier, 'How Denying Moral Standing Violates Human Dignity', in *Humiliation, Degradation, Dehumanization: Human Dignity Violated*, eds. Paulus Kaufmann, Hannes Kuch, Christian Neuhäuser and Elaine Webster (Berlin: Springer, 2011), 101–17, at 102.

[7] Donatella De Cesare, *Tortura* (Torino: Bollati Boringhieri, 2016); Jay M. Bernstein, 'Améry's Devastation and Resentment: An Ethnographic Transcendental Reduction', *Tijdschrift voor Filosofie* 76, no. 1 (2014): 5–30.

concentration camps, Auschwitz among others. After the liberation, Améry returned to Belgium where he would pursue a literary career. He committed suicide in 1978.[8]

Améry aims to give a phenomenology of the victim, whose situation he describes as a '*conditio inhumana*'.[9] In terms of style, Améry's essays are rather loose, combining 'the concrete with the philosophical and the common with the personal'.[10] As a reflection on an experienced reality, he gives us a phenomenological exploration of 'the existence of the victim'.[11] This does not contradict the statement in the academic literature that Améry offers us a phenomenology of torture.[12] It merely highlights that to Améry torture is not one among many atrocities committed by the Nazis. Torture is rather the culmination of the whole Third Reich,[13] which he characterised as 'the rule of the antiman' for its hatred of the word 'humanity'.[14]

The condition of the victim of the Nazis as Améry describes it consists of an enduring experience of dehumanisation understood as the triple loss of trust in the world, home and dignity. Since these three aspects form part of one and the same experience, they cannot be separated and Améry frequently uses them interchangeably. One could say that they are all three constitutive elements of the experience of dehumanisation. Nevertheless, there is reason to draw the distinction, for it helps to grasp what the experience of dehumanisation consists of. Furthermore, in speaking of the *conditio inhumana*, Améry did not only stress the enduring nature of the experience of dehumanisation, but he also hinted at the importance of time as a key theme in his text, more generally. This will become clearer when I turn to the competing conceptions of time of the victim and society, while discussing resentment.[15]

The horror of torture begins with the very first blow, causing the victim to lose their trust in the world.[16] Améry argues that this entails what one might call a double boundary transgression: of the body and of the self.[17] The boundary violation – one's skin feels something it does not want to feel – reduces the victim of torture to nothing but a body.[18] With the infringement of his body, the victim of torture – to his own amazement – also finds himself with a

8 Sidney Rosenfeld, 'Afterword. Jean Améry: The Writer in Revolt', in Jean Améry, *At the Mind's Limits: Contemplations by a Survivor on Auschwitz and Its Realities*, trans. Sidney Rosenfeld and Stella P. Rosenfeld (Bloomington, IN: Indiana University Press, 1980), 104–11 at 106–7.

9 Jean Améry, *At the Mind's Limits: Contemplations by a Survivor on Auschwitz and its Realities*, trans. Sidney Rosenfeld and Stella P. Rosenfeld (Bloomington, IN: Indiana University Press, 1980), vii.

10 Thomas Brudholm, 'A Confiscated Past: Jean Améry on Home and Exile', *The Hedgehog Review* 7, no. 3 (2005): 7–19 at 9.

11 Améry, *At the Mind's Limits*, ix. 12 De Cesare, *Tortura*, 101–5.

13 Améry, *At the Mind's Limits*, 24 and 30. 14 Améry, *At the Mind's Limits*, 31.

15 Cf. Chapter 5 of this book on imprescriptibility.

16 As Améry was a male, I will mostly use the male forms (he/his) throughout this chapter.

17 Améry, *At the Mind's Limits*, 28. 18 Améry, *At the Mind's Limits*, 33.

destructed soul and identity, thus questioning the strict distinction between a violation of the body and a violation of the person.[19]

Importantly, Améry stresses the temporal dimension of torture. It does not stop when the actual act of torture is over. On the contrary, one is a victim of an ongoing torture.[20] The suffering remains and trust in the world is lost forever. Améry himself uses the concept of alienation to describe this loss.[21] The victim, having been confronted with the untrustworthy other, is alienated, unable to share their experiences. The tortured person will always find themselves confronted with 'a foreignness in the world'.[22] Subsequent communication with fellow human beings will never be able to undo this alienation: the torturer has once and for all exercised his power over his victim, thus casting the latter 'from the world into agony and death'.[23]

Améry also characterises his experience of torture as a loss of home. What does he mean when he speaks of home? In short: home is security.[24] Speaking of a loss of home, Améry mentions a loss of security and a loss of community. Home is a place without disorientation, confusion or disorder, where nothing really strange can occur.[25] Later, he goes so far as to argue that this kind of security can only be found within the land of one's childhood and youth, and that losing this land entails an irredeemable loss of self.[26] Crucially, the loss of home has a strong affective dimension. The victim of torture feels fear, shame and resentment because of their inability 'to feel at home in the world'.[27] The loss has to do with the impossibility of belonging to a 'we' and the loneliness that results from this. Accordingly, the need for home – something specifically argued for by Améry – is felt both on an existential and on a political level.

Interestingly, Améry himself explicitly poses the question 'How much home does a person need?'[28] Also in this context, he uses the concept of alienation in order to capture his homesickness as a Jew, more precisely he speaks of an 'alienation from the self', for 'the past was buried and one no longer knew who one was'.[29] Uprooted, Améry found himself unable to say 'we', an individual without a community and without a self.[30] Even if he admits readily that homelessness can also have positive consequences, Améry points out the paradox that only those who have a home are in a condition where one may not need it.[31] The need for a home is undeniable for Améry. It cannot be quantified how much home is needed.[32] Yet, the need itself is fundamental to the human condition.

[19] Bernhard Waldenfels, *Bruchlinien der Erfahrung. Phänomenologie, Psychoanalyse, Phänomenotechnik* (Frankfurt am Main: Suhrkamp, 2002), 93.
[20] Améry, *At the Mind's Limits*, 36.
[21] Améry, *At the Mind's Limits*, 39.
[22] Améry, *At the Mind's Limits*, 39.
[23] Améry, *At the Mind's Limits*, 40.
[24] Améry, *At the Mind's Limits*, 47.
[25] Améry, *At the Mind's Limits*, 47.
[26] Améry, *At the Mind's Limits*, 48.
[27] Améry, *At the Mind's Limits*, 40.
[28] Améry, *At the Mind's Limits*, 41.
[29] Améry, *At the Mind's Limits*, 43.
[30] Améry, *At the Mind's Limits*, 44–45.
[31] Améry, *At the Mind's Limits*, 46.
[32] Améry, *At the Mind's Limits*, 60.

Against (simplistic forms of) cosmopolitanism,[33] Améry defends home as a place where one can read the signs, speak one's mother tongue, orient oneself through the senses, thus picking up the stories and the memories the things tell.[34] The security of home is thus intrinsically connected to one's bodily existence. It is the familiarity and the experiential primacy of what within a Husserlian tradition of phenomenology has been called a 'homeworld' in the specific sense of 'an intersubjective sphere of ownness, as it were, our world. (…) A homeworld is privileged because it is that through which our experiences coalesce as our own and in such a way that our world structures our experience itself'.[35] A loss of home accordingly occurs when 'the sense of the homeworld is no longer appropriated, when it is no longer identifiable as *our* world'.[36]

Améry suffers from a paradoxical kind of homesickness: he longs for a place that, in hindsight, has never been his. In other words, the loss has a retroactive effect.[37] Améry desires to return to 'a past that has never been present'.[38] As this longing cannot ever be fulfilled – one cannot make a new place home – the homelessness is irreversible.[39] Understanding homesickness on a phenomenological and ontological level, one may link this experience to the work of several philosophers.[40] The impoverished world of the new home where one is unable to pick up the signs or understand the language is in its indifference and uncanniness akin to some of Martin Heidegger's descriptions of boredom.[41] The embodied nature of the sense of home and the primordial security it gives us, embodied creatures, is very close to the phenomenology and ontology of Maurice Merleau-Ponty and ought to be grasped first and foremost as bodily integrity.[42] Following this line of thought, this wholeness may be understood in the key of the '*harmonie préetablie*' that exists between my body and the world, a primordial bond that makes me (bodily) belong to the world.[43]

Améry later argues that a homeland presupposes what he calls a 'fatherland' in the specific sense of a 'shelter in an autonomous social body representing an independent government entity'.[44] No homeland without a fatherland: no

[33] Améry, *At the Mind's Limits*, 56. [34] Améry, *At the Mind's Limits*, 48, 51, and 57.

[35] Anthony J. Steinbock, *Home and Beyond. Generative Phenomenology after Husserl* (Evanston, IL: Northwestern University Press, 1995), 232.

[36] Steinbock, *Home and Beyond*, 235. [37] Brudholm, 'A Confiscated Pas', 13.

[38] Maurice Merleau-Ponty, *Phenomenology of Perception*, trans. Colin Smith (London: Routledge, 2003), 282.

[39] Brudholm, 'A Confiscated Past', 16–17.

[40] Martin Shuster, 'A Phenomenology of Home: Jean Améry on Homesickness', *Journal of French and Francophone Philosophy – Revue de la philosophie française et de langue française* 24 (2016): 117–27, at 118–25.

[41] Martin Heidegger, *The Fundamental Concepts of Metaphysics: World, Finitude, Solitude* (Bloomington, IN: Indiana University Press, 2001), 137–39.

[42] Shuster, 'A Phenomenology of Home', 119.

[43] Maurice Merleau-Ponty, *The Visible and the Invisible*, trans. Alphonso Lingis Evanston (Evanston, IL: Northwestern University Press, 1968), 223.

[44] Améry, *At the Mind's Limits*, 54.

secure place without being part of a social and political community. In this socio-political understanding of home, Améry is close to Hannah Arendt and her 'right to have rights' when he gives his notion of home a more fundamental political meaning with the notion of 'fatherland'.[45] Here, with Arendt, one can say that only within a political community in which one can appear as one of the citizens in the public sphere while acting in concert with one's peers, so only when one possesses a fatherland, one can truly say that one has a home.[46] Améry is extremely bleak about the prospects of those who lost their original home to find a new one, since the condition of the exile remains that of loss.[47]

Finally, the dehumanisation of which he was a victim assaults Améry's dignity. To him, dignity is a societal concept.[48] It can be bestowed and as a consequence be taken away by society only.[49] Central to Améry's description of suffering is that he emphasises time and again that the crimes were committed by society as a whole and how he thus lost his sense of home amidst the people who supported a regime that wanted him 'to disappear from the surface of the earth'.[50] The loss of dignity seems to encompass at least three aspects. It is the loss of some kind of societal recognition as a member of society. It is the loss of the status of legal subject and equal citizen as the consequence of the Nuremberg Laws.[51] It is the loss of the acknowledgement as a fellow human being as a result of the first punch of the torturer. I will later come back to dignity. First, however, I will explore the notion of alienation.

4.3 Alienation: Towards a Critical Theory of Dehumanisation

Having sketched Améry's experience of the dehumanisation of torture, I will now seek to deepen the analysis by confronting it with the notion of alienation. Can an account of alienation help shed light on the experience of dehumanisation? The concept of alienation has a long and interesting history within European continental philosophy.[52] It plays, moreover, a crucial role in the work of Hegel and Marx, and via them in the tradition of critical theory.[53] Contemporary scholars within this tradition have taken up the concept and given it an important role in their respective theories.[54] Hartmut Rosa, for

[45] Shuster, 'A Phenomenology of Home', 124–25.
[46] Hannah Arendt, *The Origins of Totalitarianism* (San Diego: Harcourt 1973), 296–97.
[47] Shuster, 'A Phenomenology of Home', 123. [48] Améry, *At the Mind's Limits*, 89.
[49] Améry, *At the Mind's Limits*, 89.
[50] Améry, *At the Mind's Limits*, 86. For more on societal suffering, see Chapter 6.
[51] Améry, *At the Mind's Limits*, 86; Brudholm, 'A Confiscated Past', 12.
[52] Rahel Jaeggi, *Alienation*, trans. Frederick Neuhouser and Alan E. Smith (New York: Columbia University Press, 2016), 6–21.
[53] Axel Honneth, 'Foreword', in *Alienation*, trans. Frederick Neuhouser and Alan E. Smith (New York: Columbia University Press, 2016), vii–x, at vii.
[54] Stefano Petrucciani, 'Alienazione: un concetto da rivisitare?', *Etica and Politica/Ethics and Politics* 18 (2016): 109–19.

example, uses the notion within his broader framework of the social acceleration of society within late modernity.[55] Here, I will draw on the work of Rahel Jaeggi, more specifically on her monograph on alienation. One of the most interesting features of Jaeggi's book is that it combines the conceptual analysis of alienation with the (phenomenological) study of concrete cases of (self-) alienation.

Traditionally, alienation presupposed a true self: an essence from which someone is alienated. With the crumbling of the belief in essences, the concept of alienation also lost its appeal. Jaeggi aims at a redefinition of the concept beyond its essentialist interpretation, to make it useful for contemporary discourse and philosophical analysis. She characterises alienation as 'a relation of relationlessness',[56] or 'as an *impairment of acts of appropriation* (or as a *deficient praxis* of appropriation)'.[57] Alienation comes about because of a failure to appropriate oneself and/or the world. Crucially, then, also the relation to the self appears as always in between own and alien.[58] Distinct from a Kantian conception of autonomy, Jaeggi defends a more phenomenologically oriented understanding of the relationship between self and world, which is characterised by a fundamental intertwinement. Hence, alienation from oneself implies alienation from the world and vice versa.[59]

It is this intertwinement, moreover, that makes alienation a powerful concept for social criticism, since it highlights how alienation is always bound up with social conditions and institutions.[60] Alienated relations are deficient or impoverished relations with self, world and others.[61] In this context, Jaeggi takes on board two basic tenets of Heidegger's ontology, namely its antidualism and the priority of praxis.[62] The first denotes our intertwinement, or entanglement, in the world. Related to this, the second aspect characterises our relationship with the world as primarily practical: we act and live our lives in the world with others. Things in the world do not primarily appear as objects of (scientific) knowledge but rather as instruments or tools to perform a specific action: not to think about but rather to engage with and act upon.

Alienation is a concept with both a descriptive and a normative side.[63] The notion is used to describe accounts of alienated relations. Importantly, it is also utilised to give a normative evaluation of these relationships. This evaluation is a negative one. While the analysis may differ depending on which aspect one emphasises, an alienated relation is crucially one of unfreedom, because of a loss of meaning and/or a loss of power.[64] In this respect, the emphasis lies on the intrinsic relation between a world that appears as meaningful to me and as a field for my action. Only such a world is my 'own' in the strong reflexive sense in which Jaeggi uses the term in her key concept of appropriation. The

[55] Hartmut Rosa, *Social Acceleration: A New Theory of Modernity*, trans. Jonathan Trejo-Mathys (New York: Columbia University Press, 2013).

[56] Jaeggi, *Alienation*, 1. [57] Jaeggi, *Alienation*, 36. [58] Jaeggi, *Alienation*, 39 and 49.

[59] Jaeggi, *Alienation*, xxi. [60] Jaeggi, *Alienation*, xxii. [61] Jaeggi, *Alienation*, 5–6.

[62] Jaeggi, *Alienation*, 18. [63] Jaeggi, *Alienation*, 26. [64] Jaeggi, *Alienation*, 22–23.

meaning and freedom of an unalienated relation to the world entail that 'only a world that I can make "my own" – only a world I can identify with (by appropriating it) – is a world in which I can act in a self-determined manner'.[65]

Appropriation is to be understood as 'a way of establishing relations to oneself and to the world, a way of dealing with oneself and the world and of having oneself and the world at one's command'.[66] Appropriation is a complex notion. It presupposes, first of all, a concept of freedom that is both formal and positive.[67] It is formal, for it concerns the 'how' and not the 'what' of the willing.[68] It is positive in the sense of one being able to act as a responsible agent according to one's own plan. This becomes impossible when appropriation fails. Appropriation refers, moreover, to the practical relationship between self and world.[69] As a process, appropriation unfolds in time, making sense of one's past and writing one's future.[70] Finally, appropriation is a productive process, since 'what is appropriated is, at the same time, a result of the process of appropriation'.[71] More concretely, appropriation involves a process of seizing possession and leaving one's mark on a given content.[72] In this tension – between the alienness and the accessibility of an object – appropriation unfolds as 'a permanent process of transformation in which what is appropriated first comes to be through its appropriation, without one needing to fall back into the myth of a *creatio ex nihilo*'.[73] Alienation may, consequently, be understood as the result of failed or deficient appropriation.[74]

To what extent does the notion of alienation capture the experience of dehumanisation? As I have pointed out earlier, Améry uses the notion of alienation on several occasions in his text when describing his loss of trust, home and dignity. In the chapter on torture, he writes: 'The Gestapo tortures. But that was a matter until now for the somebodies who were tortured and who displayed their scars at antifascist conferences. That suddenly you yourself are the Somebody, is grasped only with difficulty. That, too, is a kind of alienation'.[75] Here, alienation seems to consist in the inability – of the person tortured – to believe that this is actually happening to them. The intellect, or mind, seems unable to grasp it. The feeling is one of astonishment, Améry tells us, at the fact that such a terrible thing is happening to oneself, has happened to oneself while one manages to endure, somehow.

Does the experience of dehumanisation amount to a 'relation of relationlessness'? In torture, one's mind is unable to grasp what happens to one's body. Or, in less dualistic terms, one is unable to understand what happens to oneself. While being tortured, one relates to oneself by not being able to relate to oneself. This alienation returns in the relation with the world: the experience of dehumanisation transforms the victim into someone who remains forever

[65] Jaeggi, *Alienation*, 23. [66] Jaeggi, *Alienation*, 36. [67] Jaeggi, *Alienation*, 30–35.
[68] Jaeggi, *Alienation*, 34. [69] Jaeggi, *Alienation*, 37. [70] Jaeggi, *Alienation*, 178.
[71] Jaeggi, *Alienation*, 37. [72] Jaeggi, *Alienation*, 38–39. [73] Jaeggi, *Alienation*, 39.
[74] Jaeggi, *Alienation*, 36. [75] Améry, *At the Mind's Limits*, 39.

lonely, a foreigner within the world. The primordial bond that exists between self, world and others is broken. While he continues to live and have contact with others, he wanders around in fear, as if dead. The astonishment may also be understood as disbelief and foreignness.[76] This foreignness, or lack of trust in the world, is something of which Améry says that it never passes.

Neither the complete astonishment nor the foreignness in the world described by Améry seems to immediately fit the cases of alienation discussed by Jaeggi; neither does homelessness.[77] The notion seems to presuppose a previously existing home to which one wants and can return and hence falls prey to the kind of essentialist thinking that Jaeggi wants to bid goodbye to. Indeed, the concept of homelessness seems to rely upon exactly this type of metaphysics, since it is easily associated with 'a nostalgic longing for premodern unalienated conditions',[78] against which she wants to reconceptualise the concept of alienation. Nevertheless, she does seem to recognise homelessness as a form of alienation.[79] Jaeggi associates homelessness with the 'detachments of one's social involvements' and 'rootlessness' and immediately links it to conservative cultural critics of modernity.[80]

Améry is surely not engaged in a conservative critique of modernity. His conception of homelessness is not so much cultural but rather ontological and embodied and – understood at the deeper level as the absence of a fatherland – political. Hence, the question is whether his experience of homelessness can be caught as a specific form of alienation in the sense of Jaeggi. Améry does relate his loss of home to (self)alienation: 'my, our homesickness was alienation from the self. Suddenly, the past was buried and one no longer knew who one was'.[81] With the loss of home comes a loss of self, something which he reiterates when he describes himself as 'completely uprooted'.[82] The only roots he does seem to have are those inscribed on his body.[83] His being alone and alien as a Jew is, Améry realises, existential to his personality: paradoxically, it is 'an inalienable possession'.[84]

Homelessness because of dehumanisation entails that although the victim settles in a particular place, it will never ever become home to him. At an existential level, it remains strange. Améry fails to grasp all the nuances in his new language, to read its signs, as he puts it. He experiences this impoverishment as a loss of self. Furthermore, Améry no longer feels secure. Here, as we have seen, he captures the political aspect of home with the notion of a fatherland. While, after the war, he no longer fears prosecution, he fails to find the same shelter in his new country of residence as he had in the country of his childhood.

Does Améry envision possibilities for appropriation? At first sight, one might be tempted to answer this question affirmatively. Améry rejected his

[76] Améry, *At the Mind's Limits*, 39. [77] Jaeggi, *Alienation*, 51–150. [78] Jaeggi, *Alienation*, 23.
[79] Jaeggi, *Alienation*, 3. [80] Jaeggi, *Alienation*, 4. [81] Améry, *At the Mind's Limits*, 43.
[82] Améry, *At the Mind's Limits*, 45. [83] Améry, *At the Mind's Limits*, 94.
[84] Améry, *At the Mind's Limits*, 95.

condition as a passive victim. Only by taking up his fate and revolting against it is Améry able to restore his dignity.[85] More concretely, Améry writes how a punch he gave to the prisoner foreman Juszek gave him back his dignity.[86] Dignity thus becomes an embodied notion, or an '*idée sensible*' in the words of Merleau-Ponty, these ideas 'could not be given to us *as ideas* except in a carnal experience'.[87] Indeed, they only exist within this specific body and it is exactly this embodiment that makes them vulnerable.[88] In Améry's writing there is a notion of appropriation at work that is fundamentally embodied. Alienation – here understood as the loss of dignity – may be reappropriated by bodily taking up one's situation and rebelling against it.[89] An appeal to abstract humanity is traded for concrete bodily action in a given situation. The punch back is a case in point. Améry takes up his situation of a Jew – that is, of a victim – and makes it his own. He thus takes the position of 'a rebelling Jew', and of 'a person'.[90] This moment of becoming a person is that of becoming a responsible agent who is able to lead his own life. One could certainly argue that it constitutes an act of appropriation. Améry accepts his paradoxical fate of impossible and necessary Jew as his own and the rebelliousness is not a pose but an embodied taking up of his fate.

This is, however, not an easy task. Améry also stresses how he finds himself haunted by fear and consumed by resentment, without trust in the world and utterly alone.[91] As he ultimately defines dignity as 'the right to live granted by society',[92] he characterises his condition as one of '*social* unrest'.[93] In emphasising the social and physical nature of his unrest, Améry points to the relationlessness of his state. The reappropriation of his dignity seems to lie in a transformation of fear into anger.[94] Yet, with the passing of time, society seems to leave increasingly less space for this anger and resentment.[95]

Améry's resentment questions any real possibility of appropriation.[96] More concretely, one may ask whether Améry's dehumanisation does not confront us with a case where appropriation seems impossible. Yes, Améry did punch back. However, the temporal structure underlying his experience of torture and his resentment seems to confront us with the limits of appropriation. Appropriation is, Jaeggi stresses, an *ongoing* process.[97] While the punch back might be the first step, it alone can never be a sufficient action in which dignity

[85] Améry, *At the Mind's Limits*, 89. [86] Améry, *At the Mind's Limits*, 90.

[87] Merleau-Ponty, *The Visible and the Invisible*, 150.

[88] Rudi Visker, *The Inhuman Condition. Looking for Difference after Levinas and Heidegger* (Berlin: Springer, 2004), 138–39.

[89] Améry, *At the Mind's Limits*, 91. [90] Améry, *At the Mind's Limits*, 91.

[91] Améry, *At the Mind's Limits*, 94–95. [92] Améry, *At the Mind's Limits*, xiv.

[93] Améry, *At the Mind's Limits*, 100. [94] Améry, *At the Mind's Limits*, 100.

[95] Améry, *At the Mind's Limits*, 70–71.

[96] For an in-depth analysis of Améryan *ressentiments*, see Thomas Brudholm, 'Revisiting Resentments: Jean Améry and the Dark Side of Forgiveness and Reconciliation', *Journal of Human Rights* 5, no. 1 (2006): 7–26.

[97] Jaeggi, *Alienation*, 39 and 176.

is regained once and for all. The process of appropriation is severely jeopardised by Améry's resentment. While the punch back puts Améry in the position of an agent, his resentment establishes him as a victim.[98] While the punch back belongs to a situation in which the field of action is opened and the future is an important temporal dimension, his resentment is a 'retrospective grudge'.[99] While the punch back gives him access to the world where he can live a life with others, his resentment confronts him with his 'extreme *loneliness*'.[100]

4.4 The Normative Challenge of the Experience of Dehumanisation

Let me retrace our steps. In Section 4.3, I have elucidated the experience of dehumanisation by linking it to alienation. There are indeed similarities between Améry's description of the experience of dehumanisation and Jaeggi's understanding of alienation. Nevertheless, it is the complete and irretrievable loss of trust in the world, home and dignity, and the disordering nature of resentment that calls the success of appropriation into question. In other words, Améry is unable to overcome the alienation of his situation. The *conditio inhumana* as he describes it from the first-person perspective is an experience of dehumanisation that cannot be appropriated. As a result of his torture, he loses trust in the world 'every day anew'.[101] This disruption is something that keeps occurring, thus destabilising his relationships with self, world and others. The process of appropriation is stopped in its tracks: it barely started and is already interrupted. Hence, the experience of dehumanisation as described by Améry may be understood as a radical case of alienation, one in which appropriation remains impossible. In order to distinguish this experience of Améry from the one Jaeggi discusses, I will refer to Améry's dehumanisation as an experience of estrangement.[102]

In this section, I argue that the estrangement experienced by the victim of dehumanisation confronts legal theory with a number of normative challenges. More specifically, the victim's estrangement questions important concepts and claims of the international legal discourse on (the aftermath of) atrocity crimes. It might, at first, be surprising to assign normativity to an experience. Nevertheless, ever since Husserl, phenomenologists have pointed out how normativity should already be located on the level of (perceptual) experience, a view that can be supported by empirical evidence from neuroscience and psychology.[103] What is normative is always linked to what is considered normal: prescribing a habitual

[98] Améry, *At the Mind's Limits*, 63. [99] Améry, *At the Mind's Limits*, 63.
[100] Améry, *At the Mind's Limits*, 70. [101] Améry, *At the Mind's Limits*, 94.
[102] See for a related notion of estrangement in a legal setting: Hans Lindahl, *Fault Lines of Globalization: Legal Order and the Politics of A-legality* (Oxford: Oxford University Press, 2013), 156–63.
[103] This paragraph is based on Maren Wehrle, 'Normality and Normativity in Experience', in *Normativity in Perception*, eds. M. Doyon and T. Breyer (Basingstoke: Palgrave McMillan, 2015), 128–40. See this chapter for examples of empirical evidence backing up the claims of phenomenology.

way of experiencing. In its turn, normality comes about in an ongoing process of normalisation guided by a normative but historically and culturally embedded ideal, reliant on the typical perception of a normally functioning body. As such, normality is constitutive for a unified and coherent perception of the world.

Now, pathological cases, and Améry's may certainly be considered one, show a break or gap in the concordant experience of the world. Since these cases transgress the very normality presupposed, they pose a *normative* challenge: questioning the boundaries of what is deemed normal, thus disrupting expectations. As a result of his experience of dehumanisation, Améry's bodily integrity is forever interrupted. I have argued that Améry experiences a triple loss: unable to fall back on a familiar lifeworld or on the habitually embodied cultural norms (recall his inability to 'read the signs'). This explains his estrangement: in his case, the process of normalisation has failed. Améry's account shows the fragility of this process, that is, how the abnormal persists as a shadow of normality.

In the remainder of this section, I will show how the experience of dehumanisation questions central concepts of theories and debates on (the aftermath of) atrocity crimes. As mentioned earlier, at first, dehumanisation appears to be at the heart of some important domains of international law (human rights law, international criminal law, humanitarian law) and yet, one can hardly say dehumanisation is a concept central to international legal discourse. The prohibition of torture is a case in point. Article 2 (2) of the Torture Convention prohibits torture under all circumstances. It bases this prohibition on the 'inherent dignity of the person'. The name of the Convention points to a conceptualisation of the term as a special case of 'cruel, inhuman or degrading treatment or punishment'. In the case law of the European Court of Human Rights on article 3 of the European Convention on Human Rights, the technical term used is degradation.[104] As such, dehumanisation seems to be a threshold experience: both inside and outside the legal order and challenging its boundaries.[105] More precisely, I will now demonstrate how the experience of dehumanisation poses a challenge in three interrelated but distinguishable ways: in terms of time, truth and dignity.

Challenge 1: 'Give me my time'.

Even though it was specific to his particular situation, I argue that Améry's resentment has an important lesson to teach us with regard to the experience of dehumanisation in general. For this purpose, it is crucial to grasp its

104 Elaine Webster, 'Degradation: A Human Rights Law Perspective', in *Humiliation, Degradation, Dehumanization: Human Dignity Violated*, eds. Paulus Kaufmann, Hannes Kuch, Christian Neuhäuser and Elaine Webster (Berlin: Springer, 2011), 67–84.

105 Nanda Oudejans and Anthony Pemberton, 'Broken Rules, Ruined Lives. Een verkenning van de normativiteit van de onrechtservaring', *Netherlands Journal of Legal Philosophy* 48, no. 1 (2019): 66–84.

temporal structure. The traumatic experience of torture has a profound effect on the victim's sense of time, making it impossible for them to write their own future because of the 'sense of foreshortened future', entailing that a loss of trust in the world and others implies a loss of a meaningful future.[106] Améry's resentment points to the tension between justice and survival, in the sense that it was pitted against 'the priority of the (quasi-)natural survival of the nation over the sake of justice'.[107] The tension becomes manifest in the different perspectives of society and the victim. It comes to the fore in the radically different conceptions of time that are at work. There is the natural notion of time of the torturers and society, on the one hand.[108] In contrast, there is the victim's moral sense of time, their own temporality understood as 'time insofar it manifests itself in human existence'.[109] Society – the social body – is basically interested in its own survival only. Accordingly, one encounters here the motive of self-preservation, central to modern philosophy.[110] Society wants to look forward and prefers reconciliation. Legally, this appears in the establishment of a statute of limitations and the (implicit) conviction that time heals all wounds.[111] The time at stake here is clock time, that is, the measurable 'flow of uninterrupted transition'.[112] Améry dismisses this sense of time as anti-moral.[113] He argues for making 'the crime become a moral reality for the criminal, in order that he be swept into the truth of his atrocity'.[114]

Resentment disorders the natural flow of time, even to the degree that moral protest consists in the resistance against the natural and wound-healing flow and the plea for the annulment of (clock) time.[115] Améry rebels against society for it wants the victims to forgive and pressures them towards reconciliation.[116] He seems rather pessimistic about the chances of society recognising his position. He fears both the relativisation of his suffering in a 'Century of

[106] For a discussion of the traumatic effects of torture on the victim's temporal experience, see Ratcliffe, Matthew, Mark Ruddell, and Benedict Smith, 'What Is a "Sense of Foreshortened Future?" A Phenomenological Study of Trauma, Trust, and Time', *Frontiers in Psychology* 5 (2014): 1–11.

[107] Theo de Wit, 'The Boundaries of Transitional Justice: Jean Améry and Johan Degenaar on the Tension between Survival and Justice', *Stellenbosch Theological Journal* 3, no. 1 (2017): 69–87, at 71.

[108] As De Wit puts it: 'What a conciliatory-minded post-Hitler society and the Nazi's former henchmen have in common, is the primacy both give to the purely physical event and the natural sense of time'. See De Wit, 'The Boundaries of Transitional Justice', 74.

[109] D. C. Hoy, *The Time of Our Lives: A Critical History of Temporality* (Cambridge, MA: The MIT Press, 2009), xiii.

[110] Dieter Henrich, 'The Basic Structure of Modern Philosophy', *Cultural Hermeneutics* 2, (1974): 1–18. For the relationship between self-preservation and security, see M. Besters, '*A Politics of (In)Security: A Philosophical Analysis of Collective Security*' (PhD diss., Tilburg University, 2016).

[111] Améry, *At the Mind's Limits*, 70–71. See also Chapter 5 of this book on imprescriptibility.

[112] Hoy, *The Time of Our Lives*, 157. For a concise overview of the differences between clock time and temporality, see p. 92.

[113] Améry, *At the Mind's Limits*, 72.

[114] Améry, *At the Mind's Limits*, 70.

[115] Améry, *At the Mind's Limits*, 72.

[116] Améry, *At the Mind's Limits*, 70 and 75.

Barbarism',[117] and the complaint of society that victims are simply irreconcilable and are looked upon with disapproval. He notes in this respect that the time dimensions are far from neutral: from the perspective of natural time, the future will always be more valuable than the past.[118]

The challenge of resentment that Améry puts forward is of a moral nature.[119] Resentment is exactly the precondition of a reconstitution of moral community.[120] He contrasts this with society's need to focus on the future. The ultimate indifference of both perpetrators and society towards his suffering are in fact one and the same when it comes to their insistence on clock time vis-à-vis Améry's reliance on a moral sense of time.[121] His rejection of forgiveness should also be grasped in this vein: forgiving is a form of forgetting, it turns away from the past towards the future – thus following the natural course of time.[122] This notion of time does not do justice to the continuing torture that Améry experiences and is even 'radically alien to morality'.[123] The impossible wish of the victim of dehumanisation is that their suffering is remembered since only in that case the moral community of victims and perpetrators may be constituted anew 'in explicit acknowledgement of the devastations that expelled them as what should never have occurred to them, and so as what the Germans themselves must wish that never should have happened'.[124] Améry's impossible 'moral time' wants to both erase events and to keep them in the mind of the guilty collective.[125] Améry himself already admits that his resentment is problematic. Accordingly, there is no question of directly transposing and keeping this sentiment within the legal order. Rather, the normative challenge of the temporal division between victims on the one hand, society, and perpetrators on the other hand, lies in tempering too enthusiastic celebrations of forgiveness and reconciliation. The experience of dehumanisation lays a claim on the legal order not to forget the suffering and sacrifice it for its own self-preservation and need for peaceful existence. Against the time of law and order with its emphasis on the future, the victim of dehumanisation lays claim to their own time.

Challenge 2: 'Hear my truth'.

Améry's experience of dehumanisation puts emphasis on suffering as a valuable truth, in the sense of the story of the victim that they regard as more real

117 Améry, *At the Mind's Limits*, 80. 118 Améry, *At the Mind's Limits*, 76.

119 Bernstein, 'Améry's Devastation and Resentment', 12; Brudholm, 'Revisiting Resentments', 21.

120 Bernstein, 'Améry's Devastation and Resentment', 15–16; Brudholm, 'Revisiting Resentments', 16.

121 Bernstein, 'Améry's Devastation and Resentment', 14–15.

122 Bernstein, 'Améry's Devastation and Resentment', 20.

123 Minkkinen speaks in this regard about Améry's 'anti-humanism'. See Panu Minkkinen, 'Ressentiment as Suffering: On Transitional Justice and the Impossibility of Forgiveness', *Law and Literature* 19, no. 3 (2007): 513–31, at 525.

124 Bernstein, 'Améry's Devastation and Resentment', 29.

125 De Wit, 'The boundaries of transitional justice', 74–75.

than any objective legal or institutional truth. This is a truth that the victim needs to tell, even if social institutions do not always allow for it to be heard. In general, when dealing with suffering, social institutions play an ambiguous role: while they include and help some victims, they exclude and cast aside others, thus aggravating their suffering.[126] Furthermore, even those who are included are not welcomed to tell their own stories. Because the infringement of the legal order takes central stage within (international) criminal law, the victim and their experience are pushed to the edge.[127] Therefore, there is always the danger of secondary victimisation.[128] From the perspective of society, however, the possibility of revenge remains a risk to its (presumably) rational order, that is why the law either excludes the victims from the trial or accepts them only on its own terms.[129] At the very origin of the legal order, the experience of the victim (of dehumanisation) escapes the legal order and questions it.[130]

Within international criminal law, this problem surfaces in the context of the ICC and the victim when it comes to the search for truth. Recently, and as a result of the influence of international human rights law, the right to truth for victims has been recognised in the field of international criminal law.[131] Even though the ICC claims to engage in a victim-centred practice and is committed to the victim's search for truth, the model of the ICC does not recognise the victim as a full party to the trial.[132] Problems occur in at least three domains: with regard to information and clarification, to contextualisation and to acknowledgement.[133] Seeking to clarify the experience of suffering, one immediately encounters the inexpressibility of suffering and the inability to share it with others.[134] Victims of mass atrocities have stressed, time and again, this failure of language.[135]

Moreover, whereas the stories of suffering shed light on the gravity of the offences, they do not provide information regarding the question of individual legal responsibility of suspects.[136] It is only this latter question, however, that

[126] Arthur Kleinman, '"Everything That Really Matters": Social Suffering, Subjectivity, and the Remaking of Human Experience in a Disordering World', *Harvard Theological Review*, vol. 90 (1997), pp. 315–35, at 321.

[127] Oudejans and Pemberton, 'Broken Rules, Ruined Lives', 69.

[128] Leora Bilsky, 'The Right to Truth in International Criminal Law', in *The Oxford Handbook of International Criminal Law*, eds. Kevin Jon Heller et al. (Oxford: Oxford University Press, 2020), 473–93, at 482.

[129] Oudejans and Pemberton, 'Broken Rules, Ruined Lives', 71–72.

[130] Oudejans and Pemberton, 'Broken Rules, Ruined Lives', 75.

[131] For a critical overview, see Leora Bilsky, 'The Right to Truth in International Criminal Law', 473–93.

[132] Leora Bilsky, 'The Right to Truth in International Criminal Law', 479.

[133] Sofia Stolk, 'The Victim, the International Criminal Court and the Search for Truth. On the Interdependence and Incompatibility of Truths about Mass Atrocity', *Journal of International Criminal Justice* 13, (2015), 973–94, at 980.

[134] Stolk, 'The Victim, the International Criminal Court and the Search for Truth', 985.

[135] Oudejans and Pemberton, 'Broken Rules, Ruined Lives', 79–80.

[136] Stolk, 'The Victim, the International Criminal Court and the Search for Truth', 986.

the judges of the ICC are to answer.[137] Regarding contextualisation, a similar picture of incompatibility between the stories of the victims and what the Court is after emerges. Again, different discourses clash, since the Court does not take suffering seriously *as* suffering.[138] Even when suffering is represented within the ICC, it remains *a-topos*: uncomfortable and uncertain of its place.[139]

Finally, the last dimension regards acknowledgement of suffering as a story that must be told and heard, for its own sake.[140] Notwithstanding the potential benefits for victims, the Court and society at large, a criminal tribunal does not seem to be the adequate site to listen to this story: 'truth-telling as a purely intrinsic act with acknowledgment as its main goal disrupts the logic of a criminal trial',[141] whose primal aim is to establish whether or not the defendant committed a crime.[142] Court and victim seem to operate in different truth regimes.[143] One may conclude that, regardless of the fact that the ICC claims and tries to give the victim's voice centre stage, 'the Court can barely deal with what that voice is telling'.[144] While the experience of dehumanisation is a truth that the victim wants and desperately needs to tell, it registers in the courtroom as 'an objection that cannot be heard', thus questioning its very legitimacy.[145]

Challenge 3: 'Let me embody my dignity'.

Through his experience of dehumanisation, Améry questions the well-known idea of the liberal subject as a complete and whole self, unattached to the world or others. Dehumanisation is so devastating because it cuts the ontological bonds or attachments between me, others and the world, thus rendering me radically alone.[146] Accordingly, the experience of dehumanisation sheds light on the human condition as profoundly social and embodied. In this sense, it questions the view of the human being as it is central to liberal theories. For according to the latter perspective, the human being who takes central stage is the autonomous and independent subject. While the

137 Bilsky explains how it is not entirely clear how the vital role that the Rome Statute gives to victims relates to procedural aspects of a criminal case and the ICC's mandate, see Leora Bilsky 'The Right to Truth in International Criminal Law', 477–90.
138 Stolk, 'The Victim, the International Criminal Court and the Search for Truth', 989.
139 Stolk, 'The Victim, the International Criminal Court and the Search for Truth', 986.
140 Oudejans and Pemberton, 'Broken Rules, Ruined Lives', 82–83.
141 Stolk, 'The Victim, the International Criminal Court and the Search for Truth', 992.
142 Stolk, 'The Victim, the International Criminal Court and the Search for Truth', 991.
143 For this use of the term truth regime, see Leora Bilksy, 'The Right to Truth in International Criminal Law'.
144 Stolk, 'The Victim, the International Criminal Court and the Search for Truth', 993.
145 Emilios Christodoulidis, 'The Objection that Cannot Be Heard: Communication and Legitimacy in the Courtroom', in *The Trial on Trial Volume 1: Truth and Due Process*, eds. Anthony Duff, Lindsay Farmer, Sandra Marshall and Victor Tadros (Oxford: Hart, 2004), 79–202.
146 Oudejans and Pemberton, 'Broken Rules, Ruined Lives', 78–79.

notion of human dignity is interpreted in a wide variety of ways and plays different functions, within liberal theories dignity is usually understood as an abstract and disembodied notion referring to respect for the intrinsic worth of an individual human being as a fundamental norm for morality, politics and law.[147]

The experience of dehumanisation is marked by the breaking of the fundamental bonds or attachments because of the transgression of self and body. These attachments are also crucial in understanding dignity. Améry's dehumanisation became an integral part of himself, constitutive of who he was. Yet, it remained a part he was never able to appropriate completely, an unhealable wound. As such, one may speak here of his dehumanisation as the inhuman core of his dignity: Améry was 'attached to something that is neither a thing nor a nothing, from which he or she cannot break loose (detach oneself) nor have access to (know it, appropriate it, reduce it to meaning)'.[148] Améry's inability to appropriate life was rooted in the impossibility to appropriate the inhuman part of himself. Paradoxically, it was exactly this inhumanity that made him into the unique human being he was.

What does this teach us about human dignity? Writing on the lived experience of dehumanisation, a focus on a concrete case has unveiled the pivotal role of the body.[149] Such an approach accomplishes a demystification of embodiment.[150] Victims of dehumanisation feel alienated from the world and suffer a loss of identity that violates their agency.[151] Drawing on the accounts of victims, one may stress the corporeal nature of this process of dehumanisation as one of a loss of autonomy, expropriation and loss of voice.[152] In view of that, dignity should be understood as embodied self-esteem, that is, 'a highly vulnerable and, therefore, threatened capability to lead a life worth living [with others] in self-esteem'.[153] As we have seen, only by bodily taking up his situation as a victim of dehumanisation and rebelling against it, Améry is able to rediscover something of his dignity. The experience of dehumanisation questions the liberal idea of an abstract and inalienable norm of dignity replacing it with an embodied and essentially vulnerable notion.[154]

147 For a concise overview of dignity within international law, see Ginevra Le Moli, 'The Principle of Human Dignity in International Law', in *General Principles and the Coherence of International Law*, eds. M. Endenas et al. (Leiden: Brill Nijhoff, 2019), 352–68.

148 Rudi Visker, 'The Inhuman Core of Human Dignity: Levinas and Beyond', *Levinas Studies* 9 (2014): 1–21, at 17.

149 Sophie Oliver, 'Dehumanization: Perceiving the Body as (In)Human', in *Humiliation, Degradation, Dehumanization: Human Dignity Violated*, eds. Paulus Kaufmann, Hannes Kuch, Christian Neuhäuser and Elaine Webster (Berlin: Springer, 2011), 85–97, at 85.

150 Oliver, 'Dehumanization', 86. 151 Oliver, 'Dehumanization', 87–89.

152 Oliver, 'Dehumanization', 90–91.

153 Pollmann, 'Embodied Self-Respect and the Fragility of Human Dignity', 244–45. I deviate from Pollman by emphasising the intersubjective dimension and by replacing self-respect by self-esteem. With both points, I follow Paul Ricoeur, *Oneself as Another*, trans. Kathleen Blamey (Chicago and London: University of Chicago Press, 1994).

154 Améry, *At the Mind's Limits*, 91.

4.5 Conclusion

This chapter has analysed the experience of dehumanisation from a first-person perspective. Starting from a paradigmatic case of dehumanisation, Améry's account of his torture, the experience is characterised as involving the triple loss of home, dignity and trust in the world. Subsequently, this analysis was deepened by confronting it with recent work on alienation. The result of this confrontation was that one can understand dehumanisation as a radical form of alienation, where no possibilities of appropriation exist. Accordingly, the experience of dehumanisation does not fit the vocabulary of alienation as established by critical theory, one of the traditions within continental philosophy that has devoted most attention to alienation. I have reserved the concept of estrangement for this experience. Finally, I have argued that the experience of dehumanisation challenges important concepts that figure prominently in debates on (the aftermath) of atrocities. This has resulted in three normative challenges: in terms of time, truth and dignity. Consequently, and notwithstanding the legal attempts to grasp processes of dehumanisation, the analysis in this chapter has shown how the experience of dehumanisation remains a *Fremdkörper* in the international legal order.

Using the central concept of this book, the dehumanised person may therefore be qualified as inhuman, as Améry has also done when he speaks of the '*conditio inhumana*'.[155] The inhuman is not something or someone existing completely outside of the order. As we have seen, law has taken dehumanisation seriously and this has resulted in various legal measures. These can be understood as legal attempts to include the dehumanised person. Nevertheless, what lies at the beginning of dehumanisation – the experience of the victim itself – remains elusive to law. What is inhuman appears as existing at the very heart of an international legal order that invokes humanity, while escaping integration within this order. Améry already pointed at the normative challenge of his own experience. If we transpose it to the present discourse on (the aftermath of) atrocities, we may formulate them as follows. While international human rights law, international criminal law and processes of transitional justice claim to make time for those who are dehumanised, accommodate their truth, and restore their dignity, an analysis of the experience of dehumanisation has shown how they ultimately fail in this attempt. In Chapters 5 and 6, I will further scrutinise the nature of this normative challenge and consider what the legal order can and cannot do.

[155] Minkkinen speaks in this regard of Améry's 'Anti-humanism'. See Panu Minkkinen, 'Ressentiment as Suffering: On Transitional Justice and the Impossibility of Forgiveness', *Law and Literature* 19, no. 3 (2007): 513–31, at 524.

5

Law, Time and Inhumanity

Judging the Imprescriptible

5.1 Introduction

The crimes known as the core or atrocity crimes, such as crimes against humanity and genocide, are imprescriptible, that is, no time bars apply to their prosecution. Ever since the atrocities of the Second World War, the notion of imprescriptible crimes has become synonymous with the law's dealing with heinous acts. Not only lawyers but also philosophers have reflected on the theme and related concepts such as forgiveness, reconciliation and revenge. In criminal law, imprescriptible crimes form an exception. Normally, alleged criminal behaviour is subject to a statute of limitations. These are

> statute(s) providing for a timeframe within which criminal proceedings must be instituted. Statutes of limitation provide for a non-exculpatory defense to a criminal defendant. Accordingly, even if the accused is allegedly culpable, a statute of limitations will bar prosecution if an action is not timely commenced. Statutes of limitation appear not only in criminal law, but in international, civil, administrative, or tax law as well.[1]

These statutes tend to 'limit two types of action: limitations to criminal actions and limitations to the enforcement of sentences'.[2] In other words, the passage of time affects the question of whether or not a crime can be prosecuted. Time thus co-determines whether something is a matter of law. As said, the absence of such a statute of limitations is in contradiction to the normal situation in criminal law, in which crimes are (basically) all subject to a statute of limitations. The especially shocking nature of atrocity crimes is usually regarded as the justification for this exception.

In this chapter, I will concentrate on the various timelines involved in the question of the imprescriptibility of international crimes. Because of its focus on the temporal dimension, this chapter is a *prolegomenon* to the question regarding the desirability of imprescriptibility. In the wider argument of

[1] Ruth A. Kok, *Statutory Limitations in International Criminal Law* (The Hague: TMC Asser Press, 2007), 13. In this chapter, I only discuss the imprescriptibility of the atrocity crimes and do not consider the imprescriptible nature of other crimes or violations.

[2] Kok, *Statutory Limitations*, 14.

this book, this chapter is a first attempt to articulate inhumanity's normative implications for the legal order. It does this by taking the perspective of the judge called upon to represent the normative community of humanity while judging the imprescriptible. The chapter is structured as follows. In Section 5.2, I will first give a brief outline of the key legal issues concerning imprescriptibility in international criminal law. Then, I will elaborate on the relationship between imprescriptibility and the unforgiveable by revisiting the positions of Vladimir Jankélévitch, Hannah Arendt and Jacques Derrida. Within continental philosophy, these authors are among the most important ones in the discussion on imprescriptibility. After that, I will distinguish four timelines involved in imprescriptibility and assess these timelines from the viewpoint of legal philosophy. Finally, I will take the perspective of the judge and spell out what is at stake in the judgement on an imprescriptible international crime.

5.2 The Law of Imprescriptibility

The core or atrocity crimes are the ones for which the International Criminal Court (ICC) holds jurisdiction under article 5 of the Rome Statute, that is, genocide, crimes against humanity; war crimes; and the crime of aggression. The imprescriptibility of these crimes is now uncontested from a legal point of view.[3] An individual does not possess the right to prescription, not even as part of the right to a fair trial as protected by article 6 ECHR.[4] When it comes to international documents, two treaties explicitly prohibit states from making the core crimes prescriptible under domestic law.[5] These international treaties are the Convention on the Non-Applicability of Statutory Limitations to War Crimes and Crimes Against Humanity of 1968 of the United Nations and the European Convention on the Non-Applicability of Statutory Limitations to Crimes against Humanity and War Crimes of 1974 of the Council of Europe.[6] The problem is, however, that both treaties were ratified by very few countries. Notwithstanding the small number of ratifications, Hessbruegge points out that the 1968 Convention 'set in motion a process of gradual crystallization of the imprescriptibility principle into a customary norm as an increasing number of states introduced the principle of imprescriptibility of core crimes into their national laws'.[7] This development culminated in the Rome Statute of the ICC of 1998. Confining ourselves to international crimes, one may say that with the adoption of the Rome Statute of the ICC, the uncertainty about the existence of a uniform

[3] Jan Arno Hessbruegge, 'Justice Delayed, Not Denied: Statutory Limitations and Human Rights Crimes', *Georgetown Journal of International Law* 43, no. 4 (2012): 346: 'international law, as it stands today, prohibits all states from making these core crimes subject to prescription under domestic statutes of limitations'.
[4] Hessbruegge, 'Justice Delayed', 347.
[5] Hessbruegge, 'Justice Delayed', 348.
[6] Hessbruegge, 'Justice Delayed', 348.
[7] Hessbruegge, 'Justice Delayed', 352.

state practice ceased to exist: a great number of states now acknowledge the imprescriptibility of the core crimes.[8] Indeed,

> [a] constant, uniform state practice to abolish statutes of limitations for genocide, crimes against humanity, and war crimes has emerged that is grounded in the sense of legal obligation (*opinio juris*) necessary to establish the 'general practice accepted as law' that gives rise to a norm of customary international law according to Article 38(1) (b) of the Statute of the International Court of Justice.[9]

Directly related to their imprescriptibility, core crimes also require specific behavior from states. What emerged is 'an international obligation to either prosecute suspects of genocide, crimes against humanity and war crimes found on their territory or to surrender them to a third state wishing to exercise jurisdiction (*aut dedere aut judicare*). This obligation is now recognised as peremptory law (*jus cogens*) that overrides conflicting norms'.[10]

Article 29 of the Rome Statute contains the imprescriptibility of the international core crimes. It reads: 'The crimes within the jurisdiction of the Court shall not be subject to any statute of limitations'. The provision thus establishes a categorical exception to the governing rule of criminal law. From the temporal perspective I take in this chapter, it is interesting to look at the justification for this exception. In this regard, a hint seems to be given in the Preamble to the Rome Statute, which opens as follows:

> The States Parties to this Statute,
>
> Conscious that all peoples are united by common bonds, their cultures pieced together in a shared heritage, and concerned that this delicate mosaic may be shattered at any time,
>
> Mindful that during this century millions of children, women and men have been victims of unimaginable atrocities that deeply shock the conscience of humanity,
>
> Recognizing that such grave crimes threaten the peace, security and well-being of the world,
>
> Affirming that the most serious crimes of concern to the international community as a whole must not go unpunished and that their effective prosecution must be ensured by taking measures at the national level and by enhancing international cooperation,
>
> Determined to put an end to impunity for the perpetrators of these crimes and thus to contribute to the prevention of such crimes, ...[11]

While the legal value of the preamble of a treaty is disputable, it often contains important political and even moral messages. In this regard, (the Preamble of) the Rome Statute shows how international criminal law imagines

[8] Kok, *Statutory Limitations*, 2. Kok uses the term 'core international crimes' for what throughout this book I have called the core or atrocity crimes.

[9] Hessbruegge, 'Justice Delayed', 353. [10] Hessbruegge, 'Justice Delayed', 354.

[11] Text of the Rome Statute circulated as document A/CONF.183/9 of 17 July 1998 and corrected by process-verbaux of 10 November 1998, 12 July 1999, 30 November 1999, 8 May 2000, 17 January 2001 and 16 January 2002, preamble.

itself as law against inhumanity. To do so, it takes three steps: it places the ICC within a specific time frame, it imagines the unimaginable atrocities and it introduces the need to attain justice in the future. I will now look at each of these steps in more detail.

The first move which is of interest in the Preamble is the way in which it places the ICC within a specific time frame. Starting from 'common bonds' of all peoples, it seems to refer to times immemorial, a kind of origin of mankind. In the very same consideration, however, it highlights the vulnerability of this bond mentioning a 'delicate mosaic' that may be 'shattered at any time'. The following consideration refers to a much more recent past: the terrible events of the twentieth century: 'unimaginable atrocities that deeply shock the conscience of humanity'. The next two considerations link the acknowledgement of these atrocities to the will to punish them and put an end to impunity. A later consideration will add that the establishment of the ICC is done 'for the sake of present and future generations'.

In this way, the establishment of the ICC is linked to a past (marked by atrocities that threaten common bonds), a present (in which the vulnerability of these bonds has moved the international community to end impunity) and a future (for the generations to come). Thus, the establishment of the ICC is placed within a specific narrative. The purpose of this narrative seems to be to legitimise the ICC: given the terrible events of the past and the need to protect future generations, the present demands the establishment of the ICC. Or, broader, given the inhumanity of which human beings are capable, we need law to combat this inhumanity and a tribunal to ensure that the law is actually respected.

The second step is that the international community provides us with the legal image of the very atrocities it deems unimaginable. It 'imagines the unimaginable' by giving legal definitions of the crimes for which the ICC has jurisdiction.[12] Of course, it needs to define them in order for the ICC to do its job. Nevertheless, it remains remarkable how quickly the unimaginable nature of the atrocities is traded for legal definitions that are sometimes disputed.[13]

Third, justice is procured for the generations to come by stretching the reach of the law as far as possible. Here imprescriptibility enters the scene, for as one can read in article 29 of the Rome Statute, no statute of limitation is applicable to the core crimes of international criminal law, the ones for which the ICC has jurisdiction.[14] Thus, the notion of imprescriptibility is inextricably linked with that of inhumanity as it occurs in the core or atrocity crimes. In other words, imprescriptibility seems to be a legal reaction to inhumanity: when faced with atrocity crimes, the law assumes authority to judge regardless of how much time has passed.

[12] I am grateful to Wouter Werner for pointing this out to me.

[13] This is related to the discussion on selectivity to which I will turn in Chapter 6.

[14] Article 29 of the Rome Statute says: 'The crimes within the jurisdiction of the Court shall not be subject to any statute of limitations'.

5.3 Imprescriptibility and the Unforgiveable

From the perspective of the victims, Vladimir Jankélevitch arguably presents the most passionate case against the application of statutory limitations. In this section, I will discuss his views and Jacques Derrida's critical appraisal of his ideas in his work on forgiveness and the unforgiveable. For Jankélévitch, there is an unbreakable unity formed by the concepts of legal time bars, pardon and forgetting. In short, he argues that statutory limitations are not to be applied to the crimes associated with the Holocaust because this would amount to pardoning the perpetrators and forgetting about their deeds. This should not be done for several reasons. First, it is not for the survivors but for the victims to pardon. Furthermore, time might have a hold on ordinary crimes; it certainly does not have it on the extraordinary horrors of the Holocaust. More in general, we have a duty towards the past to remember. Let me briefly explain these reasons, paying special attention to the temporal dimension of the argument.

Jankélevitch holds that it is not for the survivors to pardon because the crime is unforgiveable and only the victims may pardon. He sees the application of statutory limitations as the legal and therefore official acceptance of amnesia concerning the Holocaust.[15] Jankélevitch argues that the Holocaust is of an extraordinary and unfathomable nature. To express this, he uses such characterisations as 'unspeakable', a 'shameful secret', the 'product of pure wickedness', a 'metaphysical crime', 'immense', a 'truly infinite crime', 'inexpiable and monstrous', 'unmentionable', a 'work of hatred', 'incommensurable'.[16] Jankélevitch qualifies the Holocaust as a crime against humanity and gives a particular meaning to this concept: it targeted 'the "hominity" of human beings in general. (…) It was the very being of humanity, *esse*, that racial genocide attempted to annihilate in the suffering flesh of these millions of martyrs'.[17]

For Jankélevitch, statutory limitations are entirely beside the point, since the horror of Auschwitz only continues to grow.[18] Linking this argument directly to imprescriptibility, he states:

> The time that dulls all things, the time that uses up sorrow as it erodes mountains, the time that favors pardon and forgetfulness, the time that consoles, settling and healing time, does not diminish in the least the colossal slaughter; on the contrary, it never ceases to revive its horror. (…) Crimes against humanity are *imprescriptible*, that is, the penalties against them *cannot* lapse; time has no hold on them. (…) It is in general incomprehensible that time, a natural process

15 Vladimir Jankélevitch, 'Should We Pardon Them?' trans. Ann Hobart, *Critical Inquiry* 22, no. 3 (Spring 1996): 552–72, at 566.

16 Jankélevitch, 'Should We Pardon Them?', 554–63.

17 Jankélevitch, 'Should We Pardon Them?', 555. Note that 'hominity' seems to mean 'humanness' here. The English translation remains close to the French original that reads: 'contre l' "hominité"' de l'homme en general'. Vladimir Jankélevitch, *L'Imprescriptible* (Paris: Seuil, 1986), 22.

18 Jankélevitch, 'Should We Pardon Them?', 553.

without normative value, could have a diminishing effect on the unbearable horror of Auschwitz.[19]

Against time bars, pardon and forgiveness, Jankélevitch strongly pleads for imprescriptibility, not forgiving and remembering. Legally, as we have seen, this entails the lifting of time bars and prosecution of the crimes.[20] In this context, he introduces the notion of the unforgiveable:

> The extermination of the Jews was not, as was the massacre of the Armenians, a sudden outbreak of violence; it was doctrinally founded, philosophically explained, methodically prepared, and systematically perpetrated by the most pedantic dogmatists that ever existed. It fulfills an intention to exterminate that was long and deliberately matured; it is the application of a dogmatic theory that still exists and is called anti-Semitism. I would also willingly say, reversing the terms of the prayer that Jesus addresses to God in the Gospel according to Luke: Father, do not forgive them, for they know precisely what they do.[21]

This, therefore, culminates in a duty towards the past, a duty to remember.[22] In a temporal key, the argument of Jankélevitch may be summarised as follows: the Holocaust is an extraordinary crime whose horror only grows and deepens with time. Hence, there is no place for legal time bars (it is an imprescriptible crime), nor for pardon or forgiveness (it is an unforgivable crime). The application of time bars and pardoning would, Jankélevitch seems to imply, amount to forgetting. Instead, we have a duty to remember, to prosecute, not to forgive.

Jacques Derrida develops his ideas on forgiveness and the unforgiveable through a critical discussion with Jankélévitch and Hannah Arendt. I will briefly discuss Derrida's views since they bring to the fore important aspects for a philosophical understanding of imprescriptibility. Derrida distinguishes between the logic of forgiveness and the logic of exchange.[23] He juxtaposes the conditional, economic logic of exchange with the unconditional logic of forgiveness. The proper place of the latter is not so much the economic or political domain but rather 'Ethics beyond ethics'.[24] For Derrida, the central mistake of Jankélevitch is a philosophical one: 'the common or dominant axiom of the tradition, finally, and to my eyes the most problematic, is that forgiveness must have a meaning. (…) From the inexpiable or the irreparable, Jankélévitch concludes the unforgivable. And one does not forgive, according to him, the unforgivable. This connection does not seem to me to follow'.[25]

[19] Jankélevitch, 'Should We Pardon Them?', 556–57.

[20] Jankélevitch, 'Should We Pardon Them?', 562: 'The natural impulse of a person of feeling is to become indignant and to fight passionately against forgetfulness and to pursue the criminals, as the judges of the Allied Tribunal at Nuremberg promised, to the ends of the earth'.

[21] Jankélevitch, 'Should We Pardon Them?', 564.

[22] Jankélevitch, 'Should We Pardon Them?', 571.

[23] Jacques Derrida, 'On Forgiveness', in *On Cosmopolitanism and Forgiveness*, by Jacques Derrida, trans. Mark Dooley and Michael Hughes (London and New York: Routledge, 2001), 34.

[24] Derrida, 'On Forgiveness', 36. [25] Derrida, 'On Forgiveness', 36.

Here, Derrida submits, Jankélévitch follows Arendt. Dependent on human plurality, the faculty of forgiving is of crucial importance to her notion of action: 'Without being forgiven, released from the consequences of what we have done, our capacity to act would, as it were, be confined to one single deed from which we could never recover'.[26] There is, however, a limit to forgiveness, according to her and it resides in the fact

> that men are unable to forgive what they cannot punish and that they are unable to punish what has turned out to be unforgivable. This is the true hallmark of those offenses which, since Kant, we call 'radical evil' and about whose nature so little is known, even to us who have been exposed to one of their rare outbursts on the public scene.[27]

In his interpretation of these passages, Derrida stresses two points: '1 Forgiveness must rest on a *human possibility* (…) 2 This human possibility is the correlate to the possibility of punishment'.[28] Stressing the unconditional nature of forgiveness, Derrida seeks to keep it away from law and politics (and their economic, conditional logic of exchange).[29] Against Jankélevitch and Arendt, he points to the aporia of forgiveness: 'If there is something to forgive, it would be what in religious language is called mortal sin, the worst, the unforgivable crime or harm. From which comes the aporia, which can be described in its dry and implacable formality, without mercy: forgiveness forgives only the unforgivable'.[30]

What does this entail for the related but distinct concept of the imprescriptible? For Derrida, the imprescriptible in law gestures towards 'ahistoricity':

> a sort of beyond the law in the law. The imprescriptible, as a juridical notion, is certainly not the unforgivable; we have just seen why. But the imprescriptible, I come back to this, signals toward the transcendent order of the unconditional, of forgiveness and the unforgivable, toward a sort of ahistoricity, even eternity and the Final Judgement, goes beyond history and the finite time of the law: for ever, 'eternally', everywhere and always, a crime against humanity will always be subject to judgment, and it will never be effaced from the judicial archive.[31]

Here, interestingly, Derrida refers to the time of judgement on imprescriptible crimes as a 'beyond the law in the law'. He highlights the odd nature of imprescriptibility, a concept that is both part of positive law and gestures beyond it. It is exactly this place of the concept, on the threshold between inside and outside the law, that makes it fascinating but also problematic. The problematic nature of imprescriptibility is connected to different temporal perspectives one can take on it. These perspectives are dependent on underlying legal values. In Section 5.4, I discuss the different timelines implicit in the

[26] Hannah Arendt, *The Human Condition* (Chicago and London: The University of Chicago Press, 1958), 237.
[27] Arendt, *The Human Condition*, 241. [28] Derrida, 'On Forgiveness', 37.
[29] Derrida, 'On Forgiveness', 39. [30] Derrida, 'On Forgiveness', 32.
[31] Derrida, 'On Forgiveness', 53.

concept of imprescriptibility. In this way, the legal values and their underlying tensions will become clearer, improving our understanding of what is at play in imprescriptibility.

5.4 The Time of Imprescriptibility

Jan Arno Hessbruegge casts the debate on imprescriptibility as a clash between two legal values: justice and legal certainty. He makes it quite evident where he himself stands in this controversy: 'Justice delayed is no longer justice denied. When it comes to prosecuting crimes of the utmost gravity, considerations of material justice for the victims now prevail over formalistic notions of legal certainty'.[32] And yet, this is not the whole story. Even Hessbruegge implicitly admits that there is a connection between the two values when he links the case for time bars with the notion of procedural *justice*.[33] A more complete view of the different interests and legal values involved in imprescriptibility may be gained when focusing on the temporal dimension of the issue. The historian Antoon De Baets distinguishes between four timelines involved in the problem of imprescriptibility. These are those of perpetrators, victims, society at large and historians.[34] Central to all four timelines is the relationship between time and justice. I will first explain these timelines and then relate them to the legal values in the philosophy of Gustav Radbruch.

The first timeline centres on the suspects and (alleged) *perpetrators* of international crimes. From their perspective, justice appears as the wish to receive a fair trial. Here, imprescriptibility may run counter to the presumption of innocence. With regard to this timeline, De Baets discusses two arguments against and two arguments supporting imprescriptibility.[35] Starting with the arguments against imprescriptibility, one could, first, point out that the passing of time may negatively influence the quality of evidence and the credibility of the witnesses, thus jeopardising the fair trial of a suspect. This occurred, famously, in the various cases against John Demjanjuk. Second, against imprescriptibility, the argument has been raised that there is a risk of a 'memory trial': legal tribunals trying to write history by not confining themselves to (the acts of) the suspects but judging an entire regime. In order to rebuke these arguments, De Baets points out that with the passing of time the quality of evidence may also improve, for example, by the opening up of archives.[36] When it comes to the second argument, De Baets holds that the existence of legal time

[32] Hessbruegge, 'Justice Delayed', 385. [33] Hessbruegge, 'Justice Delayed', 339.

[34] Antoon De Baets, 'Historical Imprescriptibility', *Storia della Storiografia*, no. 60 (2011): 142–48.

[35] De Baets, 'Historical Imprescriptibility', 142–44.

[36] Kok also points to the beneficial role of technology in this regard: Kok, *Statutory Limitations*, 243–45.

bars may often seriously impair constructing a complete picture of what has actually happened. Another argument against imprescriptibility concentrates on the suspect's ability to stand trial. Often, (s)he is so old that this is physically (almost) impossible.

Turning to the second timeline, De Baets stipulates that from the perspective of the *victims*, one might argue that not prosecuting suspects of the core crimes flies in the face of 'the laws of humanity'.[37] De Baets understands these in accordance with the famous Martens Clause.[38] Thus, De Baets seems to say that since the victims are under the protection of the laws of humanity, not prosecuting suspects of these crimes would be a violation of these laws. In general, victims do feel the need for the (legal) recognition of their suffering and regard the trial as a stage where they can share their experiences and tell their stories.

The third timeline is that of *society*. The value at stake here is that of social peace, or closure. Society may have less interest in prosecution, or, even worse, prosecution may be an obstacle in attaining reconciliation and social peace.[39] There are, De Baets tells us, 'three defenses to this powerful argument: continuity of obligations, public interest in the truth, and remembrance'.[40] In short, De Baets points to the fact that investigating gross human rights violations is a duty and may even be connected to the right to truth, which also has a social dimension with repercussions for the field of history.[41] Remembrance then ties in with what was discussed earlier under the heading of humanity but may also be linked to the desire of 'never again': 'the rights to mourn and to remember are essential for the symbolic reparation of historical injustice, and as such, for restoring the dignity of deceased victims and for dealing appropriately with the past. Dignified commemoration is also a confirmation of humanitarian norms and in doing so it helps prevent the repetition of repression in the future'.[42]

Finally, De Baets points to the timeline of *historians* who have an epistemological interest. Here, the danger is that of anachronism and the solution may be found in retrospection. Whatever one chooses, De Baets points out the political stakes involved. Victims have a right to the truth, entailing that they have a right to know what has happened in case of gross human rights

37 De Baets, 'Historical Imprescriptibility', 144.

38 Convention (II) with Respect to the Laws and Customs of War on Land (The Hague, 29 July 1899), preamble:

> Until a more complete code of the laws of war has been issued, the High Contracting Parties deem it expedient to declare that, in cases not included in the Regulations adopted by them, the inhabitants and the belligerents remain under the protection and the rule of the principles of the law of nations, as they result from the usages established among civilized peoples, from the laws of humanity, and the dictates of the public conscience.

39 De Baets, 'Historical Imprescriptibility', 145.

40 De Baets, 'Historical Imprescriptibility', 145.

41 De Baets, 'Historical Imprescriptibility', 146.

42 De Baets, 'Historical Imprescriptibility', 146.

violations.[43] Hence, 'failing to deal properly with historical injustice is an injustice *in itself*.'[44]

To tease out the legal values at play in these timelines, I now turn to the work of Radbruch. In his legal philosophy, the idea of law, Justice, is of a multifaceted nature.[45] It consists of the following three values: distributive justice, legal certainty and expediency or purposiveness. Distributive justice should be understood in the classical sense of *suum cuique tribuere* (to give each their own). This presupposes the standpoint of a third party C (e.g., the state) in a vertical relationship vis-à-vis parties A and B whose relationship is a horizontal one. Radbruch stresses that this horizontal, that is, equal, relation between parties within a state (e.g., citizens) is not natural. Indeed, in nature, no two parties are equal. Consequently, equality between people is always *legal* equality, that is, equality established by law.[46]

The expediency, or purposiveness, of law (*Zweckmässigkeit*) stipulates that law always has a purpose. Such a purpose is given by politics; hence, it depends on the ideology of the ruling party which purpose the law is set to pursue. Purposiveness unveils how law is (also) always a means to obtain social ends: it is an instrument in the hands of politics to bring about social change or maintain the status quo. Legal certainty, finally, demands that the law put an end to social uncertainty. The law ends conflicts within society peacefully, through a procedure that results in a final verdict between parties. This verdict is based on laws that are publicly promulgated beforehand, thus making it foreseeable what the state will do and enabling citizens to adapt their behaviour accordingly. Also, procedures ought to be clear beforehand and should be applied to all equally.

If we try to connect the four timelines of De Baets with Radbruch's three components or values of the idea of law, we can see that the interest of the suspects in a fair trial is basically an interest in a just criminal procedure, that is, one in which their rights (as they are summarised in article 6 ECHR, for example) are respected. In this timeline, legal certainty takes precedence over the

[43] This right was developed in the context of the UN. A 2006 study on the subject concludes that

> the right to the truth about gross human rights violations and serious violations of human rights law is an inalienable and autonomous right, linked to the duty and obligation of the State to protect and guarantee human rights, to conduct effective investigations and to guarantee effective remedy and reparations. This right is closely linked with other rights and has both an individual and a societal dimension and should be considered as a non-derogable right and not be subject to limitations.

See E/CN.4/2006/91 of 8 February 2006, *Study on the right to the truth. Report of the Office of the United Nations High Commissioner for Human Rights*, 2.

[44] De Baets, 'Historical Imprescriptibility', 149.

[45] Gustav Radbruch, 'Legal Philosophy', in *The Legal Philosophies of Lask, Radbruch, and Dabin*, trans. Kurt Wilk (Cambridge: Harvard University Press, 1950), 45–224, at 72–112. I use Justice as the name of the idea of law and (distributive) justice as that of one of its three components.

[46] For a similar argument regarding equality and rights, see Hannah Arendt, *The Origins of Totalitarianism* (San Diego: Harcourt, 1976), 301.

two other values. The interests of the victims, their need for legal recognition of their suffering, correspond with the value of justice. Finally, the interest of society is captured under the value of expediency. To move on, a society might need to close the books and could decide to grant amnesty, to forget what has happened. However, there might also be political reasons to make crimes imprescriptible, for example, when the new regime (thinks it) needs to bring members of the old regime to trial to start a new chapter. Here, in cases of dealing with historical injustice, politics takes the guise of a politics of memory.

As the reader will have noticed, I have refrained from assigning a place to the timeline of the professional historian within the philosophy of Radbruch. The reason for this is that he does not seem to have a proper place for it within his philosophy, which is a philosophy of *law*. Recall that De Baets linked the timeline of the historian with an interest in truth. This is the truth from a historical perspective. The historian, looking at past events from a certain distance and detached from the need to pass judgement, may take her time to consider all the relevant sources to reach the highest possible level of objectivity. Writing history might thus be seen as the preliminary result in an ongoing discussion. The truth of law and a legal trial is of a different nature. In a criminal trial, only that which may be legally proven may count as evidence and thus play a role in the construction of a legal truth.[47] It might even be dangerous to make a trial into a quest for the historical truth for this may transform it into a 'show trial'.[48] Furthermore, the legal discussion – unlike the one on (the interpretation of) history – does have an endpoint. Law introduces a constructed end to the endless discussion on history. This constructed endpoint can be found in the finality and finitude of legal judgement, an issue I will return to in Sections 5.5 and 5.6.

From the perspective of Radbruch's philosophy, imprescriptibility may be seen as a case where the other values give way to justice. The grave nature of the atrocity crimes seems to be the central reason why they are imprescriptible. Accordingly, it would be unjust to make prosecution impossible for reasons of legal certainty, or more instrumental reasons. In the words of Paul Ricoeur: 'Imprescriptibility signifies that the principle of prescription has no reason to be invoked. It suspends a principle that itself consists in an obstacle to the exercise of public action. (…) Fundamentally, it is the extreme gravity of the crimes that justifies tracking down the criminals without any time limit'.[49]

Importantly, Radbruch denies the possibility of a perfect solution.[50] His philosophy is interesting in how it envisions the relationship between the

[47] On legal truth versus the truth of the victim, see also Chapter 4.

[48] On the topic of show trials and political trials in an international setting, see, for example, Hannah Arendt, *Eichmann in Jerusalem: A Report on the Banality of Evil* (New York: Viking Press, 1963) and Martti Koskenniemi, 'Between Impunity and Show Trials', *Max Planck Yearbook of United Nations Law* 6 (2002): 1–35.

[49] Paul Ricoeur, *Memory, History, Forgetting*, trans. K. Blamey and D. Pellauer (Chicago and London: The University of Chicago Press, 2004), 472.

[50] Gustav Radbruch, 'Legal Philosophy', in *The Legal Philosophies of Lask, Radbruch, and Dabin*, trans. by Kurt Wilk (Cambridge: Harvard University Press, 1950), 109–12.

three elements of the idea of law. The three components are antinomies. This entails that they, at the same time, need each other and exclude each other. Furthermore, there is no fourth element above the three components in which the tensions between the elements can be solved once and for all and some sort of synthesis may be reached. Whatever route one takes, one is forced to give precedence to one of the three components of law. Hence, every legal solution regarding a problem will necessarily bring to the foreground one or two of the elements making it vulnerable to criticism of the remaining one(s). *Mutatis mutandis*, one cannot but give more weight to one of the timelines of De Baets. This entails that any solution may be criticised from the perspective of the remaining components or timelines and corresponding interests. There is no higher point where all tensions may be *aufgehoben*. Every way of dealing with past injustices remains contingent and contestable. What might work at one time and/or place might not be the best solution for another time and/or place.[51]

5.5 The Time of Judgement

Let us recap. In Section 5.2, I have sketched the legal and institutional framework of the imprescriptibility of international core crimes. I have shown how the ICC's jurisdiction of these crimes is legitimised through a specific narrative in which past, present and future converge in the establishment of the ICC. Then, in Section 5.3 of this chapter, I have discussed Jankélévitch's and Derrida's views on the (im)possibility of forgiving the most heinous crimes. In Section 5.4, drawing on the work of De Baets, I distinguished between four timelines involved in the notion of imprescriptibility and analysed them with the help of Radbruch's philosophy. Now, I turn to the perspective of the judge. For imprescriptibility entails that law is called upon to judge, that a judgement remains possible and is even asked for. Which temporalities are involved in this possibility of judgement?

Drawing on the work of Ricoeur, one can make more sense of the *finality* involved in the act of judging. Conceiving of the judgement as the intervention in a deliberation, the ending of a social conflict, Ricoeur submits that 'it is a

[51] Besides their relation, there is also the question of the order of the three components. In this regard, usually a distinction is drawn between the early Radbruch (pre-Second World War) and the late Radbruch (post-Second World War). The early Radbruch stresses the equal weight of the three elements. Nevertheless, Radbruch argues that providing legal certainty is the first task of the law. *That* there is order is ultimately more important than the just quality of the order. Stability and predictability are to be valued *per se*, since they protect us from disorder and uncertainty. See Radbruch, 'Legal Philosophy', 118. After the Second World War, Radbruch seems to reconsider the order of the three values in what has become known as his formula, see Gustav Radbruch, 'Statutory Lawlessness and Supra-Statutory Law (1946)', *Oxford Journal of Legal Studies* 26, no. 1 (2006): 1–11. There is a scholarly debate on the question whether Radbruch really changed his views, see Stanley L. Paulson, 'Radbruch on Unjust Laws: Competing Earlier and Later Views', *Oxford Journal of Legal Studies* 15 (1995): 489–500. I will not enter this debate here.

characteristic of judgment on the judicial plane to interrupt the back-and-forth play of arguments by giving them an endpoint, even if this latter is provisory, at least so long as the ways of appeal remain open. But there will ultimately be a place or moment where a final ruling is sanctioned by public force'.[52] Now, interestingly, Ricoeur draws a distinction between two kinds of finality. Short-term finality concerns the particular dispute, and the parties involved: it ends their uncertainty and 'expresses the force of law; what is more, it states the law in terms of a singular situation'.[53]

Yet, this type of finality does not exhaust the act of judging, '[b]ecause the trial process itself is only the codified form of a broader phenomenon, namely that of conflict. It is a question therefore of replacing the trial process, with its precise procedures, against the background of the broader social phenomenon inherent in the functioning of civil society and situated at the origin of public discussion'.[54] This background, Ricoeur argues, is ultimately formed by the specific way in which a society deals with conflict, namely through discourse and the institution of a trial instead of through violence in the guise of vengeance. Hence, judging should be understood within the framework of distributive justice.[55] As the German *Ur-teil* still expresses, there is a direct link between judging and giving each their own (*suum cuique tribuere*).[56] Accordingly, the ultimate or long-term finality of judging is 'the contribution of a judgment to public peace'.[57]

In a move typical for his work, Ricoeur puts this goal in the key of mutual recognition:

> I think that the act of judging reaches its goal when someone who has, as we say, won his case still feels able to say: my adversary, the one who lost, remains like me a subject of right, his cause should have been heard, he made plausible arguments and these were heard. However, such recognition will not be complete unless the same thing can also be said by the loser, the one who did wrong, who has been condemned. He should be able to declare that the sentence that condemns him was not an act of violence but rather one of recognition.[58]

This leads to a vision of society in which shared values take central stage and in which there is an intrinsic connection between judging and sharing: 'the act of judging has as its horizon a fragile equilibrium of these two elements of sharing: that which separates my share or part from yours and that which, on the other hand, means that each of us shares in, takes part in society'.[59]

To evaluate what we can learn from Ricoeur, it is useful to consider what he said about finality by using the terms of Radbruch. With Ricoeur we may grasp the relationship between what in the terminology of Radbruch are called legal

[52] Paul Ricoeur, *The Just*, trans. David Pellauer (Chicago and London: The University of Chicago Press, 2000), 128.
[53] Ricoeur, *The Just*, 129. [54] Ricoeur, *The Just*, 130. [55] Ricoeur, *The Just*, 129.
[56] Ricoeur, *The Just*, 130. [57] Ricoeur, *The Just*, 127. [58] Ricoeur, *The Just*, 131–32.
[59] Ricoeur, *The Just*, 132.

certainty and expediency. Both these values have to do with the finality of the act of judging. The former with short-term, the latter with long-term finality. Legal certainty seems primarily concerned with particular legal disputes. It asks the law to bring these disputes to an end by an authoritative decision. As we have seen, expediency has many guises, depending on the specific socio-political goal pursued through the means of law. It is connected to long-term finality, since what is considered is the broader societal interest in a peaceful ending of conflicts, namely the avoidance of violence.

Furthermore, the act of judging is also understood by Ricoeur against the background of distributive justice. Also here, Ricoeur and Radbruch seem to concur. Yet, the connection Ricoeur stipulates between distributive justice and mutual recognition is not altogether convincing. Mutual recognition is recognition between equals. This entails that we are dealing with a horizontal relationship. Distributive justice, however, is justice done from the viewpoint of a third instance (e.g., the State). Hence, distributive justice implies a vertical relationship. In short, distributive justice precedes mutual recognition because the verticality involved in the former determines the horizontality of the latter. Before the sharing can begin, one needs to determine among whom to share, that is, who is equal to whom. Since equality is never a given but results from an abstraction of given inequalities, it always rests on a political decision.[60] *Pace* Ricoeur, distributive justice is not only about sharing. Deciding precedes sharing, and inclusion and exclusion precede distribution. Assuming an immediate link between distributive justice and mutual recognition begs the question.[61]

How can this question be formulated within the context of our inquiry into imprescriptibility? It is the question of the self of a community, the question of the 'we', more specifically in this book 'we, humanity'.[62] This is not simply a normative but a reflexive question. In his famous book *Oneself as Another*, Ricoeur discusses this reflexive question on the level of the individual.[63] With regard to the plural level, Ricoeur also seems aware of it. However, he immediately links it to national reconciliation, amnesty and forgetting – notions which he rejects.[64] His main problem with amnesty seems to be that he regards it as a politically motivated command for amnesia with the aim 'to wipe away the traces of public discord'.[65]

60 Radbruch, 'Legal Philosophy', 75.

61 Interestingly, Ricoeur seems to be aware of this problem in other work. See the critical discussion of Rawls in Paul Ricoeur, *Oneself as Another*, trans. Kathleen Blamey (Chicago and London: The University of Chicago Press, 1992), 227–39.

62 On the constitution of 'we, humanity', see Chapter 2.

63 Paul Ricoeur, *Oneself as Another*, trans. Kathleen Blamey (Chicago and London: The University of Chicago Press, 1992), 113–39.

64 Ricoeur, *The Just*, 143: 'What is at issue here? Certainly, national reconciliation. And in this regard, it is perfectly legitimate to seek to mend things by forgetting the tears in the social fabric. But we may worry about the price of this reaffirmation (which I have called magical and desperate) of the indivisible character of the sovereign political body'.

65 Ricoeur, *The Just*, 143–44.

Ricoeur juxtaposes amnesty with pardon. For the latter, memory constitutes a precondition. In one sense, Ricoeur argues, pardon is of an extra-legal nature both in terms of its logic and in terms of its end: '[p]ardon is a kind of healing of memory, the end of mourning. Delivered from the weight of debt, memory is freed for great projects. Pardon gives memory a future'.[66] And yet, pardon may – indirectly – influence the legal order. It calls to mind the equity or fairness demanded from judgement: 'pardon constitutes a permanent reminder that justice is the justice of human beings and that it must not set itself up as the final judgment'.[67] Ultimately, its meaning should be placed on the symbolic level: 'On the deepest symbolic plane, what is at stake is the separation between *Dike*, the justice of the humans, and *Themis*, the ultimate and shadowy refuge of the equation of Vengeance (with a capital V) and Justice (with a capital J)'.[68]

Note that for Ricoeur, both the final judgement and the act of pardon or forgiveness are connected to the same narrative about the *end* of time.[69] Temporally, they are situated not on the last day but on the day after the last day. In this regard, Bert van Roermund speaks of a 'time beyond time' as the proper time of forgiveness:

> forgiveness can only be thought in a time beyond time, in the optative mode of wish and hope rather than in the indicative mode of description or the imperative mode of prescription. For this anticipation of a memory that will once turn out be unequivocally 'blessed,' Ricoeur uses the theological term 'eschatology', though in a radically philosophical (rather than a theological) sense.[70]

Van Roermund complements this narrative with a second one. This second narrative talks about the *beginning* of time and the coming into being of the human condition: 'why would we be interested in forgiveness in the first place? (…) Answering these and similar questions amounts to narrating a beginning of time that is unimaginable and yet undeniable; a story of how the human condition came about'.[71] In doing this, he points to the (proto-)political origins of (public) forgiveness and reconciliation in the Arendtian notion of natality. Recall that Arendt introduces the concept of natality as follows:

> The life span of man running toward death would inevitably carry everything human to ruin and destruction if it were not for the faculty of interrupting it and beginning something new, a faculty which is inherent in action like an ever-present reminder that men, though they must die, are not born in order to die but in order to begin. (…) The miracle that saves the world, the realm of human affairs, from its normal, 'natural' ruin is ultimately the fact of natality, in which the faculty of action is ontologically rooted.[72]

66 Ricoeur, *The Just*, 144. 67 Ricoeur, *The Just*, 145. 68 Ricoeur, *The Just*, 145.

69 Ricoeur uses pardon and forgiveness as synonyms. I will follow him in this respect.

70 Bert van Roermund, 'Time beyond time – time before time: Comments on Ricoeur', in *Public Forgiveness in Post-Conflict Contexts*, eds. Bas van Stokkom, Neelke Doorn and Paul van Tongeren (Cambridge and Antwerp: Intersentia, 2012), 92.

71 Van Roermund, 'Time beyond Time', 97. 72 Arendt, *The Human Condition*, 246–47.

Natality is intimately connected to forgiveness. This becomes clear when we consider how forgiveness for Ricoeur is about a fundamental *dissociation* in which the agent is separated from the act: 'Everything, finally, hangs on the possibility of separating the agent from the action. (…) The guilty person, rendered capable of beginning again: this would be the figure of unbinding that commands all the others'.[73] At this point, Arendt and Ricoeur meet for the

> concept of 'natality' points to the kind of dissociation that Ricoeur is (rightly) demanding. (…) For Arendt it is part of a political anthropology or protology, one might say – while Ricoeur refers it to a realm beyond the political, to a time beyond time that is the ultimate perspective of morality. But note that natality as a protological concept is as much about dissociation as the eschatological account of forgiveness can be.[74]

Accordingly, dissociation is the term that links forgiveness to natality: because you forgive me, a new beginning is possible for us, together. With natality, we are at the very heart of politics – and of the human condition, one may add:

> Something new can be expected from individual men, precisely because they are held to account not only by those who are present (their fellow human beings), not only by one who remains absent (a transcendental God), but also, and even primarily, by those who are present in their absence (those who gave them birth and those to whom they will give birth). Again, this makes natality more rather than less political.[75]

Interpreting forgiveness from the viewpoint of natality unveils its revolutionary and disruptive nature as 'the unprecedented claim, the altering demand, the possible transformative impulse for any established democratic politico-legal order. As it is, such an element does not already have its place inside the order as in this case it would represent no real challenge or disturbance, nor is it irreducibly outside the order'.[76] Forgiveness appears as a strange event on the threshold of the order, not unlike revolutions. Just like public forgiveness and reconciliation, revolutions are about the re-constitution of the polity.[77] In other words, all these political beginnings are about saying 'we' again.[78]

[73] Paul Ricoeur, *Memory, History, Forgetting*, trans. K. Blamey and D. Pellauer (Chicago and London: The University of Chicago Press, 2004), 490.

[74] Van Roermund, 'Time beyond Time', 100–1. [75] Van Roermund, 'Time beyond Time', 101.

[76] Ferdinando G. Menga, 'Antagonism, Natality, A-Legality: A Phenomenological Itinerary on the Democratic Transgression of Politico-Legal Orders', *Ratio Juris* 31, no. 1 (March 2018): 100–19, at 113–14.

[77] For this interpretation of revolutions, see Luigi Corrias, 'Revolution, Authority and the Institution of Legal Order: Phenomenological Reflections', *Archiv für Rechts- und Sozialphilosphie* 100, no. 3 (July 2014): 295–307.

[78] Van Roermund, 'Time beyond Time', 103.

5.6 Conclusion

In this chapter, the imprescriptibility of the core crimes has been analysed from a philosophical point of view and with a special focus on the temporal dimensions. Some philosophers link imprescriptibility to the concept of the unforgiveable. Several timelines have been discerned both in the justificatory narrative in the preamble of the Rome Statute of the ICC and in the academic debate on imprescriptibility. Whether or not one finds imprescriptibility desirable and/or defensible depends on which timeline is given precedence. Since these timelines correspond to irreconcilable legal values, no ultimate answer is available. Yet, a legal judgement is called for. The judge cannot forgive and should not force the victims to forgive, but what role is there for the judge to play?

It is time to return to the constructed endpoint of the law. In this regard, I would like to draw a distinction between finality and finitude. Whereas the finality of the judgement may be linked to legal certainty and to social peace as ends of the law, the finitude of the judgement reflects the act of judging as an administration of human justice. As an act of justice pronounced *in the name of humanity*, the judge should remember their role as a representative of the legal order, also when this order is instituted, indeed constructed, in the name of 'we, humanity'. One could say that there is a moment of inhumanity at the very birth of the community of humanity. This marks the order by contingency from its very beginning.[79] The contingency of the legal order is irreducible, for its very birth is a process of in- and exclusion that founds and therefore precedes the justice administered by the legal order. Accordingly, recognising the finitude of the act of judgement reflects the contingency of the legal order it speaks for and the relativity of the rightness of the community it represents. In this respect, Ricoeur points to the consideration owed to the guilty, even to those guilty of atrocity crimes.[80] With Gadamer, we may also call to mind the time-honoured tradition of equity which seeks to 'refrain from applying the full rigor of the law'.[81]

As an act of *human* justice, the act of judgement should stay away from all absolute or eternal claims to justice, visions that can be provoked by the notion of imprescriptibility, as we have seen.[82] In this regard, Ricoeur sees in pardon

[79] Bernhard Waldenfels, *Phenomenology of the Alien: Basic Concepts*, trans. Tanja Stähler and Alexander Kozin (Evanston, IL: Northwestern University Press, 2011), 11.

[80] Paul Ricoeur, *Memory, History, Forgetting*, trans. K. Blamey and D. Pellauer (Chicago and London: The University of Chicago Press, 2004), 473–74.

[81] Hans-Georg Gadamer, *Truth and Method*, trans. Joel Weinsheimer and Donald G. Marshall (London: Continuum Books, 2011), 316. See also Ricoeur, *The Just*, 145.

[82] See for a critical reaction Tzvetan Todorov, *Hope and Memory: Lessons from the Twentieth Century*, trans. David Bellos (London: Atlantic Books, 2003), 212: 'Imprescriptibility is the legal translation of eternity – and eternity has no place in human jurisprudence. The absolute, the sacred, and the eternal are not subject to the law, which deals with finite, imperfect, and relative beings'.

a role to play in the juridical realm as a bulwark against a superhuman justice on the one hand and vengeance on the other hand.[83] He stresses that pardon may only be carried out by the victim and therefore 'pardon is never owed. Not only can it not be expected, but such an expectation can be legitimately refused. To this extent, pardon must first have run into the unpardonable, that is, the infinite debt, the irreparable wrong'.[84] The human judgement of an infinite debt can only be finite – it can never exhaust the debt, never do absolute justice to the wrong suffered. It thus not only relativizes the extent to which justice may be obtained, it also points to the limits of law.

What can the judge do? The judge should always leave room for the unexpected event of reconciliation and forgiveness by acknowledging the finitude of their judgement. There seems to be no right time for the judgement. It hovers between a time before time and a time beyond time. And yet, between these two unattainable moments, legal finitude has a role to play as a complement to both natality and imprescriptibility. For law not to freeze into a final word of power, it needs to remain open for an interruption by the unexpected. Natality – and forgiveness should be understood through this lens – is quintessentially about these unexpected beginnings. Imprescriptibility suspends the legal principle of prescription, it puts on hold the effect of time. Acknowledging legal finitude suspends or puts on hold the effects of imprescriptibility, it defers or postpones (*post-ponere*) laying down (*ponere*) the law.

[83] Ricoeur, *The Just*, 145. [84] Ricoeur, *The Just*, 144.

6

Silent Claims and the Limits of International Criminal Law

6.1 Introduction

In Chapter 5, I took the perspective of imprescriptibility to ask normative questions regarding the relationship between the international legal order and the perpetrator of atrocity crimes. I argued for a modesty of law enforcement vis-à-vis the perpetrator, emphasising how human justice should stay away from universal or eternal pretensions of justice. This chapter turns to normative questions related to the victim. In Chapter 4, I discussed that while international criminal tribunals increasingly welcome victims to participate within trials, this does not always lead to satisfactory results. In this chapter, I inquire more generally into the normative relationship between victim and international legal order. This perspective is opened through the notion of suffering.

References to 'humanity' in international law are often bound up with suffering and the call to end it. Apart from the Preamble to the Rome Statute of the ICC quoted in earlier chapters, take the following examples. In its resolution 96 (I) of 11 December 1946, the General Assembly of the United Nations holds:

> Genocide is a denial of the right of existence of entire human groups, as homicide is the denial of the right to live of individual human beings; such denial of the right of existence shocks the conscience of mankind, results in great losses to humanity in the form of cultural and other contributions represented by these human groups, and is contrary to moral law and to the spirit and aims of the United Nations. Many instances of such crimes of genocide have occurred when racial, religious, political and other groups have been destroyed, entirely or in part. The punishment of the crime of genocide is a matter of international concern.[1]

In its preamble, the Genocide Convention of 12 January 1951 states that the crime of genocide is 'condemned by the civilized world', 'has inflicted great losses on humanity' and thus calls 'to liberate mankind from such an odious scourge'.[2]

[1] UN General Assembly, *The Crime of Genocide*, 11 December 1946, A/RES/96.

[2] Convention on the Prevention and Punishment of the Crime of Genocide. Adopted by the General Assembly of the United Nations on 9 December 1948.

The closest textual link between suffering and international law may be found in the Torture Convention of 1984. In its preamble, it explicitly refers to human rights and recognises that they 'derive from the inherent dignity of the human person'.[3] The Convention does not only ban torture but also 'other cruel, inhuman or degrading treatment or punishment'.[4] In article 1 of the Convention, torture is directly linked to the intentional infliction of pain or suffering.[5] What does humanity, or inhumanity, refer to in this context? At first sight, the text of the Convention seems to stipulate that the treatment or punishment may become inhuman. Yet, what exactly makes the treatment inhuman? The underlying argument seems to be that torture disrespects the inherent dignity of the human person. As such, torture might be described as a form of inhumanity that leads to suffering. So, the act of torture (or other acts of degrading treatment) leads to the inhuman suffering of the victim. The victim's humanity is denied (the victim is dehumanised, one might say).

What interests me in this chapter is the question of what kind of claim suffering makes on the (international) legal order. Section 6.2 introduces the distinction between human and inhuman suffering and shows its centrality within international criminal law (ICL). Section 6.3 discusses forms of suffering that are not recognised by ICL. Section 6.4 builds on the notion of alienness to characterise unrecognisable forms of suffering. In Section 6.5, I introduce the key notion of silent claim to outline what sort of demand unrecognisable suffering poses to the international legal order. I also discuss a political action taken in the name of humanity as an example of a silent claim.

6.2 Varieties of Suffering

What exactly is the relationship between suffering and the legal order? Talal Asad turns our attention to distinct types of suffering, indeed *hierarchies* of suffering, inherent in international law. Even while nowadays presented as a universal norm in, for example, the Torture Convention, Asad argues that the modern rejection of cruel and degrading treatment or punishment is actually a particular standard based on a secular idea of what it means to be truly human.[6]

[3] Convention against Torture and Other Cruel, Inhuman or Degrading Treatment or Punishment. Adopted by the General Assembly of the United Nations on 10 December 1984.

[4] Convention against Torture and Other Cruel, Inhuman or Degrading Treatment or Punishment. Adopted by the General Assembly of the United Nations on 10 December 1984.

[5] Article 1: 1. For the purposes of this Convention, the term 'torture' means any act by which severe pain or suffering, whether physical or mental, is intentionally inflicted on a person for such purposes as obtaining from him or a third person information or a confession, punishing him for an act he or a third person has committed or is suspected of having committed, or intimidating or coercing him or a third person, or for any reason based on discrimination of any kind, when such pain or suffering is inflicted by or at the instigation of or with the consent or acquiescence of a public official or other person acting in an official capacity. It does not include pain or suffering arising only from, inherent in or incidental to lawful sanctions.

[6] T. Asad, 'On Torture, or Cruel, Inhuman, and Degrading Treatment', *Social Research* 63, no. 4 (Winter 1996): 1081–109, at 1082.

This measure or standard goes back to the colonial project of European rulers creating 'new human subjects' by outlawing uncivilised customs.[7] In this humanising project, a key distinction between necessary and unnecessary suffering was at work.[8] The former form of suffering was regarded as measurable and as an inevitable consequence of the civilising process. Consequently, this suffering – deemed necessary in making colonial subjects fully human – was not to be regarded as punishable by law. Necessary suffering fits in a specific conception of development, or teleology of progress, that is rooted in a liberal Western conception of civilisation.

This was different with unnecessary or inhuman suffering. This referred to a kind of suffering that was both excessive and gratuitous: '*Inhuman* suffering, typically associated with barbaric behavior, was a morally insufferable condition for which someone was therefore responsible; those requiring it (themselves inhuman enough to cause it to be inflicted) must be made to desist and, if necessary, punished'.[9] Inhuman suffering is unnecessary because, instead of being a consequence of a humanising practice, it rather results from a 'barbaric custom' that needs to be left behind to become truly human.[10] Because it is unnecessary, it is illegal and may be punished.[11] In short, what is inhuman needs to be punished, according to this line of reasoning. The inhuman is included in international law's reach but only as punishable behaviour.[12] Hence, Asad's conclusion is that 'the modern hostility is not simply to pain, it is to pain that does not accord with a particular conception of being human – *and that is therefore in excess*. "Excess" is a concept of measure. An essential aspect of the modern attitude to pain rests on a calculus that defines appropriate actions'.[13] Excessive suffering is inhuman. Note that excessive does not simply mean 'more than the appropriate measure'. Rather, 'excessive' points to what is immeasurable.

However, one can question whether law succeeds in grasping what is immeasurable. In Chapter 2, we have already seen that law grapples with a perpetrator (Ongwen) who is deemed inhuman, situated inside and outside ICL. Academics, novelists and survivors have also pointed out the immeasurable nature of the suffering involved in atrocity crimes. Primo Levi, for example, turns the reader's attention from the very outset to the unbelievable nature of what he has to tell: 'many survivors (…) remember that the SS militiamen cynically enjoyed admonishing the prisoners: "However this war may end, we have

[7] Asad, 'On Torture', 1091. [8] Asad, 'On Torture', 1092–93. [9] Asad, 'On Torture', 1092.

[10] For an explanation of how this originates in Enlightenment thought on humanity, see Robert Legros, *L'idée d'humanité: Introduction à la phénoménologie*. Coll. «Le Collège de philosophie» (Paris: Grasset & Fasquelle, 1990), 13–49.

[11] This same discourse underlies (*a contrario*) the notion of 'military necessity' in modern warfare, regarded as an acceptable reason for suffering. Asad, 'On Torture', 1098.

[12] Sinja Graf, *The Humanity of Universal Crime: Inclusion, Inequality, and Intervention in International Political Thought* (Oxford: Oxford University Press, 2021). See Chapter 1 for a discussion of Graf's argument.

[13] Asad, 'On Torture', 1103.

won the war against you; none of you will be left to bear witness, but even if someone were to survive, the world would not believe him. (…)'"[14] And indeed, Levi describes a nightmare, mentioned in many memoirs of survivors, in which they who 'had returned home and with passion and relief were describing their past sufferings, addressing themselves to a loved person, and were not believed, indeed were not even listened to'.[15] The dream points out, Levi comments, 'how both parties, victims and oppressors, had a keen awareness of the enormity and therefore the non-credibility of what took place in the Lagers'.[16]

Scott Veitch describes the problem in the following way:

> The horrors of the twentieth century and the difficulty in attempting to understand them are marked symptomatically by the limits of language in comprehending the scale and nature of suffering. This limit is one with which we have become familiarised through phrases commonly found in that century's literature: the 'untold' suffering; the 'unspeakable' truths; the 'unimaginable' horrors. These and many other similar expressions together bear witness to the failure of language and imagination to come to terms with the extensive experience of suffering. And that failure of language is replicated in the realm of normative response; it is in fact bound up with it. (…) Somehow, trying to grapple with and give *measure* to the horrors seems to do them injustice: what balances *could* be made that would be proportionate to 'untold' suffering?[17]

There is, accordingly, a double problem. Just as Levi, Veitch highlights how suffering lays bare the limits of language. Furthermore, this leads to a normative limit in terms of the failure of law to recognise certain forms of suffering. However, Veitch questions the normative response and goes on to argue that, when one looks closer, law is actually complicit in much suffering: 'with respect to certain instances of mass suffering, what is often seen to be an excess has its basis in the "normal," in legal norms themselves' (…) and, consequently, 'the excess is not beyond law, but has its roots *within* law; what is *deemed* immeasurable has its roots within the measurable'.[18] Veitch complicates the picture sketched by Asad: it is law itself that causes excessive suffering as a system of 'organized irresponsibility'.[19] Following this line of thought, one may ask how this plays out in ICL: what types of suffering are recognised by ICL and what types are not?

6.3 Suffering within and beyond International Criminal Law

This is the problem of selectivity and the way in which modern ICL and its predecessors have included some forms of suffering in their ambit while

[14] Primo Levi, *The Drowned and the Saved* (New York City, NY: Simon and Schuster, 2017), 1.
[15] Levi, *The Drowned and the Saved*, 2. [16] Levi, *The Drowned and the Saved*, 2.
[17] Scott Veitch, *Law and Irresponsibility: On the Legitimation of Human Suffering* (Abingdon: Routledge, 2007), 8.
[18] Veitch, *Law and Irresponsibility*, 2 and 10. [19] Veitch, *Law and Irresponsibility*, 1.

excluding other forms.[20] Here, I would like to make a related point: how ICL's focus on 'core' or 'atrocity' crimes, also followed in this book, while constructing the immeasurability of certain types of suffering, at the same time hides other forms of suffering from view. In an ideological critique of ICL, Tor Krever argues that this is a result of ICL's focus on the individual.[21] As a consequence, political-economic roots of violence are pushed aside. In particular, structural forms of violence are excluded from ICL.[22] Krever takes the conflict in the former Yugoslavia as an example where 'violence and war were no less a product of external forces, including the economic, political, and legal intervention of international institutions, and systemic political-economic forces manipulated by these institutions'.[23] Yet, because of its individualistic setup, ICL remains concerned with 'the *abnormality* of conjunctural violence, rather than with the *normality* of the forces – including economic and legal structures – that lurk beneath. The former is subjected to war crimes trials and hailed as an example of what needs to be addressed while the other is obscured and legitimised as a permanent, even beneficent, trait of international life'.[24]

Christine Schwöbel-Patel points out how the label 'core crimes' itself already frames some crimes as more important than others.[25] In particular, and here the analysis approaches the one of Talal Asad, by distinguishing between 'civilised' and 'uncivilised' countries, by deeming global political-economic inequalities less important and by upholding specific images of both victims and perpetrators, the core crimes tell a specific narrative of ICL.[26] This story benefits some and comes at the expense of other forms of suffering: 'Tropes and images of racialization, barbarism, backwardness, and economic marginalisation in the global order have organising effects on which

[20] Robert Cryer, *Prosecuting International Crimes: Selectivity and the International Criminal Law Regime*. Cambridge Studies in International and Comparative Law 41 (Cambridge: Cambridge University Press, 2005), 72: 'Who should be prosecuted, for which crimes, according to what law, with what defences, by whom, sentenced to what and, indeed, prosecuted for what purpose, are questions which have been answered differently at different times by different people'. For a fine-grained typology of selectivity, see Asad Kiyani, 'Group-Based Differentiation and Local Repression: The Custom and Curse of Selectivity', *Journal of International Criminal Justice* 14, no. 4 (2016): 939–57, at 942–51.

[21] Tor Krever, 'International Criminal Law: An Ideology Critique', *Leiden Journal of International Law* 26, no. 3 (2013): 701–23, at 711.

[22] Cryer, *Prosecuting International Crimes*, 330: 'The ambit of international criminal law has never been apolitical. (…) International criminal law is also largely blind to the issues of structural violence that cause misery around the world. Famine, a lack of clean water and basic medical care kill millions of people per year, yet remain for the most part outside of the criminal ambit of international law'.

[23] Krever, 'International Criminal Law', 701–23, at 715.

[24] Krever, 'International Criminal Law', 701–23, at 722.

[25] Christine Schwöbel-Patel, 'The Core Crimes of International Criminal Law', in *The Oxford Handbook of International Criminal Law*, eds. Kevin Jon Heller, Frédéric Mégret, Sarah Nouwen, Jens David Ohlin, and Darryl Robinson (Oxford: Oxford University Press, 2018), 768–90, at 775.

[26] Schwöbel-Patel, 'The Core Crimes of International Criminal Law', 768–70, at 784–90.

crimes are considered as "core." Such biases also have material-distributive effects, ultimately benefiting economically powerful states and individuals over others'.[27]

It is not surprising that authors who take the perspective of the Global South have pointed out what suffering ICL cannot grasp. Kamari Clarke is one of the most original thinkers on the limits of international criminal justice, more specifically with regard to how power works through specific representations or spectacles.[28] On the side of the perpetrators, that is the picture of the African warlord while also drawing on the representation of specific individual victims in order to ground its moral authority.[29] Clarke calls this '"a fiction of justice" – the creation and codification of a regime of truth that concerns itself with only some crimes and that celebrates the achievement of punishment and its symbolic potential to deter future crimes, rather than addressing some of the contests at the heart of violent struggles'.[30]

Focusing on the Special Court for Sierra Leone (SCSL), Clarke argues that due to a legal device such as command responsibility, systemic reasons for violence and suffering remain hidden while individuals are targeted.[31] The SCSL managed to uphold the story of 'an end to impunity' while making the suffering of concrete victims secondary to a global neoliberal economic logic that has led to the abuse of workers' rights, the plunder of national resources and unfair competition.[32] Through this vocabulary, the African victim can only appear as the one that needs to be 'saved', thus reigniting the old humanitarian logic while forgetting the everyday problems of concrete individuals.[33]

Asad Kiyani voices more explicitly a critique of ICL from the perspective of Third World approaches to international law (TWAIL). Selectivity in enforcement, suppressing local and non-legal forms of transitional justice, leaving in place the global status quo and not taking on board voices from the Global South are just a few of the points of critique that he raises.[34] ICL suffers from 'the unwillingness and inability to recognise violence beyond particular forms of bodily harm, notably the structural or slow violence that conditions the day-to-day realities of violence in the postcolonial state, all the while intersecting with transnational economic forces'.[35]

[27] Schwöbel-Patel, 'The Core Crimes of International Criminal Law', 768–90, at 790.
[28] Kamari Maxine Clarke, 'The Rule of Law through Its Economies of Appearances: The Making of the African Warlord', *Indiana Journal of Global Legal Studies* 18, no. 1 (2011): 7–40, at 8.
[29] Clarke, 'The Rule of Law', 7–40, at 11–12. In a similar vein with regard to the victim, see Christine Schwöbel-Patel, 'The "Ideal" Victim of International Criminal Law', *European Journal of International Law* 29, no. 3 (2018): 703–24.
[30] Clarke, 'The Rule of Law', 7–40, at 13. [31] Clarke, 'The Rule of Law', 7–40, at 15–7.
[32] Clarke, 'The Rule of Law', 7–40, at 32–34. [33] Clarke, 'The Rule of Law', 7–40, at 38–40.
[34] Asad G. Kiyani, 'Third World Approaches to International Criminal Law', *American Journal of International Law* 109, (2015): 255–59, at 255–56.
[35] Kiyani, 'Third World Approaches', 255–59, at 258–59.

Another example of unrecognisable suffering concerns the way in which abuses of social rights relate to ICL.[36] Evelyne Schmid has shown that despite the lack of attention to social rights in ICL, certain abuses of social rights may fall under current definitions of international crimes. Concretely, we are speaking here of how mass atrocities lead to a denial of access to education, food, health, water, work and so on. Because of ICL's focus on individual criminal responsibility, it is not surprising that there is very limited case law where social rights are explicitly mentioned.[37] Nevertheless, social rights may be of relevance to ICL in the following ways: (1) because of overlap between abuse of a social right and an international crime; (2) because abuses of social rights are a cause of international crimes; (3) because international crimes trigger the abuse of social rights; (4) because of consequences – positive and negative – of criminal prosecutions and other transitional justice mechanisms on social rights.[38] While a consensus is growing that social rights ought to play a (bigger) role in ICL or transitional justice more generally, it would at the same time be naive to expect that the ICC could play a major part in protecting social rights.[39] Nevertheless, Schmid contends that more attention to abuses of social rights by international tribunals could have strong expressive effects sending the message that abuses of social rights will not be tolerated.[40]

Harm to the environment is a final example of unrecognisable suffering that I would like to mention here. With the attention to environmental harm, climate change and mass extinction, culminating in the new geological era of the Anthropocene, the campaign for the introduction of the crime of ecocide seems to have gained momentum.[41] This has led to the draft of a new international crime in the Rome Statute of the ICC as formulated by the International Expert Panel (IEP) of the Stop Ecocide Foundation, which has defined ecocide as 'unlawful or wanton acts committed with knowledge that there is a substantial likelihood of severe and either widespread or long-term damage to the environment being caused by those acts'.[42] Given the potential scale and repercussions of environmental harm, the ICC also seems to be the right place for prosecutions: 'The ICC is held up as the natural location from which to prosecute these global crimes, a global court being called upon to protect and bring justice for our common planet, responding to the call of a humanity brought together by

[36] In speaking of 'abuses', I follow Schmid, see: Evelyne Schmid, 'International Criminal Law and Social Rights', in *Research Handbook on International Law and Social Rights*, eds. Christina Binder, Flavia Piovesan, Amaya Úbeda de Torres and Jane Hofbauer (Cheltenham, UK: Edward Elgar Publishing Ltd, 2020), 519–34, at 524.

[37] Schmid, 'International Criminal Law and Social Rights', 523.

[38] Schmid, 'International Criminal Law and Social Rights', 524.

[39] Schmid, 'International Criminal Law and Social Rights', 531–32.

[40] Schmid, 'International Criminal Law and Social Rights', 534.

[41] Adam Branch and Liana Minkova, 'Ecocide, the Anthropocene, and the International Criminal Court', *Ethics and International Affairs* 37, no. 1 (2023): 51–79, at 52.

[42] Branch and Minkova, 'Ecocide', 51–79, at 51–52.

the existential threat it faces today'.[43] As a matter of fact, Extinction Rebellion might have thought the same as it occupied the ICC and demanded the recognition of ecocide as an international crime.[44]

Apart from being unrecognisable, what do these forms of suffering have in common? They are all forms of social suffering caused by structural or slow violence. This type of suffering escapes ICL and its liberal focus on the individual perpetrator, which makes it impossible to take structural causes of violence into account.[45] Often these causes are connected to global systems of economic and environmental exploitation, rooted in the ongoing consequences of colonialism and imperialism.[46] In not recognising these forms of suffering, ICL fails on two distinct but related accounts. First, ICL fails to recognise the suffering of specific victims. Persons in the Global South and the environment are examples. Second, ICL usually holds specific (types of) perpetrators responsible while failing to call those responsible for 'slow violence' to account. While the 'African warlord' is punished, those responsible for environmental harm or economic exploitation walk away. With these two failures, ICL leaves global inequalities and hierarchies intact.

6.4 Strange Suffering

International criminal law conditions who can suffer and what counts as suffering within its legal order. Despite that ICL recognises some forms of suffering and discards other ones as irrelevant to ICL, one can inquire into the relationship between unrecognisable suffering and the legal order. I will start this inquiry by first explaining a type of criticism of the law's inability to deal with suffering, before turning to the strange character of suffering in relation to the legal order.

In a short text, Emmanuel Levinas argues that suffering is useless. For an order that pretends to incorporate everything, suffering registers as 'at once what disturbs the order and this disturbance itself'.[47] Thus, suffering is both a

[43] Branch and Minkova, 'Ecocide', 51–79, at 52.

[44] https://extinctionrebellion.nl/22-rebels-arrested-during-icc-protest-to-criminalise-ecocide/ (visited 20 March 2024). Branch and Minkova point out that making ecocide a crime is problematic regarding such issues as intentionality, the determination of environmental harm, striking a proper balance between the interests of the environment and those of society, blaming individuals while eschewing the role of structural factors and so on. Furthermore, ecocide and its underlying concept of nature fall prey to the politics that have also been employed with the concept of humanity. See Branch and Minkova, 'Ecocide', 51–79, at 53–72. For a critique of making ecocide an international crime from a political-economic point of view arguing that international law also enables forms of structural violence, see Eliana Cusato and Emily Jones, 'The "Imbroglio" of Ecocide: A Political Economic Analysis', *Leiden Journal of International Law* 37, no. 1 (2024): 42–61.

[45] Martti Koskenniemi, 'Between Impunity and Show Trials', *Max Planck Yearbook of United Nations Law Online* 6, no. 1 (2002): 1–35, at 11–19.

[46] Kamari Clarke, 'Rethinking Africa through Its Exclusions: The Politics of Naming Criminal Responsibility', *Anthropological Quarterly* 83, no. 3 (2010): 625–51.

[47] Emmanuel Levinas, 'Useless Suffering', trans. Richard Cohen, in *The Provocation of Levinas*, eds. Robert Bernasconi and David Wood (Abingdon: Routledge, 1988), 156–67, at 156.

given that cannot be grasped through the categories of order and the way in which this 'unassumability' registers.[48] Therefore, Levinas characterises suffering as 'for nothing'. Arguing that it can never be captured by law or legal order, he instead suggests an ethical approach to suffering. The normative or even ethical truth of suffering could be summarised as follows: 'a residue will always remain after the law has attempted to bring meaning to the atrocities committed through its causal narratives. The suffering of the individual will, in the end, remain expressionless, meaningless, and "for nothing." As such, its appeal calling for my response is much louder than anything the trial will invoke through its choreographed proceedings'.[49] According to Levinas, suffering seeks help, seeks the other.[50]

Levinas says that law is never able to do justice to suffering. He is right. The suffering of the victim cannot completely be recognised by law. Yet, perhaps this is a good thing: for it avoids a total juridification of life and of the concrete experience of suffering. Moreover, the legal order does not 'help', even if the ICL's institutions sometimes claim to do so. Law is no charity. What can the law do? With the development of ICL after the Second World War, the legal instruments to prosecute the suspects of atrocity crimes have been called into being: treaties have been signed and tribunals have been established. A legal language and a range of legal institutions are put into place to grasp the atrocities and punish those responsible for them, thus opening the possibility to use arguments within that language to recognise suffering. Is the legal recognition of the existence of suffering not a symbolic way of capturing it?[51] Law cannot help, but it might be a way to 'appreciate' the suffering by giving it recognition in the symbolic language of the law.[52]

Moreover, what transpired is that some persons are not regarded as fully human in the specific sense that their suffering is taken for granted, as an inevitable cost of the march of progress. The colonial subjects discussed by Talal Asad are a case in point. As many contemporary scholars have argued, this type of logic can explain certain characteristics of ICL, even if the language of civilisation has subsided. Furthermore, the problem with the ethical approach is that it individualises suffering. In this way, it also depoliticises it. Therefore, the collective or social origins of suffering disappear from view. These social origins correspond to what critics of ICL bring forward.

48 Levinas, 'Useless Suffering', 156.

49 Panu Minkkinen, 'The Expressionless: Law, Ethics, and the Imagery of Suffering', *Law and Critique* 19, no. 1 (2008): 65–85, at 84. Minkkinen seems to follow Levinas but also moves beyond the latter's framework, even if he does not acknowledge this. By showing how art can 'enchant' the expressionless (i.e., suffering) in a way that makes art show its own essence, Minkkinen makes clear that suffering is not 'for nothing'.

50 Levinas, 'Useless Suffering', 158–59.

51 See Rudi Visker, *The Inhuman Condition. Looking for Difference after Levinas and Heidegger* (Dordrecht: Springer, 2004), 297–98, footnote 9, where such a process of symbolisation is explained for the public sphere. I believe law works in a similar way; see also what I have said about the symbolic order of humanity in Chapter 2.

52 Visker, *The Inhuman Condition*, 175.

Judith Butler makes an interesting remark regarding the relationship between suffering and the collective. She phrases it in terms of loss and catastrophe:

> If catastrophe is not representable according to the narrative explanations that would 'make sense' of history, then making sense of ourselves and charting the future are not impossible. But we are, as it were, marked for life, and that mark is insuperable, irrecoverable. It becomes the condition by which life is risked, by which the questions of whether one can move, and with whom, and in what way are framed and incited by the irreversibility of loss itself.[53]

Butler seems to say that there is a primacy of catastrophe: that there is a suffering from which the collective springs, as from an origin that it cannot ever recover from but to which it remains bound. Law and legal order appear as a reaction to what cannot be recuperated within the order. With Butler, I argue that, in a certain sense, suffering produces the ICL legal order. The ICL legal order is the 'product' of the unimaginable suffering: it is called into being to do justice to it. This suffering, constitutive for the legal order, lies not only at its origin but stays with it as its shadow. Because of the law's failure to grapple with suffering, it haunts the legal order. The phrase of Butler puts us on track with the strange that lingers at the threshold of the order. While Levinas is right that suffering might not have meaning, he does not seem to reckon with the possibility of something to which the order needs to respond even if it is not within the realm of the meaningful. While it is 'useless' from one perspective, that is, the logic in which the legal order is regarded primarily as an instrument to end social conflict in a peaceful way,[54] I argue that it can still be 'of value' to address the legal order. More precisely, suffering can be valuable within political struggles. The normative reflection on social suffering and systemic violence acts as a bridge between the individual experience and the social analysis of the institution, in this case the legal order.[55]

To develop a deeper understanding of the relationships between claims of suffering vis-à-vis the legal order, I draw on the responsive phenomenology of Bernhard Waldenfels. Interestingly, Waldenfels starts from the phenomenon of order. One fundamental distinction in this respect is that between the pre-modern and the modern order. The pre-modern conception of order, exemplified by the cosmos as developed in ancient Greek philosophy, has no outside.[56] The cosmos is conceived as a total order in which everything forms part of one,

[53] Judith Butler, 'Afterword: After Loss, What Then?', in *Loss: The Politics of Mourning*, eds. David L. Eng and David Kazanjian (Berkeley: University of California Press, 2003), 467–73, at 472.

[54] Minkkinen, 'The Expressionless', 65 and 70.

[55] Emmanuel Renault, 'A Critical Theory of Social Suffering', *Critical Horizons* 11, no. 2 (2010): 221–41, at 230–31.

[56] Bernhard Waldenfels, *Phenomenology of the Alien: Basic Concepts* (Evanston, IL: Northwestern University Press, 2011), 10.

integrated whole.[57] In contradistinction to this complete conception of order, any legal order is a modern order in the specific sense of a bounded whole. This means that legal orders are established in a process of self-inclusion and exclusion wherein 'the own' is delineated by drawing boundaries. Hence, the establishment of modern (legal) orders should be interpreted from a first-person perspective, as a process of self-establishment, or self-constitution. As I have argued throughout this book, this is a first-person *plural*, in this case 'we, humanity'. Importantly, drawing boundaries (1) hides the act of drawing from the order drawn, as an origin that cannot fully be recovered and (2) comes about from an inside distinguishing itself from an outside, thus giving rise to a 'preference in the difference'.[58]

The self-establishment of orders, and this is crucial for our argument, marks them as radically contingent: they can always be different from what they are.[59] This gives every order something arbitrary that points to a blind spot of the order, that is, 'something unordered that does not merely constitute a deficit'.[60] Indeed, by the process of self-inclusion and exclusion, by the very process of constitution, the possibilities of strange transgressions are opened up.[61] What is excluded from the order of the self is not the other but the strange or the alien.[62] Hence, the alien is what does not fit the order, the strange or extra-ordinary.[63] This blind spot of the order – the non-place of the alien, which finds no place within the order – does not disappear but remains related to it. Attached to the order from its very constitution, the alien comes to the fore whenever the order is shaken by particular events or experiences that take the form of 'withdrawal, expropriation, displacement, differing'.[64] Alien is what escapes or disrupts orders: their fissures, borders, boundaries, limits and fault-lines. What is alien confronts the order with its non-coincidence with itself and with its fundamental contingency.[65]

57 Bernhard Waldenfels, *Order in the Twilight* (Athens, OH: Ohio University Press, 1996), 53–54.

58 Waldenfels, *Phenomenology of the Alien*, 15.

59 Waldenfels, *Phenomenology of the Alien*, 11.

60 Waldenfels, *Phenomenology of the Alien*, 13. For the notion of a blind spot of legal order, see also Hans Lindahl, *Fault Lines of Globalization: Legal Order and the Politics of A-Legality* (Oxford: Oxford University Press, 2013), 248. Norm Friesen, 'Waldenfels' Responsive Phenomenology of the Alien: An Introduction', *Phenomenology and Practice* 7, no. 2 (2014): 68–77, at 69.

61 Friesen, 'Waldenfels' Responsive Phenomenology of the Alien', 71.

62 Waldenfels, *Phenomenology of the Alien*, 16. Hans Lindahl has extensively worked on the notion of 'the strange' in legal philosophy. See, for example, Hans Lindahl, 'Intentionality, Representation, Recognition: Phenomenology and the Politics of A-Legality', in *Political Phenomenology*, eds. Thomas Bedorf and Steffen Herrmann (London: Routledge, 2019), 256–76.

63 Bernhard Waldenfels, 'From Intentionality to Responsivity', in *Phenomenology Today: The Schuwer Sepp Lectures*, 1998–2002, eds. Rudolf Bernet and Daniel J. Martino (Pittsburg: Duquesne University, 2003), 23–35, at 24.

64 Ferdinando G. Menga, 'Guest Editor's Preface: The Experience of the Alien and the Philosophy of Response', *Etica and Politica/Ethics and Politics* XIII, no. 1 (2011): 7–15, at 10.

65 Menga, 'Guest Editor's Preface', 10–11.

The alien questions the order giving rise to a need to respond.[66] As a result of such a provocation, the order responds.[67] For Waldenfels, responding means 'the genuine way in which we encounter the alien as alien'.[68] The order responds to the questioning of the alien, as it is affected by it.[69] In this respect, Waldenfels speaks of a radical or original passivity of the order, since the primacy lies with the alien.[70] Importantly, the demand or call of the alien is of a double nature presenting both 'an appeal that is directed at someone and a claim or pretension to something'.[71] This combination of appeal and claim is crucial: 'In the appeal that I receive, there arise claims that demand something from me. Incorporated into the situation, such demands precede every moral or legal claim'.[72] As a claim, the call corresponds to a specific content.[73] However, the call cannot be exhausted by this or that content. For as an appeal, the call singles me out as responsible, urging me to respond. Suffering makes such a demand on the legal order, confronting it with a need to respond.

How to respond to the demand of the alien without betraying its radical strangeness? Importantly, the response always starts from the alien, as it is a reaction to the latter's demand. Yet, paradoxically, responding is the privileged site at which the alien can appear, as the alien by its very nature does not register on the order's own terms.[74] A response, therefore, has the key characteristics of being limited, unavoidable, asymmetrical and creative.[75] The response is limited because it fails to ever exhaust the demand of the alien. The response is unavoidable because even the refusal to answer or keeping silent is already a response. The response is asymmetrical because there is no third instance that can represent own and alien as comparable. The response is creative because it is always made up in (and not available before or apart from) the actual practice of responding. The primacy of the appeal over the claim is reflected in the excess of responding over a given response: 'the very *event of*

[66] Menga, 'Guest Editor's Preface', 7–15, at 11: '[T]he alien (…) can be conceived of as the extraordinary, which exceeds, surmounts and, therefore, can constantly put into question the order itself, by maintaining alive its contingent structure and its impossibility to give itself as a totality'.

[67] Friesen, 'Waldenfels' Responsive Phenomenology of the Alien', 73.

[68] Waldenfels, 'From Intentionality to Responsivity', 23.

[69] Waldenfels, *Phenomenology of the Alien*, 27–28.

[70] Waldenfels, *Phenomenology of the Alien*, 29.

[71] Waldenfels, *Phenomenology of the Alien*, 37.

[72] Waldenfels, 'From Intentionality to Responsivity', 31.

[73] Waldenfels, *Phenomenology of the Alien*, 37–38. Waldenfels, 'From Intentionality to Responsivity', 30.

[74] Menga, 'Guest Editor's Preface', 10. See also at 13:

> Responding, in fact, on one side, has the capability of not robbing the alien of its goad, as the response itself starts not from a subjective or thematising act by the own self, but always in delay and as a pathic experience, that is, exactly from the same request of the alien, to which the answer is called to reply. On the other side, however, response can be interpreted as originally indispensable and this in the Derridian sense of an original supplementary structure, since response is the only place where the request of the alien can come into appearance at all.

[75] Menga, 'Guest Editor's Preface', 14–15.

responding is in no way exhausted by this [answer content] (...) Responding in its full sense does not give what it has, but rather what it finds and invents in responding. (...) Giving an answer is not exhausted by the answer given'.[76] So, responding is a creative act; it has the structure of a creative expression in the sense of Merleau-Ponty.[77]

6.5 Silent Claims

This understanding of order and alien has an important consequence for law. Understood as an instance of the third, the viewpoint of law is indispensable.[78] This position has often been equated with that of the judge as the third adjudicating the conflict between two parties. But the judge is never only third but also the representative of a first-person plural: as we have seen, international criminal tribunals speak in the name of, or represent, 'we, humanity'.[79] Yet, by judging the demand of the alien 'by a universal law and by thus *equalizing what is not equal*, justice always contains a moment of injustice'.[80] This injustice does not simply disappear. It is what remains unsaid in every saying in the name of justice. In words that seem to echo the ones of Butler, Waldenfels submits: 'That from which our speech and discourse begins, and has always begun, cannot be observed, judged or managed as something lying before our eyes or in our hands. It only comes to light *while* we say and do something. It is dependent upon an indirect manner of speaking and communicating which remains connected to silence'.[81]

Here, I introduce the notion of a silent claim. I argue that unrecognisable suffering can have a 'value' as it bears upon the order and makes a claim on it.[82] Yet, this claim can only register because it is located neither inside nor completely outside the order. Rather, the claim comes from the threshold. In this sense, one may say that the victim appears as a transitional figure, a dweller of a legal and a non-legal world,[83] both as a figure constructed by the legal order and as a concrete and embodied person. Unrecognisable suffering constitutes a silent claim. The silent claim is an 'interruptive silence' recalling the order to its origins in a wound.[84] A silent claim is a demand to the legal

[76] Waldenfels, 'From Intentionality to Responsivity', 31.

[77] Waldenfels, 'From Intentionality to Responsivity', 35. For the concept of creative expression in Merleau-Ponty and its value for legal philosophy, see Luigi Corrias, *The Passivity of Law: Competence and Constitution in the European Court of Justice* (Berlin: Springer Science & Business Media, 2011).

[78] Waldenfels, 'From Intentionality to Responsivity', 35.

[79] See especially Chapter 2 of this book.

[80] Waldenfels, 'From Intentionality to Responsivity', 35.

[81] Waldenfels, 'From Intentionality to Responsivity', 33–34.

[82] Visker, *The Inhuman Condition*, 4, 6–7, 175.

[83] Bernhard Waldenfels, 'Responsive Ethics', in *The Oxford Handbook of Contemporary Phenomenology*, ed. Dan Zahavi (Oxford: Oxford University Press, 2012), 423–41, at 439.

[84] Minkkinen, 'The Expressionless', 84.

order in which an appeal to acknowledge the sufferer is combined with a claim to recognise the suffering.

Acknowledgement in this context does not imply including those who were previously excluded. As we have seen, ICL includes some *only as sub-human capable of breaking the law*. In that sense, the words of Danielle Allen regarding racial discrimination in the US also hold for ICL:

> This discourse of exclusion and inclusion has for a long time been the basic strategy for dealing with the failings of liberalism's supposed commitments to universal rights. When universal institutions prove to be otherwise, get everyone included and then we can move on with our lives. But two generations of scholarship in history and political philosophy have shown that the inclusion/exclusion paradigm is inadequate to reality. Our problem is not exclusion, to be solved by inclusion. Our problem is domination, to be solved by non-domination.[85]

Accordingly, acknowledgement has to do with the practical political relationship between equals under condition of non-domination. This requires a practical attitude towards the other and cannot be reduced to mere knowledge: 'acknowledgement "goes beyond" knowledge, not in the order, or as a feat, of cognition, but in the call upon me to express the knowledge at its core, to recognise what I know, to do something in the light of it, apart from which this knowledge remains without expression, hence perhaps without possession'.[86]

On the other hand, I argue that a silent claim still seeks a form of recognition from the legal order. This recognition can take different forms. In the case of environmental harm and the consequences of structural violence, victims might still seek to have their suffering included within the ICL legal order, for example, by the introduction of new crimes. Yet, there are also situations where legal inclusion is, indeed, not the solution. At such moments, the law should exercise a form of self-restraint, take a step back and admit that there is behaviour that goes beyond its ambit. Such a silence of the legal order – a *juris silentium*, to use the felicitous phrase of Mark Drumbl[87] – can also be a possible response to a silent claim.

[85] D. Allen, 'Danielle Allen Response to Ferguson Forum', *Boston Review*, 14 March 2023, www.bostonreview.net/forum_response/danielle-allen-danielle-allen-response-ferguson-forum/.

[86] Stanley Cavell, *Must We Mean What We Say? A Book of Essays* (Cambridge: Cambridge University Press, 1969), 257.

[87] Mark A. Drumbl, 'The Kapo on Film: Tragic Perpetrators and Imperfect Victims', *Griffith J.L. & Human Dignity* 6, no. 1 (2018): 229–71, at 232:

> Ultimately, identifying the logics and aesthetics of criminal law and literature to be in tension on this subject, I urge a *juris silentium* – that is, for criminal law to recede rather than always to regale. I recommend that it is best for certain actors, survivors, and perpetrators to lie beyond criminal law's remit and, hence, to remain non-justiciable. A *juris silentium* is not a world without sound or speech or image. It is a space shorn of the at times domineering fix-it commands of criminal law. This space, however, remains crimped so long as the accoutrements of the criminal law – courtrooms, verdicts, and jailhouses – expand as the iconic way in which to imagine post-conflict justice and solemnly authenticate the past. Law's restraint, then, might encourage other voices to fill the space – lively, animated voices.

In the remainder of this section, I discuss one concrete case of the way in which a silent claim can be made. I have decided to discuss this specific example for several reasons. First, the silent claim was formulated 'in the name of humanity'. While this is not a prerequisite of a silent claim, it does fit well with the overall theme of the book. Second, the silent claim is discussed extensively in an academic publication. Finally, the claim has an interesting form, underscoring the strange character of a silent claim, both inside and outside the legal order.

Ayça Çubukçu provides an example of the possibilities and perils of legal-political mobilisation in the name of humanity. Çubukçu participated in and analysed the World Tribunal on Iraq (WTI), a people's tribunal that protested against the invasion and occupation of Iraq by 'the coalition of the willing'. She poses and answers a fundamental question: '*why* do we care about justice, about the freedom and the happiness, the life and the death of each other, here and there? An answer offered by the World Tribunal on Iraq could be: for the love of humanity'.[88] The aim of the tribunal was to hold those responsible to account, former US President G. W. Bush and former British Prime Minister T. Blair, first of all. The idea of a 'tribunal' was crucial in this movement that tried to be a network without a centre.[89] The tribunal gave a specific form connected to reclaiming justice; a concept associated with a constituency; a memory of the famous Russell Tribunal; and the stage, indeed a global public space, where the global network and their stories could appear.[90]

A large part of Çubukçu's argument involves setting out the tension between legal approaches and political approaches to the WTI. The former argue that the WTI should take the ICC as its model, thus asserting that international law could act as a neutral and universal framework, a view summarised under the headings 'legal cosmopolitanism' or 'law's empire'.[91] The violence inherent in 'law's empire' entails that it cannot be distinguished from 'empire's law'.[92] In this regard, Çubukçu is critical of the Iraqi High Tribunal and NGOs such as AI and HRW that failed to unmask it as an occupation tribunal.[93] Therefore, what was hidden from view was the violence of hanging Saddam Hussein as an 'enemy of humanity'.[94]

Rejecting the legal perspective, Çubukçu argues in favour of a political one. This view rejects a neutral position and the abstract principles of international law among which (legal) accountability.[95] The political approach wants to

[88] Ayça Çubukçu, *For the Love of Humanity: The World Tribunal on Iraq* (Philadelphia, PA: University of Pennsylvania Press, 2018), 7.

[89] Çubukçu, *For the Love of Humanity*, 20. [90] Çubukçu, *For the Love of Humanity*, 20–21.

[91] Çubukçu, *For the Love of Humanity*, 21–27.

[92] Çubukçu, *For the Love of Humanity*, 126–57, which is a critical assessment of the writings of Habermas on the legitimacy of international law. For a similar critique, see Sinja Graf, *The Humanity of Universal Crime: Inclusion, Inequality, and Intervention in International Political Thought* (Oxford: Oxford University Press, 2021), 113–67.

[93] Çubukçu, *For the Love of Humanity*, 80.

[94] Çubukçu, *For the Love of Humanity*, 82–82 and 89.

[95] Çubukçu, *For the Love of Humanity*, 30–34.

question legal institutions and political structures through 'the *act* of holding to account' thus establishing 'an unmediated, direct relationship between the judging and the judged'.[96] In this way, the WTI as global network or multitude entailed

> a powerful critique of the notion of *representational legitimacy*, while recasting the question on an imminent plane: thus, the legitimacy of political action would not be constituted by its capacity to represent or speak in the name of an 'other' who would structurally remain absent. Instead, the legitimacy of political action would be constituted through the practice of a political subject being 'identical' to itself, as it were, or as a *manifestation* of what the subject already does.[97]

Çubukçu argument here is one of participation in an already existing global antiwar movement.[98]

How is humanity invoked in the work of the WTI? From the political perspective, it is important to pose the question of humanity beyond the framework of nation-states.[99] What stood out for those participating in the WTI is that 'humanity' was the community violated by the war in Iraq, so at stake was not a 'national self' but rather a 'human self'.[100] The network form of the WTI might be able to provide that because it couples representation with 'implication' in the network.[101] Admittedly, this could only be done through a 'negative signature', entailing that no one could speak in its name.[102] What transpires from the analysis is the profound ambiguity of collective action 'for the love of humanity'. Çubukçu's position is best summarised in the last thesis of her afterword: 'The WTI was conducted from the perspective of humanity, for the love of humanity. This was its animating energy, its strength, its weakness'.[103]

Coming back to the notion of a silent claim, I argue that the WTI makes such a claim by holding political leaders to account and questioning legal institutions in the name of humanity. I believe that one cannot escape the logic of (political) representation. This also goes for the WTI: the novelist Arundhati Roy acted as the spokesperson of the WTI's Jury of Conscience that declared both Bush and Blair guilty.[104] The suffering caused by the crimes of Bush and Blair is not recognised under ICL. Yet, the WTI rejects the neutrality and universality of ICL and refuses inclusion. Here, it links up with alter-globalisation movements.[105]

Furthermore, the WTI's silent claim, voiced 'for the love of humanity', seeks acknowledgement of 'humanity' as a harmed party. It does this by showing how inhumanity is always already implicated within humanity.

[96] Çubukçu, *For the Love of Humanity*, 34. [97] Çubukçu, *For the Love of Humanity*, 37.
[98] Çubukçu, *For the Love of Humanity*, 37. [99] Çubukçu, *For the Love of Humanity*, 98.
[100] Çubukçu, *For the Love of Humanity*, 40 and 71.
[101] Çubukçu, *For the Love of Humanity*, 120–21.
[102] Çubukçu, *For the Love of Humanity*, 123–24. [103] Çubukçu, *For the Love of Humanity*, 160.
[104] Çubukçu, *For the Love of Humanity*, 3.
[105] Hans Lindahl, *Authority and the Globalisation of Inclusion and Exclusion* (Cambridge: Cambridge University Press, 2018).

Through this argument – not simply participation but implication – the WTI shows that representational legitimacy may indeed not be the whole story. Here, we can distinguish between two senses of this implication.[106] On the one hand, the WTI turns our attention to inhuman behaviour that is intermingled with the law and regarded as legal: the imperial violence associated with some forms of human rights activism, exemplified in the violence of human rights enforcement. Hence, WTI's refusal to model itself upon the ICC and ICL. On the other hand, the WTI shows how inhumanity can also be what resists inclusion into an allegedly all-encompassing legal order and opens up possibilities to challenge the claim that law is pronounced in the name of humanity. Inhumanity can be the disorder of the order, the multitude of the people and the constituent power of the constituted community. As the constituent potential of humanity, inhumanity as a silent claim opens possibilities for humanity to be imagined otherwise, seeking acknowledgement beyond domination. Tapping this abundance is the political stake of a silent claim.

6.6 Conclusion

This chapter has delved into the relationship between suffering and the legal order. I showed how international (criminal) law made a distinction between human suffering and inhuman suffering. It has been law's aim to punish behaviour that causes inhuman suffering, for this type of suffering was deemed excessive and immeasurable. This distinction foreshadowed the selection within ICL between 'core' or 'atrocity' crimes and other types of suffering. As several authors have argued, this selection leaves structural forms of suffering outside of ICL's picture. I submitted that these forms of suffering do not simply disappear but present the order with a silent claim, seeking both legal recognition of the suffering and acknowledgement of the sufferer.

Notwithstanding the development of ICL over the last decades, the international legal order cannot ever fully respond to the silent claim. While it can try to do justice to it as a legal claim by recognising suffering, it cannot do justice to appeals. The legal order cannot respond directly to silent claims as appeals because they transgress the order of law as an institution called upon to put an end authoritatively and peacefully to social conflicts. This is not a failure of law. These appeals might register indirectly in the affective response of the ICL order: recall the 'unimaginable atrocities that deeply shock the conscience of humanity' in the Preamble of the Rome Statute. In 'the shock' caused by suffering, the limits of the international legal order are uncovered: its birth in a wound it cannot unmake, as an origin it cannot ever retrieve. Therefore,

[106] Jean-François Lyotard, *The Inhuman: Reflections on Time* (Redwood City, CA: Stanford University Press, 1991).

making a silent claim should be understood as a type of *political* action by or in the name of those experiencing unrecognisable suffering. This action can take many forms, including a collective claim 'for the love of humanity', as in the case of the WTI. Yet, actions demanding concrete amendments to a legal system are also imaginable. Crucially, since it seeks acknowledgement, the silent claim as an appeal goes beyond the inclusion–exclusion dichotomy inviting ever new ways of living together.

Epilogue

This book has traced the relationship between law and inhumanity, especially how it plays out in the discourse on the so-called core or atrocity crimes. This could not be done without making sense of the concept of humanity. Indeed, in legal, moral and political discourses on atrocity crimes, humanity is often invoked, referring to different but interrelated meanings of the word. I argued how humanity, in the context of the discourse on the atrocity crimes, primarily designates a normative community. Accordingly, one should be aware of the way in which the concept of humanity appeals to a first-person plural perspective by way of the speech act 'we, humanity'. It is this communal or plural understanding of humanity – humanity as a collective subject – that takes precedence over other understandings, such as intersubjective empathy or humanity as a principle of legal interpretation.

This invocation, or claim to be speaking on behalf of humanity, has universalist pretensions but comes with its own in- and exclusions.[1] In Chapter 1, we have seen that supporters of speaking about developments in international law in terms of humanity implicitly presuppose this collective subject, while some critics of this kind of speech explicitly reject it. I argued that one cannot easily get rid of this type of speech for it is essential to grasp dehumanisation and the experience of inhumanity.

Prosecuting in the Name of Humanity

Whenever mass atrocities occur, people look expectedly at what ICL, and more specifically the ICC, can do. After a visit to the Rafah Crossing at the end of October 2023, Karim Khan, chief prosecutor of the ICC, gave a speech in which he addressed the issue of the task of the ICC:

[1] Sinja Graf, *The Humanity of Universal Crime: Inclusion, Inequality, and Intervention in International Political Thought* (Oxford: Oxford University Press, 2021), 183: 'Perhaps the most we can know about humanity is to recall that it is a *claim* to the common values and life of a universal mankind. And maybe we would do well to recall that "humanity talk" creates patterns of order amongst people around the world. And perhaps naming these orders is the most we can know about mankind'.

> We are currently experiencing a moment of profound human suffering globally. A pandemic of inhumanity has taken hold, from Darfur to Ukraine, from the plight of women and girls in Afghanistan to the seemingly forgotten voices of Rohingya refugees in Myanmar, and now the intolerable tragedy that is deepening in Israel and the State of Palestine and threatening to spread wider. These human rights emergencies are interconnected. At their heart they are driven by a common crisis: a failure to give value to the lives of all people.[2]

This book has built the conceptual framework to make sense of and critically assess this kind of discourse. Let us look at Khan's speech through that lens. Note, to begin, that Khan's speech starts with a first-person plural. Rhetoric aside, who is the 'we' here? While Khan does not answer this question directly, he seems to refer to humanity as a whole. It is humanity as a collective subject, I argue, that must be understood to experience suffering. It is this suffering that is named a 'pandemic of inhumanity'. The metaphor of the pandemic – an infectious disease threatening all – underscores that the collective subject at play is indeed humanity as a whole. Inhumanity refers to the suffering that is a consequence of violations of human rights, the laws of war and international humanitarian law, bringing forth atrocity crimes.

What role can law play? Khan answers this question as follows:

> It is in times like these, when the vulnerable feel that they may have been forgotten, that we need the law more than ever. Not the law in abstract terms, not the law as theory, but the law capable of providing tangible protection to those who need it most. People need to see that the law and human rights have a real impact on their lives. (…) It is something they should be able to cling on to and something that should shelter them from the worst elements of inhumanity. (…) To ensure that, amid conflict, amid rage, there remains a baseline of human conduct, of humanity, over which no individual may trespass. As the UN secretary general, António Guterres, said: 'Even war has rules.' This is the law of the international criminal court (ICC).[3]

Khan believes that law has quite an important task to fulfill, offering protection when atrocities occur and upholding a certain standard of behaviour when the norms of the international community are violated. As we have seen in Chapter 2, in these instances 'humanity' as a symbolic order is implicitly or explicitly invoked and law is called upon to react with punitive measures whenever the norms of this order are violated. Accordingly, inhumanity does not only refer to the suffering of the victim but also to the acts of the perpetrator. The ICL legal order tries to offer a symbolic stage where the suspect of atrocity crimes is judged, while the victim of these crimes is given voice in the procedure; at least that is the claim.

[2] Karim Khan, 'We Are Witnessing a Pandemic of Inhumanity: To Halt the Spread, We Must Cling to the Law', *The Guardian*, 10 November 2023, www.theguardian.com/commentisfree/2023/nov/10/law-israel-hamas-international-criminal-court-icc, accessed 18 March 2024.

[3] Khan, 'We Are Witnessing a Pandemic of Inhumanity'.

However, its universal assertion notwithstanding, the community or order of humanity is not all-inclusive. That is why it is crucial to trace the boundaries of this community and what it includes and excludes. I argued that the experience of inhumanity resists incorporation within the community of humanity and lingers at the threshold of the order. This experience is usually caught under the heading of dehumanisation. In Chapters 3 and 4, I have critically analysed processes of dehumanisation and (attempts at) rehumanisation as they play out in a legal case and in the account of a victim of torture, respectively. Dehumanisation, I argued, should be understood as being treated as less-than-human, or as the experience of being estranged from the world.

Chapters 5 and 6 have sketched some normative consequences of this understanding of inhumanity for ICL, both in terms of how to deal with perpetrators and with victims of dehumanisation. Chapter 5 has taken a temporal perspective on atrocity crimes in order to disentangle the different timelines of imprescriptibility, forgiveness and legal values. It argued that even when dealing with imprescriptible crimes, the law should not pretend to incorporate eternal justice. The conclusion of Chapter 5 is that modesty becomes the law. More specifically regarding ICL, this entails that one should be realistic about what the law can and cannot do and for whom. For example, can law act as a shelter, as Khan has it? I have my doubts.

Other Silences

In Chapter 6, we have seen that even when it is enforced, ICL selects, thus designating some forms of suffering as (more) important to humanity than others. Perhaps Khan is aware of this when he speaks of 'seemingly forgotten voices'. Chapter 6 has delved into the relationship between law, atrocities and suffering. As we have seen, there are forms of suffering that are silenced and remain unrecognisable to the legal order. I have argued that the latter forms of suffering do not simply disappear but may be brought to the legal order as what I called a silent claim. I coined this concept to designate a demand to the legal order in which an appeal to acknowledge the sufferer is combined with a claim to recognise the suffering.

While I analysed one case of a silent claim, there remains much work to be done in developing this concept and evaluating its value in other contexts and for different practices. In this regard, I propose to distinguish between the form and the content of silent claims. When it comes to *content*, one example of a potential silent claim is the type of suffering that is unrecognisable because of the current legal definition of genocide. As a result of this definition, cultural genocide as a collective claim for cultural restitution falls outside of the law, for instance.[4]

[4] Leora Bilsky and Rachel Klagsbrun, 'The Return of Cultural Genocide?', *European Journal of International Law* 29, no. 2 (2018): 373–96.

One obvious context where silent claims might play a role is in legal and political struggles linked to climate change. In this respect, it is interesting to witness that while 'we, humanity' is a contested category, as we have seen, it has not lost its appeal. The historian Dipesh Chakrabarty stipulates that the question of what 'we, humanity' entails has become even more pressing for us in the era of the Anthropocene, since 'climate change poses for us a question of a human collectivity, an us, pointing to a figure of the universal that escapes our capacity to experience the world. It is more like a universal that arises from a shared sense of a catastrophe'.[5] Notice how Chakrabarty refers to the human collectivity as an 'us' instead of a 'we'. By using the object pronoun, Chakrabarty seems to underline how the catastrophe of climate change casts 'humanity' first in the position of who is affected by climate change. Related to this is the question of how to envision the position of inhumanity in the Anthropocene. This is a subject that fell outside of the scope of this book, as it took the discourse on the current atrocity crimes as its starting point, yet remains an interesting avenue to explore in the future.[6]

Another important question regarding silent claims is that of the *form* that they may take. In which way may a silent claim address the legal order? Are there ways that work better than others? How to avoid cultural appropriation of suffering? These questions refer to the aesthetic dimension of silent claims, wherein imagination and creativity play important roles. Literary fiction offers rich narratives of human resilience in the face of atrocities and of how suffering may even be constitutive for community.[7] Artists may join efforts with victims whose suffering is silenced by law; re-enactments could be especially fit for this purpose.[8]

Attentiveness

As we have seen in Chapter 6, silent claims provoke a response from the legal order. Yet, how to increase the chance that silent claims are actually heard and handled well? This is a theme that also seems to resonate with Khan's words when he urges us to 'reject desensitisation' even when confronted with many

[5] Dipesh Chakrabarty, 'The Climate of History: Four Theses', *Critical Inquiry* 35, no. 2 (2009): 197–222, at 222. I cannot do justice to the debate provoked by this important article. For starters, see the critical discussion in Graf, *The Humanity of Universal Crime*, 179–83.

[6] In this respect, it is worthwhile to note that Kathryn Yussof has recently taken up the question of how to conceptualise the relationship between power, race and humanism in the Anthropocene under the heading of 'the inhumanities', see Kathryn Yusoff, 'The Inhumanities', *Annals of the American Association of Geographers* 111, no. 3 (2021): 663–76.

[7] For an interesting reading of the novel *The Plague* in this key, see Giunia Gatta, 'Suffering and the Making of Politics: Perspectives from Jaspers and Camus', *Contemporary Political Theory* 14, no. 4 (2015): 335–54.

[8] In this respect, the work of theatre director Milo Rau is interesting. See Milo Rau, 'New Realism and the Contemporary World. The Re-enactments and Tribunals of the International Institute of Political Murder', *Documenta* 34, no. 2 (2016): 121–37.

atrocities in different places in the world.[9] I would like to translate this call as a plea for attentiveness, which I interpret as a pre-condition for the responsiveness towards silent claims. One could say that attentiveness connects the imagination of concern – making us aware of suffering and vulnerability – to the imagination of solutions – moving us to act.[10] Even if real solutions may be a bridge too far, attentiveness might bring us a step closer to justice.[11]

Attentiveness, as a virtue on a personal level, ought to be practiced by all those who play a role in the process of formulating and handling a silent claim. Attentiveness has different connotations.[12] It can mean 'be careful' as in the Italian *attento*, or *fai attenzione*. It has a link with being precise, paying attention and caring, as in 'to attend to'. Attentiveness also harbours a temporal dimension in the Latin *ad-tendere*, which means to wait or pause. Finally, it can mean to keep.[13]

What I call attentiveness comes close to what Jill Stauffer describes as openness: 'If hearing is meaningful, it has to be embedded in an openness where what is said might be heard even if it threatens to break the order of the known world for those who listen'.[14] Accordingly, in attentiveness – in being sensitive to the demand of the silent claim – one puts one's own order 'we, humanity' at stake in the response to the inhuman.[15] Perhaps, all things considered, the ultimate test for a legal order that claims to judge in the name of humanity lies exactly in how it deals with inhumanity.

9 Khan, 'We Are Witnessing a Pandemic of Inhumanity'.

10 Maksymilian Del Mar, 'Jurisprudence on the Frontline', *European Journal of International Law* 19, no. 5. (2008): 1095–108, at 1107–8.

11 Here, I refer to the notion of justice as it is developed by Marianne Constable, see Marianne Constable, *Just Silences: The Limits and Possibilities of Modern Law* (Princeton, NJ: Princeton University Press, 2009), 177: 'Justice lies in stillness, awaiting the silent call to it that comes out of the human need to act and judge in a world that is *not* of one's own making'.

12 'Attentiveness', in Cambridge Dictionary Online, https://dictionary.cambridge.org/dictionary/english/attentiveness, accessed 18 March 2024.

13 'Attendere', in Wiktionary, the free dictionary, https://en.wiktionary.org/wiki/attendere#Etymology, accessed 18 March 2024.

14 Jill Stauffer, *Ethical Loneliness: The Injustice of Not Being Heard* (New York: Columbia University Press, 2015), 80.

15 Here, there are connections with what Aletta Norval requires of an aversive conception of democracy; see Aletta Norval, 'Deliberative, Agonistic and Aversive Grammars of Democracy: The Question of Criteria', in *Practices of Freedom: Decentred Governance, Conflict and Democratic Participation*, eds. Steven Griggs, Aletta J. Norval and Hendrik Wagenaar (Cambridge: Cambridge University Press, 2014), 60–84, at 82: 'Hence, an aversive conception of democracy demands: sensitivity to the expression of inchoate demands; sensitivity to the diversity of languages that may be mobilised to express such demands; responsiveness and engagement with demands; openness to appeal and counter-appeal; critical self-scrutiny and scrutiny of democratic procedures, processes and institutions'.

Bibliography

'22 Rebels Arrested during ICC Protest to Criminalise Ecocide', available at https://extinctionrebellion.nl/22-rebels-arrested-during-icc-protest-to-criminalise-ecocide/, accessed 20 March 2024.

Aksenova, Marina, 'Solidarity as a Moral and Legal Basis for Crimes against Humanity: A Durkheimean Perspective', in *Breaking the Cycle of Mass Atrocities: Criminological and Socio-Legal Approaches in International Criminal Law*, eds. M. Aksenova, E. Van Sliedregt, and S. Parmentier (London: Hart Publishing, 2019), 73–92.

Allen, D., 'Danielle Allen Response to Ferguson Forum', *Boston Review*, 14 March 2023, www.bostonreview.net/forum_response/danielle-allen-danielle-allen-response-ferguson-forum/, accessed 10 April 2024.

Améry, Jean, *At the Mind's Limits: Contemplations by a Survivor on Auschwitz and Its Realities*, trans. Sidney Rosenfeld and Stella P. Rosenfeld (Bloomington, IN: Indiana University Press, 1980).

Anghie, Antony, *Imperialism, Sovereignty and the Making of International Law*. Vol. 37 (Cambridge: Cambridge University Press, 2007).

Anghie, Antony, 'The Evolution of International Law: Colonial and Postcolonial Realities', *Third World Quarterly* 27, no. 5 (2006): 739–53.

Anghie, Antony, 'Francisco de Vitoria and the Colonial Origins of International Law', *Social & Legal Studies* 5, no. 3 (1996): 321–36.

Arendt, Hannah, 'The Eichmann Controversy: A Letter to Gershom Scholem', in *Hannah Arendt: The Jewish Writings*, eds. Jerome Kohn and Ron H. Feldman (New York: Schocken Books, 2007), 465–71.

Arendt, Hannah, 'Thinking and Moral Considerations', in *Responsibility and Judgment*, ed. Jerome Kohn (New York: Schocken Books, 2003), 159–65.

Arendt, Hannah, *The Human Condition*, 2nd ed. (Chicago: University of Chicago Press, 1998).

Arendt, Hannah, 'Organized Guilt and Universal Responsibility', in *Essays in Understanding, 1930–1954*, ed. Jerome Kohn (New York: Schocken Books, 1994), 121–32.

Arendt, Hannah, *The Life of the Mind. Part One: Thinking* (New York: Harcourt Brace, 1978).

Arendt, Hannah, *The Origins of Totalitarianism* (New York: Harcourt Brace, 1973).

Arendt, Hannah, 'On Humanity in Dark Times: Thoughts about Lessing', in *Men in Dark Times*, ed. Hannah Arendt (New York: Harcourt Brace, 1968), 3–25.

Arendt, Hannah, *Eichmann in Jerusalem: Report on the Banality of Evil* (London: Faber and Faber, 1963).

Asad, Talal, 'Reflections on Violence, Law, and Humanitarianism', *Critical Inquiry* 41 (Winter 2015): 390–427.

Asad, Talal, 'On Torture, or Cruel, Inhuman, and Degrading Treatment', *Social Research* 63, no. 4 (Winter 1996): 1081–109.

'Attendere', in Wiktionary, *The Free Dictionary*, https://en.wiktionary.org/wiki/attendere#Etymology, accessed 18 March 2024.

'Attentiveness', in Cambridge Dictionary Online, https://dictionary.cambridge.org/dictionary/english/attentiveness, accessed 18 March 2024.

Baines, Erin K., 'Complex Political Perpetrators: Reflections on Dominic Ongwen', *The Journal of Modern African Studies* 47, no. 2 (2009): 163–91.

Bassiouni, Mahmoud Cherif, 'Enslavement as an International Crime', *New York University Journal of International Law and Politics* 23 (1990): 445–517.

Berkowitz, Roger, 'Misreading "Eichmann in Jerusalem"', *New York Times*, 7 July 2013, http://opinionator.blogs.nytimes.com/2013/07/07/misreading-hannah-arendts-eichmann-in-jerusalem/?_php=true&_type=blogs&_r=1, accessed 8 March 2016.

Bernstein, Jay M., 'Améry's Devastation and Resentment: An Ethnographic Transcendental Reduction', *Tijdschrift voor Filosofie* 76, no. 1 (2014): 5–30.

Besters, Michiel, 'A Politics of (In)Security: A Philosophical Analysis of Collective Security' (PhD diss., Tilburg University, 2016).

Bilsky, Leora, 'The Right to Truth in International Criminal Law', in *The Oxford Handbook of International Criminal Law*, eds. Kevin Jon Heller et al. (Oxford: Oxford University Press, 2020), 473–93.

Bilsky, Leora, and Rachel Klagsbrun, 'The Return of Cultural Genocide?', *European Journal of International Law* 29, no. 2 (2018): 373–96.

Bouwknegt, Thijs B., and Barbora Holá, 'Dominic Ongwen: The ICC's Poster and Problem Child' (16 March 2020), www.justiceinfo.net/en/44014-dominic-ongwen-icc-poster-and-problem-child.html, accessed 11 March 2024.

Bowden, Brett, 'The Colonial Origins of International Law-European Expansion and the Classical Standard of Civilization', *Journal of the History of International Law* 7, no. 1 (2005): 1–24.

Branch, Adam, and Liana Minkova, 'Ecocide, the Anthropocene, and the International Criminal Court', *Ethics and International Affairs* 37, no. 1 (2023): 51–79.

Brudholm, Thomas, 'Revisiting Resentments: Jean Améry and the Dark Side of Forgiveness and Reconciliation', *Journal of Human Rights* 5, no. 1 (2006): 7–26.

Brudholm, Thomas, 'A Confiscated Past: Jean Améry on Home and Exile', *The Hedgehog Review* 7, no. 3 (2005): 7–19.

Butler, Judith, 'Afterword: After Loss, What Then?', in *Loss: The Politics of Mourning*, eds. David L. Eng and David Kazanjian (Berkeley: University of California Press, 2003), 467–73.

Cavell, Stanley, *The Claim of Reason: Wittgenstein, Skepticism, Morality, and Tragedy* (Oxford: Oxford University Press, 1999).

Cavell, Stanley, *Must We Mean What We Say? A Book of Essays* (Cambridge: Cambridge University Press, 1969).

Chakrabarty, Dipesh, 'The Climate of History: Four Theses', *Critical Inquiry* 35, no. 2 (2009): 197–222.

Chandler, David, *Voices from S-21: Terror and History in Pol Pot's Secret Prison* (Berkeley: University of California Press, 1999).

Christodoulidis, Emilios, 'The Objection that Cannot Be Heard: Communication and Legitimacy in the Courtroom', in *The Trial on Trial Volume 1: Truth and Due Process*, eds. Anthony Duff, Lindsay Farmer, Sandra Marshall, and Victor Tadros (Oxford: Hart, 2004), 179–202.

Clarke, Kamari, 'The Rule of Law through Its Economies of Appearances: The Making of the African Warlord', *Indiana Journal of Global Legal Studies* 18, no. 1 (2011): 7–40.

Clarke, Kamari, 'Rethinking Africa through Its Exclusions: The Politics of Naming Criminal Responsibility', *Anthropological Quarterly* 83, no. 3 (2010): 625–51.

Comaroff, John L., 'Colonialism, Culture, and the Law: A Foreword', *Law and Social Inquiry* 26, no. 2 (2001): 305–14.

Constable, Marianne, *Just Silences: The Limits and Possibilities of Modern Law* (Princeton, NJ: Princeton University Press, 2009).

Cornelissen, Wout, 'Arendt on the Activity of Thinking', in *The Bloomsbury Companion to Arendt*, eds. Yasemin Sari and Peter Gratton (London: Bloomsbury, 2020), 291–301.

Corrias, Luigi, 'Environmental Law and Youth Protests: Future Generations between Speech Acts and Political Representation', *International Journal for the Semiotics of Law-Revue internationale de Sémiotique juridique* 36, no. 2 (2023): 893–906.

Corrias, Luigi, 'Dehumanization by Law', in *The Routledge Handbook of Dehumanization*, ed. Maria Kronfeldner (Abingdon: Routledge, 2021), 201–13.

Corrias, Luigi, and Geoffrey M. Gordon, 'Judging in the Name of Humanity: International Criminal Tribunals and the Representation of a Global Public', *Journal of International Criminal Justice* 13, no. 1 (2015): 97–112.

Corrias, Luigi, 'Revolution, Authority and the Institution of Legal Order: Phenomenological Reflections', *Archiv für Rechtsund Sozialphilosphie* 100, no. 3 (July 2014): 295–307.

Corrias, Luigi, 'The Inhuman Stain: Representing Humanity in International Criminal Law', in *Humanity across International Law and Biolaw*, eds. B. van Beers, L. Corrias and W. Werner (Cambridge: Cambridge University Press, 2013), 67–86.

Corrias, Luigi, 'The Legal Theory of the Juridical Coup: Constituent Power Now', *German Law Journal* 12, no. 8 (2011): 1553–72.

Corrias, Luigi, *The Passivity of Law: Competence and Constitution in the European Court of Justice* (Berlin: Springer Science & Business Media, 2011).

Coupland, Robin, 'Humanity: What Is It and How Does It Influence International Law?', *International Review of the Red Cross* 83, no. 844 (2001): 969–89.

Cryer, Robert, *Prosecuting International Crimes: Selectivity and the International Criminal Law Regime*. Cambridge Studies in International and Comparative Law 41 (Cambridge: Cambridge University Press, 2005).

Çubukçu, Ayça, *For the Love of Humanity: The World Tribunal on Iraq* (Philadelphia, PA: University of Pennsylvania Press, 2018).

Çubukçu, Ayça, 'Thinking against Humanity', *London Review of International Law* 5, no. 2 (2017): 251–67.

Cusato, Eliana, and Emily Jones, 'The "Imbroglio" of Ecocide: A Political Economic Analysis', *Leiden Journal of International Law* 37, no. 1 (2024): 42–61.

De Baets, Antoon, 'Historical Imprescriptibility', *Storia della Storiografia* 60 (2011): 142–48.

De Cesare, Donatella, *Tortura* (Torino: Bollati Boringhieri, 2016).

De Wit, Theo, 'The Boundaries of Transitional Justice: Jean Améry and Johan Degenaar on the Tension between Survival and Justice', *Stellenbosch Theological Journal* 3, no. 1 (2017): 69–87.

Del Mar, Maksymilian, 'Jurisprudence on the Frontline', *European Journal of International Law* 19, no. 5. (2008): 1095–108.

Derrida, Jacques, *On Cosmopolitanism and Forgiveness*, by Jacques Derrida, trans. Mark Dooley and Michael Hughes (London and New York: Routledge, 2001).

Derrida, Jacques, 'Declarations of Independence', *New Political Science* 15 (1986): 7–15.

Drumbl, Mark A., 'The Kapo on Film: Tragic Perpetrators and Imperfect Victims', *Griffith J.L. AND Human Dignity* 6 (2018): 229–71.

Drumbl, Mark A., 'Victims Who Victimize', *London Review of International Law* 4, no. 2 (2016): 217–46.

Duff, Anthony, 'Authority and Responsibility in International Criminal Law', in *The Philosophy of International Law*, eds. Samantha Besson and John Tasioulas (Oxford: Oxford University Press, 2010), 589–604.

Durkheim, Emile, *The Division of Labour in Society*, trans. W. D. Halls (London: Palgrave Macmillan, 1984).

Durkheim, Emile, *The Rules of Sociological Method*, trans. W. D. Halls (New York City, NY: Free Press, 1982).

Esmeir, Samera, 'On Making Dehumanization Possible', *PMLA* 121, no. 5 (2006): 1544–51.

Eze, Emmanuel C., *Achieving Our Humanity: The Idea of the Postracial Future* (Abingdon: Routledge, 2013).

Ezra, Michael, 'The Eichmann Polemics: Hannah Arendt and Her Critics', *Democratiya* 9 (2007): 141–69.

Fassin, Didier, *Humanitarian Reason. A Moral History of the Present*, trans. R. Gomme (Berkeley, CA: University of California Press, 2012).

Feldman, Allen, 'Inhumanitas: Political Speciation, Animality, Natality, Defacement', in *In the Name of Humanity: The Government of Threat and Care*, eds. Ilana Feldman and Miriam Ticktin (Durham, NC: Duke University Press, 2010), 115–49.

Feldman, Ilana, and Miriam Ticktin, 'Introduction: Government and Humanity', in *In the Name of Humanity: The Government of Threat and Care*, eds. Ilana Feldman and Miriam Ticktin (Durham, NC: Duke University Press, 2010), 1–26.

Fine, Robert, 'Dehumanising the Dehumanisers: Reversal in Human Rights Discourse', *Journal of Global Ethics* 6, no. 2 (2010): 179–87.

Fine, Robert, 'Crimes against Humanity: Hannah Arendt and the Nuremberg Debates', *European Journal of Social Theory* 3, no. 3 (2000): 293–311.

Fitzgibbon, Will, 'Visions of Justice: Shakespeare and Duch's Proposed "Return to Humanity"', *ANU College of Law Research Paper*, no. 11–32 (2010) Electronic copy available at: http://ssrn.com/abstract=1948272 (consulted 8 March 2016).

Franck, Thomas M., 'Humanitarian Intervention', in *The Philosophy of International Law*, eds. Samantha Besson and John Tasioulas (Oxford: Oxford University Press, 2010), 531–48.

Friesen, Norm, 'Waldenfels' Responsive Phenomenology of the Alien: An Introduction', *Phenomenology and Practice* 7, no. 2 (2014): 68–77.

Gadamer, Hans-Georg, *Truth and Method*, trans. Joel Weinsheimer and Donald G. Marshall (London: Continuum Books, 2011).

Gaita, Raimond, *A Common Humanity: Thinking about Love and Truth and Justice* (Abingdon: Routledge, 2013).

Garapon, Antoine, 'Judging the Past: Three Ways of Understanding Time', in *Temporal Boundaries of Law and Politics: Time Out of Joint*, eds. L. Corrias and L. Francot (London: Routledge, 2018), 15–32.

Gatta, Giunia, 'Suffering and the Making of Politics: Perspectives from Jaspers and Camus', *Contemporary Political Theory* 14, no. 4 (2015): 335–54.

Graf, Sinja, *The Humanity of Universal Crime: Inclusion, Inequality, and Intervention in International Political Thought* (Oxford: Oxford University Press, 2021).

Hassellind, Filip Strandberg, 'The International Criminal Trial as a Site for Contesting Historical and Political Narratives: The Case of Dominic Ongwen.' *Social and Legal Studies* 30, no. 5 (2021): 790–809.

Havercroft, Jonathan, and David Owen, 'Soul-Blindness, Police Orders and Black Lives Matter: Wittgenstein, Cavell, and Ranciére', *Political Theory* 44, no. 6 (2016): 739–63.

Hayden, Patrick, 'From Political Friendship to Befriending the World', *The European Legacy* 20, no. 7 (2015): 745–64.

Hayden, Patrick, 'Systemic Evil and the International Political Imagination', *International Politics* 51, no. 4 (2014): 424–40.

Hayden, Patrick, 'The Relevance of Hannah Arendt's Reflections on Evil: Globalization and Rightlessness', *Human Rights Review* 11, no. 4 (2010): 451–67.

Heidegger, Martin, *The Fundamental Concepts of Metaphysics: World, Finitude, Solitude* (Bloomington: Indiana University Press, 2001).

Henrich, Dieter, 'The Basic Structure of Modern Philosophy', *Cultural Hermeneutics* 2, no. 1 (1974): 1–18.

Hessbruegge, Jan Arno, 'Justice Delayed, Not Denied: Statutory Limitations and Human Rights Crimes', *Georgetown Journal of International Law* 43, no. 4 (2012): 335–85.

Hobbes, Thomas, *Leviathan* (London: Penguin Press, 1968).

Honneth, Axel, 'Foreword', in *Alienation*, trans. Frederick Neuhouser and Alan E. Smith (New York: Columbia University Press, 2016), vii–x.

Howard, Matt, *Law's Memories* (London: Palgrave Macmillan, 2023).

Hoy, D. C., *The Time of Our Lives: A Critical History of Temporality* (Cambridge, MA: The MIT Press, 2009).

Jaeggi, Rahel, *Alienation*, trans. Frederick Neuhouser and Alan E. Smith (New York: Columbia University Press, 2016).

Janicaud, Dominique, *On the Human Condition* (Abingdon: Routledge, 2005).

Jankélevitch, Vladimir, 'Should We Pardon Them?' trans. Ann Hobart, *Critical Inquiry* 22, no. 3 (Spring 1996): 552–72.

Jankélevitch, Vladimir, *L'Imprescriptible* (Paris: Seuil, 1986).

Kaufmann, Paulus, Hannes Kuch, Christian Neuhäuser and Elaine Webster, eds., *Humiliation, Degradation, Dehumanization: Human Dignity Violated* (Berlin: Springer, 2011).

Khan, Karim, 'We Are Witnessing a Pandemic of Inhumanity: To Halt the Spread, We Must Cling to the Law', *The Guardian*, 10 November 2023, www.theguardian.com/commentisfree/2023/nov/10/law-israel-hamas-international-criminal-court-icc, accessed 18 March 2024.

Kiyani, Asad, 'Group-Based Differentiation and Local Repression: The Custom and Curse of Selectivity', *Journal of International Criminal Justice* 14, no. 4 (2016): 939–57.

Kiyani, Asad, 'Third World Approaches to International Criminal Law', *American Journal of International Law* 109 (2015): 255–59.

Kleinman, Arthur, '"Everything That Really Matters": Social Suffering, Subjectivity, and the Remaking of Human Experience in a Disordering World', *Harvard Theological Review*, 90, no. 3 (1997), 315–35.

Kok, Ruth A., *Statutory Limitations in International Criminal Law* (The Hague: TMC Asser Press, 2007).

Koskenniemi, Martti, 'International Law in Europe: Between Tradition and Renewal', *The European Journal of International Law* 16, no. 1 (2005): 113–24.

Koskenniemi, Martti, 'Between Impunity and Show Trials', *Max Planck Yearbook of United Nations Law* 6 (2002): 1–35.

Krever, Tor, 'International Criminal Law: An Ideology Critique', *Leiden Journal of International Law* 26, no. 3 (2013): 701–23.

Kronfeldner, Maria E. ed., *Routledge Research Handbook of Dehumanization* (Abingdon: Routledge, 2021).

Kteily, Nour, and Emile Bruneau, 'Darker Demons of Our Nature: The Need to (Re)Focus Attention on Blatant Forms of Dehumanization', *Current Directions in Psychological Science* 26, no. 6 (2017): 487–94.

Le Moli, Ginevra, 'The Principle of Human Dignity in International Law', in *General Principles and the Coherence of International Law*, eds. M. Endenas et al. (Leiden: Brill Nijhoff, 2019), 352–68.

Lefort, Claude, *Democracy and Political Theory*, trans. D. Macey (Hoboken, NJ: Wiley, 1991).

Legros, Robert, *L'idée d'humanité: Introduction à la phénoménologie*. Coll. «Le Collège de philosophie» (Paris: Grasset & Fasquelle, 1990).

Levi, Primo, *The Drowned and the Saved* (New York City, NY: Simon and Schuster, 2017).

Levinas, Emmanuel, 'Useless Suffering', trans. Richard Cohen, in *The Provocation of Levinas*, eds. Robert Bernasconi and David Wood (Abingdon: Routledge, 1988), 156–67.

Lindahl, Hans, 'Intentionality, Representation, Recognition: Phenomenology and the Politics of A-Legality', in *Political Phenomenology*, eds. Thomas Bedorf and Steffen Herrmann (London: Routledge, 2019), 256–76.

Lindahl, Hans, *Authority and the Globalisation of Inclusion and Exclusion* (Cambridge: Cambridge University Press, 2018).

Lindahl, Hans, *Fault Lines of Globalization: Legal Order and a Politics of A-Legality* (Oxford: Oxford University Press, 2013).

Luban, David, 'The Enemy of All Humanity', *Netherlands Journal of Legal Philosophy* 47, no. 2 (2018): 112–37.

Luban, David, 'Hannah Arendt as a Theorist of International Criminal Law', *International Criminal Law Review* 11, no. 3 (2011): 621–41.

Luban, David, 'A Theory of Crimes against Humanity', *The Yale Journal of International Law* 29, no. 1 (2004): 85–167.

Lyotard, Jean-François, *The Inhuman: Reflections on Time*, trans. Geoffrey Bennington and Rachel Bowlby (Redwood City, CA: Stanford University Press, 1991).

Macleod, Christopher, 'Towards a Philosophical Account of Crimes against Humanity', *European Journal of International Law* 21, no. 2 (2010): 281–302.

Maier, Andreas, 'How Denying Moral Standing Violates Human Dignity', in *Humiliation, Degradation, Dehumanization: Human Dignity Violated*, eds. Paulus Kaufmann, Hannes Kuch, Christian Neuhäuser and Elaine Webster (Berlin: Springer, 2011), 101–17.

Margalit, Avishai, *The Decent Society*, trans. N. Goldblum (Cambridge, MA: Harvard University Press, 1995).

May, Larry, *Crimes against Humanity: A Normative Account* (Cambridge: Cambridge University Press, 2005).

Mbembe, Achille, 'Necropolitics', *Public Culture* 15, no. 1 (2003): 11–40.

Menga, Ferdinando G., 'Antagonism, Natality, A-Legality: A Phenomenological Itinerary on the Democratic Transgression of Politico-Legal Orders', *Ratio Juris* 31, no. 1 (March 2018): 100–19.

Menga, Ferdinando G., 'Guest Editor's Preface: The Experience of the Alien and the Philosophy of Response', *Etica & Politica/Ethics & Politics XIII* 1 (2011): 7–15.

Merleau-Ponty, Maurice, *Phenomenology of Perception*, trans. Colin Smith (London: Routledge, 2003).

Merleau-Ponty, Maurice, *The Visible and the Invisible*, trans. Alphonso Lingis (Evanston, IL: Northwestern University Press, 1968).

Meron, Theodor, *The Humanization of International Law* (Leiden: Brill Nijhoff, 2006).

Mertens, Thomas, 'The Eichmann Trial: Hannah Arendt's View on the Jerusalem Court's Competence', *German Law Journal* 6, no. 2 (2005): 407–24.

Minkkinen, Panu, 'The Expressionless: Law, Ethics, and the Imagery of Suffering', *Law and Critique* 19, no. 1 (2008): 65–85.

Minkkinen, Panu, 'Ressentiment as Suffering: On Transitional Justice and the Impossibility of Forgiveness', *Law and Literature* 19, no. 3 (2007): 513–31.

Moreno Ocampo, L., 'The International Criminal Court: Seeking Global Justice', *Case Western Reserve Journal of International Law* 40, no. 1 (2008): 215–26.

Morera, Maria D., Maria N. Quiles, Ana D. Correa, Naira N. Delgado, and Jacques-Phillipe Leyens, 'Perception of Mind and Dehumanization: Human, Animal, or Machine?', *International Journal of Psychology* 53, no. 4 (2018): 253–60.

Nasiri, Shahin, and Leila Faghfouri Azar, 'Investigating the 1981 Massacre in Iran: On the Law-Constituting Force of Violence', *Journal of Genocide Research* 26, no. 2 (2024): 164–87.

Nimaga, Salif, 'An International Conscience Collective? A Durkheimian Analysis of International Criminal Law', *International Criminal Law Review* 7, no. 4 (2007): 561–619.

Norval, Aletta, 'Deliberative, Agonistic and Aversive Grammars of Democracy: The Question of Criteria', in *Practices of Freedom: Decentred Governance, Conflict and Democratic Participation*, eds. Steven Griggs, Aletta J. Norval and Hendrik Wagenaar (Cambridge: Cambridge University Press, 2014), 60–84.

Nouwen, Sarah M. H., and Wouter G. Werner, 'Monopolizing Global Justice: International Criminal Law as Challenge to Human Diversity', *Journal of International Criminal Justice* 13, no. 1 (2015): 157–76.

Oliver, Sophie, 'Dehumanization: Perceiving the Body as (In)Human', in *Humiliation, Degradation, Dehumanization: Human Dignity Violated*, eds. Paulus Kaufmann, Hannes Kuch, Christian Neuhäuser and Elaine Webster (Berlin: Springer, 2011), 85–97.

Oudejans, Nanda, and Anthony Pemberton, 'Broken Rules, Ruined Lives. Een verkenning van de normativiteit van de onrechtservaring', *Netherlands Journal of Legal Philosophy* 48, no. 1 (2019): 66–84.

Paulson, Stanley L., 'Radbruch on Unjust Laws: Competing Earlier and Later Views', *Oxford Journal of Legal Studies* 15, no. 3 (1995): 489–500.

Perry, John, 'Myself and I', in *Philosophie in synthetischer Absicht – Synthesis in Mind*, ed. Marcelo Stamm (Stuttgart: Klett-Cotta, 1998), 83–103.

Peters, Anne, 'Humanity as the A and Ω of Sovereignty', *European Journal of International Law* 20, no. 3 (2009): 513–44.

Petrucciani, Stefano, 'Alienazione: un concetto da rivisitare?', *Etica & Politica – Ethics & Politics* 18, (2016): 109–19.

Pieters, Nini Els, and Tonny Raymond Kirabira, '*The Ongwen Judgement at the ICC: A Missed Opportunity for Former Child Soldiers?*' (22 June 2021), https://internationallaw.blog/2021/06/22/the-ongwen-judgement-at-the-icc-a-missed-opportunity-for-former-child-soldiers/, accessed 11 March 2024.

Pollmann, Arnd, 'Embodied Self-Respect and the Fragility of Human Dignity: A Human Rights Approach', in *Humiliation, Degradation, Dehumanization: Human Dignity Violated*, eds. Paulus Kaufmann, Hannes Kuch, Christian Neuhäuser and Elaine Webster (Berlin: Springer, 2011), 243–61.

Quijano, Anibal, 'Coloniality of Power and Eurocentrism in Latin America', *International Sociology* 15, no. 2 (2000): 215–32.

Radbruch, Gustav, 'Statutory Lawlessness and Supra-statutory Law (1946)', *Oxford Journal of Legal Studies* 26, no. 1 (2006): 1–11.

Radbruch, Gustav, 'Legal Philosophy', in *The Legal Philosophies of Lask, Radbruch, and Dabin*, trans. Kurt Wilk (Cambridge: Harvard University Press, 1950), 45–224.

Rajkovic, Nikolas M., 'What Is a "Grave" International Crime? The Rome Statute, Durkheim and the Sociology of Ruling Outrages', *Loyola University Chicago School of Law Review* 16 (2020): 65–86.

Ratcliffe, Matthew, Mark Ruddell, and Benedict Smith, 'What Is a 'Sense of Foreshortened Future?' A Phenomenological Study of Trauma, Trust, and Time', *Frontiers in Psychology* 5 (2014): 1026.

Rau, Milo, 'New Realism and the Contemporary World: The Re-enactments and Tribunals of the International Institute of Political Murder', *Documenta* 34, no. 2 (2016): 121–37.

Renault, Emmanuel, 'A Critical Theory of Social Suffering', *Critical Horizons* 11, no. 2 (2010): 221–41.

Ricoeur, Paul, *Memory, History, Forgetting*, trans. K. Blamey and D. Pellauer (Chicago and London: The University of Chicago Press, 2004).

Ricoeur, Paul, *The Just*, trans. David Pellauer (Chicago and London: The University of Chicago Press, 2000).

Ricoeur, Paul, *Oneself as Another*, trans. K. Blamey (Chicago and London: The University of Chicago Press, 1992).

Rosa, Hartmut, *Social Acceleration: A New Theory of Modernity*, trans. Jonathan Trejo-Mathys (New York: Columbia University Press, 2013).

Rosenfeld, Sidney, 'Afterword. Jean Améry: The Writer in Revolt', in *At the Mind's Limits: Contemplations by a Survivor on Auschwitz and Its Realities*, trans. Sidney Rosenfeld and Stella P. Rosenfeld; ed. Jean Améry (Bloomington, IN: Indiana University Press, 1980), 104–11.

Rosenstock, Bruce, 'Against Sovereign Impunity: The Political Theology of the International Criminal Court', in *After Secular Law*, eds. Winnifred Sullivan, Robert A. Yelle, and Mateo Taussig-Rubbo (Redwood City, CA: Stanford University Press, 2011), 160–79.

Sangiovanni, Andrea, *Humanity without Dignity: Moral Equality, Respect, and Human Rights* (Cambridge, MA: Harvard University Press, 2017).

Seymour, David M., 'The Autonomy of the Political and the Dissolution of the Jews', *International Journal of Law in Context* 3, no. 4 (2007): 373–87.

Shuster, Martin, 'A Phenomenology of Home: Jean Améry on Homesickness', *Journal of French and Francophone Philosophy – Revue de la philosophie française et de langue française* 24, no. 3 (2016): 117–27.

Schmid, Evelyne, 'International Criminal Law and Social Rights', in *Research Handbook on International Law and Social Rights*, eds. Christina Binder, Flavia Piovesan, Amaya Úbeda de Torres and Jane Hofbauer (Cheltenham: Edward Elgar, 2020), 519–34.

Schmitt, Carl, *The Concept of the Political* trans. G. Schwab (Chicago and London: The University of Chicago Press, 2007).

Schwöbel-Patel, Christine, 'The Core Crimes of International Criminal Law', in *The Oxford Handbook of International Criminal Law*, eds. Kevin Jon Heller et al. (Oxford: Oxford University Press, 2018), 768–90.

Schwöbel-Patel, Christine, 'The "Ideal" Victim of International Criminal Law', *European Journal of International Law* 29, no. 3 (2018): 703–24.

Smith, David L., 'Paradoxes of Dehumanization', *Social Theory and Practice* 42, no. 2 (2016): 416–43.

Smith, David Woodruff, 'Phenomenology', in *The Stanford Encyclopedia of Philosophy* (Summer 2018 Edition), ed. Edward N. Zalta, accessed 23 March 2024, https://plato.stanford.edu/archives/sum2018/entries/phenomenology/.

Soirila, Ukri, 'Persons and Things in International Law and "Law of Humanity"', *German Law Journal* 18, no. 5 (2017): 1163–82.

Souris, Renée Nicole, 'Virtue Ethics, Criminal Responsibility, and Dominic Ongwen', *International Criminal Law Review* 19, no. 3 (2019): 475–504.

Spiegelberg, Herbert, '"We": A Linguistic and Phenomenological Analysis', in *Doing Phenomenology. Essays on and in Phenomenology* (The Hague: Martinus Nijhoff, 1975), 215–45.

Stanton, Gregory H., 'The 10 Stages of Genocide', Human Rights Watch 2006–2013, available at http://genocidewatch.net/genocide-2/8-stages-of-genocide/, accessed 2 March 2021.

Stauffer, Jill, 'Law, Politics, the Age of Responsibility, and the Problem of Child Soldiers', *Law, Culture and the Humanities* 16, no. 1 (2020): 42–52.

Stauffer, Jill, *Ethical Loneliness: The Injustice of Not Being Heard* (New York: Columbia University Press, 2015).

Steinbock, Anthony J., *Home and Beyond. Generative Phenomenology after Husserl* (Evanston, IL: Northwestern University Press, 1995).

Stolk, Sofia, 'The Victim, the International Criminal Court and the Search for Truth. On the Interdependence and Incompatibility of Truths about Mass Atrocity', *Journal of International Criminal Justice* 13, no. 5 (2015), 973–94.

Tallgren, Immi, 'The Voice of the International: Who Is Speaking?', *Journal of International Criminal Justice* 13, no. 1 (2015): 135–55.

Tallgren, Immi. 'The Durkheimian Spell of International Criminal Law?', *Revue interdisciplinaire d'études juridiques* 71, no. 2 (2013): 137–69.

Taylor, Charles, *Sources of the Self: The Making of the Modern Identity* (Cambridge: Cambridge University Press, 1989).

Teitel, Ruti, *Humanity's Law* (Oxford: Oxford University Press, 2011).

Todorov, Tzvetan, *Hope and Memory: Lessons from the Twentieth Century*, trans. David Bellos (London: Atlantic Books, 2003).

Van Beers, B., L. Corrias and W. G. Werner, eds., *Humanity across International Law and Biolaw* (Cambridge: Cambridge University Press, 2013).

Van Roermund, Bert, *Law in the First Person Plural: Roots, Concepts, Topics* (Cheltenham: Edward Elgar Publishing, 2020).

Van Roermund, Bert, *Legal Thought and Philosophy: What Legal Scholarship Is About* (Cheltenham: Edward Elgar Publishing, 2013).

Van Roermund, Bert, 'Time Beyond Time – Time before Time: Comments on Ricoeur', in *Public Forgiveness in Post-Conflict Contexts*, eds. Bas van Stokkom, Neelke Doorn and Paul van Tongeren (Cambridge and Antwerp: Intersentia, 2012), 91–105.

Van Sliedregt, Elies, 'International Criminal Law: Over-Studied and Underachieving?', *Leiden Journal of International Law* 29 no. 1 (2016): 1–12.

Veitch, Scott, *Law and Irresponsibility: On the Legitimation of Human Suffering* (Abingdon: Routledge, 2007).

Vernon, Richard, 'What Is Crime against Humanity?', *Journal of Political Philosophy* 10, no. 3 (2002): 231–49.

Visker, Rudi, 'The Inhuman Core of Human Dignity: Levinas and Beyond', *Levinas Studies* 9, (2014): 1–22.

Visker, Rudi, *The Inhuman Condition: Looking for Difference after Levinas and Heidegger* (Berlin: Springer, 2004).

Vitoria, Francisco de, 'Lecture on the American Indians', in *Political Writings*, eds. Anthony Pagden and Jeremy Lawrance (Cambridge: Cambridge University Press, 1991), 231–92.

Waldenfels, Bernhard, 'Responsive Ethics', in *The Oxford Handbook of Contemporary Phenomenology*, ed. Dan Zahavi (Oxford: Oxford University Press, 2012), 423–41.

Waldenfels, Bernhard, *Phenomenology of the Alien: Basic Concepts*, trans. Tanja Stähler and Alexander Kozin (Evanston, IL: Northwestern University Press, 2011).

Waldenfels, Bernhard, *Fremdheit, Gastfreundschaft und Feindschaft*, www.information-philosophie.de/?a=1&t=219&n=2&y=1&c=1, accessed 8 March 2024, aus: Heft 5/2006, S. 7–18.

Waldenfels, Bernhard, *Bruchlinien der Erfahrung. Phänomenologie, Psychoanalyse, Phänomenotechnik* (Frankfurt am Main: Suhrkamp, 2002).

Waldenfels, Bernhard, *Verfremdung der Moderne: Phänomenologische Grenzgänge*. Vol. 10. (Göttingen: Wallstein Verlag, 2001).

Waldenfels, Bernhard, 'From Intentionality to Responsivity', in *Phenomenology Today: The Schuwer Spep Lectures, 1998–2002*, eds. Rudolf Bernet, and Daniel J. Martino (Pittsburg: Duquesne University, 2003), 23–35.

Waldenfels, Bernhard, *Order in the Twilight* trans. David J. Parent (Athens, OH: Ohio University Press, 1996).

Webster, Elaine, 'Degradation: A Human Rights Law Perspective', in *Humiliation, Degradation, Dehumanization: Human Dignity Violated*, eds. Paulus Kaufmann, Hannes Kuch, Christian Neuhäuser and Elaine Webster (Berlin: Springer, 2011), 67–84.

Wehrle, Maren, 'Normality and Normativity in Experience', in *Normativity in Perception*, eds. M. Doyon and T. Breyer (Basingstoke: Palgrave McMillan, 2015), 128–40.

Werner, Wouter, *Repetition and International Law* (Cambridge: Cambridge University Press, 2022).

Wilson, Richard A., 'When Humanity Sits in Judgment: Crimes against Humanity and the Conundrum of Race and Ethnicity at the International Criminal Tribunal for Rwanda', in *In the Name of Humanity: The Government of Threat and Care*, eds. I. Feldman and M. Ticktin (Durham, NC: Duke University Press, 2010), 27–57.

Wittgenstein, Ludwig, *Philosophical Investigations*, trans. G. E. M. Anscombe (Oxford: Basil Blackwell, 1967).

Yusoff, Kathryn, 'The Inhumanities', *Annals of the American Association of Geographers* 111, no. 3 (2021): 663–76.

Zolo, Danilo, 'Humanitarian Militarism?' in *The Philosophy of International Law*, eds. Samantha Besson and John Tasioulas (Oxford: Oxford University Press, 2010), 549–65.

Legal Documents of the ECCC

Compilation of statements of apology made by Kaing Guek Eav alias Duch during the proceedings, available at www.eccc.gov.kh/sites/default/files/publications/Case001Apology_En_low_res.pdf (consulted 8 March 2016).

ECCC, Office of the Co-Investigating Judges, Closing Order Indicting Kaing Geuk Eav alias Duch (8 August 2008).

Law on the Establishment of Extraordinary Chambers in the Courts of Cambodia for the Prosecution of Crimes Committed during the Period of Democratic Kampuchea with inclusion of amendments as promulgated on 27 October 2004.

Transcript of Proceedings, 'Duch' Trial Public, Trial Chamber of the Extraordinary Chambers in the Courts of Cambodia, 30 March 2009, Trial Day 1.

Transcript of Proceedings, 'Duch' Trial Public, Trial Chamber of the Extraordinary Chambers in the Courts of Cambodia, 31 March 2009, Trial Day 2.

Transcript of Proceedings, 'Duch' Trial Public, Trial Chamber of the Extraordinary Chambers in the Courts of Cambodia, 8 April 2009, Trial Day 6.

Transcript of Proceedings, 'Duch' Trial Public, Trial Chamber of the Extraordinary Chambers in the Courts of Cambodia, 23 November 2009, Trial Day 73.

Transcript of Proceedings, 'Duch' Trial Public, Trial Chamber of the Extraordinary Chambers in the Courts of Cambodia, 25 November 2009, Trial Day 75.

Transcript of Proceedings, 'Duch' Trial Public, Trial Chamber of the Extraordinary Chambers in the Courts of Cambodia, 26 November 2009, Trial Day 76.

Other Legal Documents

Convention against Torture and Other Cruel, Inhuman or Degrading Treatment or Punishment. Adopted by the General Assembly of the United Nations on 10 December 1984.

Convention on the Prevention and Punishment of the Crime of Genocide. Adopted by the General Assembly of the United Nations on 9 December 1948.

Convention (II) with Respect to the Laws and Customs of War on Land (The Hague, 29 July 1899).

E/CN.4/2006/91 of 8 February 2006, *Study on the right to the truth. Report of the Office of the United Nations High Commissioner for Human Rights.*

Murphy, Sean D., 'Fourth Report of the Special Rapporteur on Crimes against Humanity' (2019) United Nations International Law Commission, A/CN.4/725.

Text of the Rome Statute circulated as document A/CONF.183/9 of 17 July 1998 and corrected by process-verbaux of 10 November 1998, 12 July 1999, 30 November 1999, 8 May 2000, 17 January 2001 and 16 January 2002.

UN General Assembly, *The Crime of Genocide*, 11 December 1946, A/RES/96.

Index

Printed by Integrated Books International,
United States of America